PERSIAN

A.M. Miandji

HIPPOCRENE BOOKS
New York

Originally published by Mehran Publications, Tabriz, Iran.

Hippocrene paperback edition, 1998.

All rights reserved.

For information, address:
HIPPOCRENE BOOKS, INC.
171 Madison Avenue
New York, NY 10016

ISBN 0-7818-0567-8

Printed in the United States of America.

CONTENTS

Preface XI
Acknowledgments XI

Part One 1

Key to the phonetic symbols 3
    Vowels/Diphthongs 3
    Consonant 4
    Farsi alphabet 5
Marks 6
Vowel points 6
Especial phonetic symbols 7
Introduction 11
    Farsi phonemics 12

Part Two 17

SECTION 1   INFORMAL TALKING 19

1-1 Ordinary conversation 21
1-2 Greeting / Farewell 33
1-3 Thanks / Congratulation 35
1-4 Apologies 37
1-5 Asking questions 39
1-6 Answers / Opinions 43
1-7 Phrases 47
1-8 Language 53

SECTION 2 GENERAL DATA	57

2-1 Numbers	59
2-2 Time	65
2-3 Seasons / Months	69
2-4 Watch	71
2-5 Direction	75
2-6 Climate	77
2-7 Age	81
2-8 Family relationships	83
2-9 Colors	87
2-10 Qualities	91
2-11 Education	95
2-12 Occupation	99

SECTION 3 ARRIVAL / DEPARTURE	103

3-1 Customs	105
3-2 Airport	109
3-3 Airport loudspeaker	115
3-4 Flight idioms	117
3-5 Inside a plane	119
3-6 Travelling by rail	121
3-7 Travelling by car	125
3-8 Garage	129
3-9 Travelling by ship	133

SECTION 4 IN TOWN	137

4-1 Taxi	139
4-2 Town (sign, address, ...)	141
4-3 Bus	149
4-4 Hotel	151
4-5 Bank / Money	155

4-6 Post	159
4-7 Telephone	161
4-8 Restaurant (menu, ...)	165
4-9 Museum	171
4-10 Factory	175

SECTION 5	GENERAL NEEDS	179

5-1 Supermarket / Grocery	181
5-2 Fruit / Vegetables	185
5-3 Clothing Shop	189
5-4 Clothing Repair	193
5-5 Hairdresser	195
5-6 Laundry / dry cleaning	199
5-7 Shoe	201
5-8 Shoe repair	203
5-9 Book / Magazine	205
5-10 Photographer	209

SECTION 6	HEALTH	211

6-1 Parts of the body	213
6-2 Doctor / Clinic	217
Medical occupations	218
Diseases	218
Examination	220
6-3 Dentist	223
6-4 Pharmacy	225

SECTION 7	AMUSEMENTS	229

7-1 Sports	231
7-2 Television / Radio	235
7-3 Cinema	239

7-4 Theatre	243
7-5 Concert	247
7-6 Hobbies	251
7-7 Mamals	255
Birds	257
Fish	258
Insects	259
Amphians / Reptiles	259

Part Three 261

SECTION I GEOGRAPHY	263
I.I General profile	265
I.II Climate	265
I.III Age Distribution	266
I.IV Language	266
I.V Occupation	266
I.VI Religion	266
SECTION II TRAVEL	267
II.I Traveling to Iran	269
Air	269
Land	269
Sea	269
II.II Inland Trips	269
By land	269
By Air	269
II.III Road and motoring	270
II.IV Transportation	270
Car	270
Train	271

Aircraft 271
II.V Adaptation and hospitality centers 271
    Hotel / Inn 271
    Hospitality centers 271
    On road 272
II.VI National Iranian dishes 272
    Dish 272
    Bread 272
    Beverage 272
II.VII Opening and closing times 273
    Local time 273
    Weekly closing day 273
    Comerical bank 273
    Comercial office 273
    Shope hours 273
    Restaurant hours 273
    Bazaar hours 273

SECTION III   SIGHTS 275

III.I Main attractions 277
III.II Azarbaijan 277
    Ahar 277
    Ardabil 277
    Jolfa 277
    Khoy 277
    Maku 277
    Maragheh 278
    Miyaneh 278
    Naghadeh 278
    Tabriz 278
    Takab 278
    Urumieh Lake 278

III.III Fars 279
   Perspolis (Takht-e-Jamshid) 279
   Shiraz 279
III.IV Hamadan 280
   Hamadan 280
III.V Ilam 280
   Ilam 280
III.VI Isfahan 280
   Isfahan 280
   Handicrafts 281
III.VII Kerman 281
   Bam 281
   Kerman 281
   Mahan 281
III.VIII Kermanshah 282
   Ancient cities 282
   Historical relics 282
III.IX Khorasan 282
   Mashhad 282
   Neishabour 283
   Tus 283
III.X Khuzestan 283
   Ahwaz 283
   Shush 283
III.XI Kordestan 283
   Sanandaj 283
   Handicrafts 283
III.XII Southern coasts and Persian-Gulf islands 284
III.XIII Tehran 284
   Tehran 284
III.XIV The Caspian coast 285
III.XV Yazd 285
   Yazd 285
III.XVI Sports 286

House of Strength	286
Wrestling	286
Climbing	286
Skiing	287
Other sports	287
III.XVII Iranian handicrafts	287
Carpet	287
Other	287

To the reader

Preface

Language is a means of communication and man is the only species, who boasts of being genetically endowed with it. Farsi, an Indo-European language, now spoken in Iran and in some Asian countries has a long literary tradition and a rich cultural inheritance. It is, therefore, understandable why most people, acquainted with Iranian literary and artworks, embark on learning Farsi in order to secure a key, so to speak, to gain access to the valuable treasure in this beautiful country.

The present book is prepared to help the reader in his pursuit of enriching his world view through learning Farsi. The book consists of three parts: 1) An introduction on phonetic symbols used, Farsi alphabet of letters and sounds. 2) Texts based on various daily-life subjects in seven chapters made up of sixty sections. 3) A tourist-guide providing useful information for the people interested in paying visits to places of historical sights, museums, art galleries...and so on.

Prepared alphabetically, the book is easy to use. The reader is assumed, through the pronunciation guide, to encounter no problem in reading the Farsi sentences and expressions given. We hope that the reader will oblige us with his constructive comments so that we can consider them for future editions.

Anooshirvan M. Miandji
September 1994

Acknowledgments

The author wishes to express his gratitude to the English Language Department of Tabriz University for their valuable recommendations on Farsi phonemic transcription; the editor, Taghi Gheisari for the critical comments on grammatical points and style consistency; Ne'mati Typesetters for their typesetting and layout; Mehran Publications for patiently managing the technical procedures of lithography, printing and binding.

Part One

KEY TO THE PHONETIC SYMBOLS
Vowels / Diphthongs

ɪ	as	it	/ɪt/	uː [2]	as	too	/tuː/
e [1]	as	ten	/ten/	ɜː	as	fur	/fɜː/
æ	as	hat	/hæt/	vː [2]	as	→p 7	
a	as	→p 7		eɪ	as	day	/deɪ/
ɒ	as	got	/gɒt/	ɔɪ	as	boy	/bɔɪ/
ʊ	as	put	/pʊt/	aɪ	as	fly	/flaɪ/
ʌ	as	up	/ʌp/	aʊ	as	now	/naʊ/
ə	as	ago	/əgəʊ/	əʊ	as	go	/gəʊ/
o [1]	as	→p 7		ɪə	as	near	/nɪər/
iː [2]	as	see	/siː/	eə	as	hair	/heər/
ɑː	as	arm	/ɑːm/	ʊə	as	pure	/pjʊər/
ɔː	as	saw	/sɔː/	ow [3]	as	→p 15F

1- Persian short vowels
2- Persian long vowels
3- Persian diphthong

Consonants

*b	as	by	/baɪ/	w	as	we	/wiː/
*d	as	do	/duː/	*j	as	yes	/jes/
*f	as	fun	/fʌn/	*z	as	zip	/zɪp/
*g	as	got	/gɒt/	*tʃ	as	chin	/tʃɪn/
*h	as	how	/haʊ/	*dʒ	as	jaw	/dʒɔː/
*k	as	cat	/kæt/	θ	as	thin	/θɪn/
*l	as	leg	/leg/	ð	as	then	/ðen/
*m	as	my	/maɪ/	*ʃ	as	she	/ʃiː/
*n	as	no	/nəʊ/	*ʒ	as	vision	/vɪʒn/
*p	as	pen	/pen/	*ŋ	as	long	/lɔːŋ/
*r	as	red	/red/	*x	as	loch	/lɒx/
*s	as	sun	/sʌn/	*ɢ	as	→ p 7	
*t	as	tea	/tiː/	*ʔ	as	→ p 7	
*v	as	voice	/vɔɪs/				

---

* Persian consonants

Key to the... 5

sound	name	alone	last	middle	first
ɒː / ʌ	/ʔalef/	ا	ـا	-	آ
b	/beː/	ب	ـب	ـبـ	بـ
p	/peː/	پ	ـپ	ـپـ	پـ
t	/teː/	ت	ـت	ـتـ	تـ
s	/seː/	ث	ـث	ـثـ	ثـ
dʒ	/dʒiːm/	ج	ـج	ـجـ	جـ
tʃ	/tʃeː/	چ	ـچ	ـچـ	چـ
h	/heː/	ح	ـح	ـحـ	حـ
x	/xeː/	خ	ـخ	ـخـ	خـ
d	/dɒːl/	د	ـد	ـد	د
z	/zɒːl/	ذ	ـذ	ـذ	ذ
r	/reː/	ر	ـر	ـر	ر
z	/zeː/	ز	ـز	ـز	ز
ʒ	/ʒeː/	ژ	ـژ	ـژ	ژ
s	/sɪn/	س	ـس	ـسـ	سـ
ʃ	/ʃɪn/	ش	ـش	ـشـ	شـ
s	/sɒːd/	ص	ـص	ـصـ	صـ
z	/zɒːd/	ض	ـض	ـضـ	ضـ
t	/tɒː/	ط	ـط	ـط	ط
z	/zɒː/	ظ	ـظ	ـظ	ظ
ʔ	/ʔajn/	ع	ـع	ـعـ	عـ
ɢ	/ɢajn/	غ	ـغ	ـغـ	غـ
f	/fɒː/	ف	ـف	ـفـ	فـ
ɢ	/ɢɒːf/	ق	ـق	ـقـ	قـ
k	/kɒːf/	ک	ـک	ـکـ	کـ
g	/gɒːf/	گ	ـگ	ـگـ	گـ
l	/lɒːm/	ل	ـل	ـلـ	لـ
m	/miːm/	م	ـم	ـمـ	مـ
n	/nʊn/	ن	ـن	ـنـ	نـ
uː /v /ow	/vɒːv/	و	ـو	ـو	و
h /e	/heː/	ه	ـه	ـهـ	هـ
j / iː / ɪ / ʔ	/jɒː/	ی	ـی	ـیـ	یـ

Table 1

MARKS

1. (ﹾ) /tanvın/ pronounced as 'an' in .... دَقیقاً/daGi:Gan/

2. (ﹽ) /taʃdi:d/ shows repetition of letter as in .... فرّار/far-rv:r/

3. (ﺀ) /hamze/ pronounced in different forms as ....
.... مطمئن/motmaʔen/ & متأسفم /motaʔassefam/

VOWEL POINTS*

1. (ﹷ) /zabar/ pronounced as 'a' in .... بَد /bad/

2. (ﹻ) /zi:r/ pronounced as 'e' in .... دِل /del/

3. (ﹹ) /piːʃ/ pronounced as 'o' in .... تُند /tond/

---

*Vowel points aren't in written Persian unless in elementary level of primary school for teaching purposes.

ESPECIAL PHONETIC SYMBOLS

1. (a) This vowel is front and open in tongue height. The lips are spread. It pronunced as (æ) but stronger. (see Fig. 1 / Table 2,3)

2. (o) This vowel is back and half-close in tongue height. The lips are rounded. (see Fig. 1 / Table 2,3)

3. (vː) This is a back long vowel but not as back as (ɑː), and diagram shows that it is open tongue height. The lips are neutral. *(NOTE* This vowel resembles the vowel (ɑː) in English and in the case of difficulty in spelling, non-native speakers may use (ɑː) instead.) (see Fig. 1 / Table 2,3)

4. (ʔ) The vocal cords can be firmly pressed togeder so that air cannot pass between them. When this happens in speech we call it a *glottal stop* or *glottal plosive*, for which we used symbol(ʔ). You can practice this by coughing gently; then practice the sequence ʔaʔaʔaʔa... . (see table 3)

5. (G) This is a uvular consonant. It pronunced as (q) but voiced. It transliterated as (gh). (see table 3)

iː = II	uː = UU	vː = ΛΛ

Table 1, Synonymous sound patterns

8 Beginner's Persian

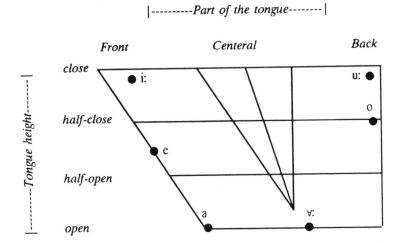

Fig. 1: Tongue position of Persian Vowels

	e	a	o	i:	u:	ɒ:	ow
short	✓	✓	✓	-	-	-	-
pure	✓	✓	✓	✓	✓	✓	-
close	-	-	-	✓	✓	-	-
open	-	✓	-	-	-	✓	-
front	✓	✓	-	✓	-	-	-
back	-	-	✓	-	✓	✓	✓
round	-	-	✓	-	✓	-	✓

Table 2: Analysis of Persian Vowel System

Place of articulation

Manner of articulation		Bilabial	Labiodental	Alveolar	Palato-alveolar	Palatal	Velar	Uvular	Glottal
		-	+	-	+	-	+	-	+	-	+	-	+	-	+
Plosive		p	b			t	d					k	g		ɢ	ʔ	
Nasal			m				n						ŋ				
Affricate								tʃ	dʒ								
Lateral		▓	▓	▓	▓		l										
Fricative				f	v	s	z	ʃ	ʒ		j	x				h	
Trill							r							▓	▓	▓	▓

Table 3: Persian Consonant Phonemes. Shaded areas denote articulations judged impossible.
- *voiceless*
+ *voiced*

Introduction

The aim of this guide book is to enable an English native or English-speaking reader to read and speak elementary Farsi within her / his trip to Iran (or even other Farsi-speaking countries). From among these readers are tourists, tradesmen, staff of foreign countries, scientific visitors and experts etc., who have to visit, stay or work for a period of time in Iran and need communicating with diverse ranks and classes of people.

In preparing the overall framework of the book, it has been considered to cover the essential categories of the social relations as well as meeting the necessity of supplying the basic needs. Thus, on the way to this objective, the categories are overlapped in some margins due to the nature of the matter.

To help the beginner to pronounce Farsi words as natural, a set of completely distinct phonetic symbols have been utilized, in addition to a brief description of the basic phonetic charecteristics of Farsi.

We have included a form for learning about your opinions on contents and overall layout of the book. Clearly discussion of these comments and suggestions will help the author to enrich the next edition and riverse the shortages.

PERSIAN PHONEMICS

To learn the basic linguistic characteristics rules, and to develope a consistent set of lingual elements of Farsi, the following comments could be helpful:

A. None of the words in Farsi has wovels as the first phonem, though it seems that in the words like «این» (this), «آن» (that), «او» (she/he), etc. the first phonem to be a vowel, one can recognize a consonant as a glottal stop *(hidden hamzeh)* preceding it. The symbol(ʔ)indicates the sounds of the mentioned hidden hamzeh in the forms of:
«آ ، اِی ، اُو ، اَ ، اِ ، اُ»

The same symbol has been used to carry the sound of "*appearant hamzeh*" «أ ، ؤ ، ء ، ئ» and (ʔajn) «ع ، ـع ، ـعـ ، عـ» which have Arabic origin and sound identically in Farsi. Note the function of hidden hamzeh, appearant hamzeh and (ʔajn) in Table 5

phonem	example	pronunciation	meaning
آ	آسمان	/ʔɒ:semʌn/	sky
ایـ، ای	ایشان	/ʔi:ʃʌn/	they
–	پارهای	/pɒ:reʔi:/	partial
او	او	/ʔu:/	she/he
اَ	اَبر	/ʔabr/	cloud
اُ	اُجاق	/ʔodʒɒ:ɢ/	fireplace
اِ	اِمروز	/ʔemru:z/	today
أ	مبدأ	/mabdaʔ/	origin
ﺄ	تأثیر	/taʔsi:r/	influence
ؤ	مسؤول	/masʔu:l/	responsible
ء	سوءظن	/su:ʔe zan/	suspicion
ئـ	قائم	/ɢɒ:ʔem/	vertical
عـ، ـعـ، ـع، ع	عالی	/ʔɒ:li:/	excellent
–	بعد	/baʔd/	then
–	مانع	/mɒ:neʔ/	obstacle
–	دفاع	/defɒ:ʔ/	defence

Table 5 *Examples of glottal stop usage*

B. The terminating «ـه» or «ه» sound both «h» and «e» depending on the word. There is no established rule for distinguishing them and one can discriminate the right sound through practice. The following examples indicate this difference in some cases:

«دَه»	/dah/	(ten)
«دِه»	/deh/	(village)
«خانه»	/xɑ:ne/	(house)
«شُده»	/ʃode/	(done)
«سایه»	/sɑ:je/	(shadow)

C. The long vowel (i:) never precede the consonant (j) in formal Farsi. For example:

«بسیار» /besıjɑ:r/   *not*   /besi:jɑ:r/ (many)
«سیاه» /sıjɑ:h/   *not*   /si:jɑ:h/ (black)

D. In Farsi phonemics a vowel cannot followed by another wovel. The basic phonemic sequence of Farsi is of CVC* type and also we can find the general form as:

CV(C(C))   (one-syllable)
CVC-CV(C(C))   (two-syllable)
... -CV(C)-CV(C)   (multi-syllable)

where the 'C's within parantheses may be ommited depending on the case. Note the following examples:

CV
ما   /mɑ:/   (we)   (1-syllable)

CVC
کار   /kɑ:r/   (work)   (1-syllable)

---

* *C=consonant, V=vowel*

CVCC
ابر   /ʔabr/   (cloud)   (1-syllable)

CV-CVC
روغن   /row-ɢan/   (oil)   (2-syllables)

CVC-CV-CV
کارخانه   /kɒ:r-xɒ:-ne/   (factory)   (3-syllables)

CV-CV-CV-VCV
کیمیاگر   /ki:-mɪ-jɒ:-gar/   (alchemist)   (4-syllables)

E. When a vowel is followed by a quiescenced *'n'*[*], the vowel decreases in lenght and the long vowels (ɒ:) , (i:) and (u:) reduces to be (ʌ) , (ɪ) and (ʊ) respectively.

نگران	/negarʌn/	not	/negarɒ:n/	(anxious)
زمین	/zamɪn/	not	/zami:n/	(earth)
صابون	/sɒ:bʊn/	not	/sɒ:bu:n/	(soap)

F. The only significant diphthong in Farsi is «ow» which mainly occures in the words with Arabic origin, however there are some original Farsi words with this diphthong like اورنگ/ʔowraŋ/

To illustrate this diphthong we can compare it with some vowels which seems could be substitued with «ow». Note the

---

[*] *Quiescened letter is a last consonant of a word without a vowel after it.*

difference between sounds in the following words:

دو	/do/	(two)
دو	/dow/	(running)
دوری	/du:ri:/	(remoteness)
دوری	/dowri:/	(dish)

Part Two

SECTION 1
INFORMAL TALKING

1-1 ORDINARY CONVERSATION
1-2 GREETINGS/FAREWELL
1-3 THANKS/CONGRATULATION
1-4 APOLOGIES
1-5 ASKING QUESTIONS
1-6 ANSWERS/OPINIONS
1-7 PHRASES
1-8 LANGUAGE

1-1
ORDINARY CONVERSATION

After you.	/be-far-mɑ:/	بفرما.
All right.	/be-sɪ-jɑ:r xu:b/	بسیار خوب.
All is yours.	/Gɑ:-be-li: na-dɑ:-rad/	قابلی ندارد.
Allow me.	/ʔe-dʒɑ:-ze be-de/	اجازه بده.
As you know ...	/ha-mʌn towr ke mi:-dɑ:-ni:/	همان طور که می‌دانی ...
As you wish.	/har towr mej-le to ʔast/	هر طور میل تو است.
Be careful!	/mo-vɑ:-zeb bɑ:ʃ!/	مواظب باش!
Believe you me.	/bɑ:-var kon/	باور کن.
Break a leg.	/mo-vaf-faG bɑ:-ʃi:/	موفّق باشی.
Bully for you.	/ʔɑ:-fa-rɪn/	آفرین.
Clear the way.	/be-ra-vi:d ken-ɑ:r/	بروید کنار.

Come again?	/tʃe gof-ti:/	چه گفتی؟
Come along.	/zu:d bɤ:ʃ/	زود باش.
Come here and sit by me.	/bɪ-jɤ: ʔɪn-dʒɤ: ke-nɤ:-ram be-ne-ʃɪn/	بیا اینجا کنارم بنشین.
Come around.	/ha-vv:-sat dʒamʔ bɤ:-ʃad/	حواست جمع باشد.
Come here.	/bɪ-jɤ: ʔɪn-dʒɤ:/	بیا اینجا.
Come in.	/bɪ-jɤ: tu:/	بیا تو.
Come near.	/bɪ-jɤ: naz-di:k/	بیا نزدیک.
Come what may.	/har tʃe bɤ:-dɤ: bɤ:d/	هر چه بادا باد.
Cool it.	/bi:-xɪ-jɤ:l/	بی‌خیال.
Dear me!	/xo-dɤ:-je man/	خدای من!
Do me a favor.	/lot-fi: be man be-kon/	لطفی به من بکن.
Do you need help?	/be ko-mak ʔeh-tɪ-jɤ:dʒ dɤ:-ri:/	به کمک احتیاج داری؟
Do your best.	/saʔ-jat rɤ: be-kon/	سعی‌ات را بکن.
Do say.	/har-fat rɤ: be-zan/	حرفت را بزن.
Do what you like.	/har tʃe du:st dɤ:-ri: be-kon/	هر چه دوست داری بکن.
Don't all speak together!	/ha-me bɤ: ham soh-bat na-ko-ni:d/	همه با هم صحبت نکنید!
Don't be angry.	/ʔa-sa-bɤ:-ni: na-ʃo/	عصبانی نشو.
Don't be funny.	/ʃu:-xi: na-kon/	شوخی نکن.
Don't be selfish.	/xod-xv:h na-bɤ:ʃ/	خودخواه نباش.
Don't care a pine.	/fek-raʃ rɤ: na-kon/	فکرش را نکن.
Don't forget to keep in touch.	/hat-man ta-mɤ:s be-gi:r/	حتماً تماس بگیر.
Don't loaf away your time.	/vaG-tat rɤ: ha-dar na-de/	وقتت را هدر نده.
Don't snap my head off.	/har-fam rɤ: Gatʔ na-kon/	حرفم را قطع نکن.
Don't sweat it.	/ne-ga-rʌn na-bɤ:ʃ/	نگران نباش.
Don't trouble yourself.	/be xo-dat zah-mat na-de/	به خودت زحمت نده.
Don't worry about it.	/ne-ga-rɤ:-ne ʔʌn na-bɤ:ʃ/	نگران آن نباش.

Informal Talking

Easy does it.	/bɒ: deɢ-ɢat ʔa-mal kon/	با دقّت عمل کن.
Enjoy!	/xoʃ bɒ:ʃ!/	خوش باش!
Everybody knows it.	/ha-me ʔʌn rɒ: mi:-dɒ:-nand/	همه آن را می‌دانند.
Everyhting is ready.	/ha-me tʃi:z ʔɒ:-mɒ:-de ʔast/	همه چیز آماده است.
Excellent!	/ʔɒ:-li: ʔast!/	عالی است!
Fancy that!	/fek-raʃ rɒ: be-kon!/	فکرش را بکن!
Far from it!	/ʔɪn-towr ni:st!/	اینطور نیست!
Fine, and you?	/xu:-bam to tʃe-tow-ri:/	خوبم، تو چطوری؟
Follow me.	/don-bɒ:-lam bɪ-jɒ:/	دنبالم بیا.
For all I care!	/ʔa-ham-mɪj-ja-ti: ne-mi:-da-ham/	اهمیّتی نمی‌دهم!
For all I know...	/tɒ: dʒɒ:-ʔi: ke mi:-dɒ:-nam/	تا جایی که می‌دانم...
Forget about it.	/fa-rɒ:-mu:-ʃaʃ kon/	فراموشش کن.
Forgot it!	/ʔa-ham-mɪj-ja-ti: na-dɒ:-rad/	اهمیّتی ندارد!
Gangway!	/ʔaz sa-re rɒ:h ke-nɒ:r bo-ro/	از سر راه کنار برو!
Get a hold on that.	/be-gi:-reʃ/	بگیرش!
Get a life!	/dʒed-di: bɒ:ʃ/	جدّی باش!
Get the message?	/mi:-fah-mi:/	می‌فهمی؟
Get a picture!	/he-sɒ:-be ha-me tʃi:z rɒ: be-kon/	حساب همه چیز را بکن!
Getting bored?	/xas-te ʃo-de-ʔi:/	خسته شده‌ای؟
Give it a try.	/saʔj kon/	سعی کن.
Give it to me.	/ʔʌn rɒ: be man be-de/	آن را به من بده.
Give me a chair.	/jek san-da-li: be man be-de/	یک صندلی به من بده.
Give me a rest!	/rɒ:-ha-tam be-go-zɒ:r/	راحتم بگذار!
Go ahead.	/ʔe-dɒ:-me be-de/	ادامه بده.
Go along with you.	/beʃ-no ʔo bɒ:-var na-kon/	بشنو و باور نکن.
Go and see.	/bo-ro be-bɪn/	برو ببین.
Good God!	/ʔej xo-dɒ:/	ای خدا!
Good heavens!	/xo-dɒ:-je man!/	خدای من!
Have a seat.	/be-far-mɒ:-ʔi:d ben-ʃi:-ni:d/	بفرمایید بنشینید.
Her/His voice has a pleasant tone.	/sa-dɒ:-jaʃ lah-ne xo-ʃɒ:-jan-di: dɒ:-rad/	صدایش لحن خوشایندی دارد.

24 Beginner's Persian

Her/His work was impressive.	/kɒ:-raʃ xej-li: gi:-rɒ: bu:d/	کارش خیلی گیرا بود.
Here's to you!	/be sa-lɒ:-ma-tɪ-je ʃo-mɒ:/	به سلامتی شما!
Hey! listen to me!	/hej be man gu:ʃ be-de/	هی! به من گوش بده!
Hold it!	/sabr kon/	صبر کن!
Hold everything!	/dast ne-gah-dɒ:r/	دست نگهدار!
Hold still!	/ha-re-kat na-kon/	حرکت نکن!
Hop to it!	/be-dʒomb/	بجنب!
How is your father?	/hɒ:-le pe-da-rat tʃe-towr ʔast/	حال پدرت چطور است؟
How nice!	/tʃe xu:b/	چه خوب!
How unpleasant!	/tʃe bad/	چه بد!
Hurry up!	/ʔa-dʒa-le kon/	عجله کن!
I agree with you.	/bɒ: ʃo-mɒ: mo-vɒ:-fe-ɢam/	با شما موافقم.
I'm always ready to help.	/man ha-mi:-ʃe ʔɒ:-mɒ:-de-je ko-mak has-tam/	من همیشه آمادهٔ کمک هستم.
I'm as tired as all get out.	/xej-li: xas-te-ʔam/	خیلی خسته‌ام.
I'm at home.	/dar xɒ:-ne has-tam/	در خانه هستم.
I'm bored.	/how-se-le-ʔam sar raft/	حوصله‌ام سر رفت.
I'm crazy about it.	/man ʔɒ:-ʃe-ɢaʃ has-tam/	من عاشقش هستم.
I'm deeply grieved.	/ʔa-mi:-ɢan mo-ta-ʔas-se-fam/	عمیقاً متأسّفم.
I'm easy.	/rɒ:-ha-tam/	راحتم.
I'm happy.	/xoʃ-hɒ:-lam/	خوشحالم.
I'm in a hurry.	/ʔa-dʒa-le dɒ:-ram/	عجله دارم.
I'm in two mind about it.	/do-del has-tam/	دودل هستم.
I'm not kidding!	/ʃu:-xi: ne-mi:-ko-nam/	شوخی نمی‌کنم!
I'm not quite sure.	/kɒ:-me-lan mot-ma-ʔen ni:s-tam/	کاملاً مطمئن نیستم.
I'm not speaking with you.	/bɒ: ʃo-mɒ: ni:s-tam/	با شما نیستم.
I'm ready.	/hɒ:-ze-ram/	حاضرم.
I'm really not in the mood.	/ʔas-lan how-se-le na-dɒ:-ram/	اصلاً حوصله ندارم.
I'm tired.	/xas-te-ʔam/	خسته‌ام.

Informal Talking

I'm too busy. .... /sa-ram xej-li: ʃuː-luːG ʔast/ سرم خیلی شلوغ است.
I'm very glad of it. .... /ʔaz bvː-ba-te ʔʌn xej-li: xoʃ-hvː-lam/
از بابت آن خیلی خوشحالم.
I ask you. .... /ʔaz ʃo-mvː miː-por-sam/ از شما می‌پرسم.
I begged her not to go. .... /ʔes-rvːr kar-dam ke na-ra-vad/
اصرار کردم که نرود.
I come to tell you. .... /ʔvː-ma-dam be ʃo-mvː be-guː-jam/
آمدم به شما بگویم.
I could use a hand. .... /miː-ta-vvː-nam ko-ma-kat ko-nam/
می‌توانم کمکت کنم.
I did it in a hurry. .... /ʔʌn rvː bvː ʔa-dʒa-le ʔan-dʒvːm dvː-dam/
آن را با عجله انجام دادم.
I didn't catch what you said. ..... /man-zuː-rat rvː ne-miː-fah-mam/
منظورت را نمی‌فهمم.
I didn't do it. .... /man na-kar-de-ʔam/ من نکردم.
I didn't know it. .../man ʔʌn rvː ne-miː-dvː-nes-tam/ من آن را نمی‌دانستم.
I didn't mean it. ..../man-zuː-ram ʔʌn na-buːd/ منظورم آن نبود.
I didn't mean to hurt you. ....
.../ne-miː-xvːs-tam ʃo-mvː rvː be-ran-dʒvː-nam/ نمی‌خواستم شما را برنجانم.
I didn't understand anything. .... /tʃiː-zi: na-fah-miː-dam/
چیزی نفهمیدم.
I don't believe this. .... /bvː-var ne-miː-ko-nam/ باور نمی‌کنم.
I don't get you. /man-zuː-rat rvː ne-miː-fah-mam/ منظورت را نمی‌فهمم.
I don't know. .... /ne-miː-dvː-nam/ نمی‌دانم.
I don't know how to say it in Farsi. ....
/ne-miː-dvː-nam tʃe-towr be fvːr-si: be-guː-jam/ نمی‌دانم چطور به فارسی بگویم.
I don't mean that. .... /man-zuː-ram ʔɪn niːst/ منظورم این نیست.
I enjoy my job. .... /man ʔaz kvː-ram laz-zat miː-ba-ram/
من از کارم لذّت می‌برم.
I gather. .... /ʔɪn towr xɪ-jvːl miː-ko-nam/ این طور خیال می‌کنم.
I got angry with him. .... /ʔaz das-taʃ ʔa-sa-bvː-ni: ʃo-dam/
از دستش عصبانی شدم.

I guess.	/hæds mi:-zæ-næm/	حدس می‌زنم.
I've done a silly thing.	/kɒ:-re ʔæh-mæ-ɢɒ:-ne-ʔi: kær-dæm/	کار احمقانه‌ای کردم.
I've wasted your time.	/mo-zɒ:-he-me vɑɢ-te-tʌn ʃo-dæm/	مزاحم وقتتان شدم.
I hear you!.	/mi:-dɒ:-næm tʃe mi:-xɒ:-hi: be-gu:-ji:/	می‌دانم چه می‌خواهی بگویی!
I hope it works.	/ʔo-mi:d-vɒ:-ræm mo-fi:d vɒ:-ɢeʔ ʃa-væd/	امیدوارم مفید واقع شود.
I hope so.	/mæn hæm ʔo-mi:d-vɒ:-ræm/	من هم امیدوارم.
I like you.	/ʔæz to xo-ʃæm mi:-ʔɒ:-jæd/	از تو خوشم می‌آید.
I lost mine.	/mɒ:-le xo-dæm rɒ: gom kær-dæm/	مال خودم را گم کردم.
I love you.	/du:-set dɒ:-ræm/	دوست دارم.
I met him/her by chance.	/ʔu: rɒ: ʔet-te-fɒ:-ɢi: di:-dæm/	او را اتّفاقی دیدم.
I need some practice.	/be kæ-mi: tæm-rɪn nɪ-jɒ:z dɒ:-ræm/	به کمی تمرین نیاز دارم.
I never mind.	/ʔæ-hæm-mɪj-jæ-ti: ne-mi:-dæ-hæm/	اهمّیّتی نمی‌دهم.
I remember it.	/be xɒ:-ter mi:-ʔɒ:-væ-ræm/	به خاطر می‌آورم.
I thank you.	/mo-tæ-ʃæk-ke-ræm/	متشکّرم.
I understand you.	/dær-ke-tʌn mi:-ko-næm/	درکتان می‌کنم.
I usually bath at night.	/mæʔ-mu:-læn ʃæb hæm-mɒ:m mi:-ko-næm/	معمولاً شب حمّام می‌کنم.
I was about to say...	/mi:-xɒ:s-tæm be-gu:-jæm/	می‌خواستم بگویم...
I wish I could.	/kɒ:ʃ-ki: mi:-tæ-vɒ:-nes-tæm/	کاشکی می‌توانستم.
I'd like to introduce a friend of mine.	/mɒ:-je-læm je-ki: ʔæz du:s-tɒ:-næm rɒ: mo-ʔær-re-fi: ko-næm/	مایلم یکی از دوستانم را معرّفی کنم.
If only she would come!	/kɒ:ʃ mi:-ʔɒ:-mæd/	کاش می‌آمد!
It's a pleasure.	/lotf dɒ:-ri:d/	لطف دارید.
It ain' no good no how.	/be hær hɒ:l xu:b ni:st/	به هرحال خوب نیست.

Informal Talking

It's about time.	/di:r ʃo-de/	دیر شده!
It's all over.	/be kol-li: ta-mʌ:m ʃod/	به کلّی تمام شد.
It's all the same to me.	/ba-rʌ:-jam far-Gi: na-dʌ:-rad/	برایم فرقی ندارد.
It's just what I wanted.	/do-rost ha-mʌn tʃi:-zi: ʔast ke mi:-xʌ:s-tam/	درست همان چیزی است که می‌خواستم.
It's no matter.	/ʔa-ham-mɪj-ja-ti: na-dʌ:-rad/	اهمّیّتی ندارد.
It's possible.	/mom-ken ʔast/	ممکن است.
It's true.	/ha-Gi:-Gat dʌ:-rad/	حقیقت دارد.
It's unknown to me.	/sar dar ne-mi:-ʔʌ:-va-ram/	سر در نمی‌آورم.
It's very sad.	/xej-li: Gam-gɪn ʔast/	خیلی غمگین است.
It must be there.	/bʌ:-jad ʔʌn-dʒʌ: bʌ:-ʃad/	باید آنجا باشد.
It was a pleasure to have you.	/ʔaz ho-zu:-re-tʌn laz-zat bor-di:m/	از حضورتان لذّت بردیم.
It was not my fault.	/taG-si:-re man na-bu:d/	تقصیر من نبود.
Just a minute.	/jek da-Gi:-Ge sabr ko-ni:d/	یک دقیقه صبر کنید.
Just tell me, what you'd like me to do.	/be-gu: be-bi:-nam hʌ:-lʌ: mi:-xʌ:-hi: tʃe kʌ:r ko-nam/	بگو ببینم، حالا می‌خواهی چه کار کنم؟
Keep talking!	/ʔe-dʌ:-me be-de/	ادامه بده!
Lend me.	/be man Garz be-de/	به من قرض بده.
Let me help you.	/ʔe-dʒʌ:-ze be-de ko-ma-kat ko-nam/	اجازه بده کمکت کنم.
Let me introduce myself.	/ʔe-dʒʌ:-ze da-hi:d xo-dam rʌ: mo-ʔar-re-fi: ko-nam/	اجازه دهید خودم را معرّفی کنم.
Let me introduce you to Mr... .	/ʔe-dʒʌ:-ze da-hi:d ʃo-mʌ: rʌ: be ʔʌ:-Gʌ:-je ... mo-ʔar-re-fi: ko-nam/	اجازه دهید شما را به آقای ... معرّفی کنم.
Let me tell you.	/ʔe-dʒʌ:-ze da-hi:d be-gu:-jam/	اجازه دهید بگویم.
Let us see.	/bɪ-jʌ:-ji:d be-bi:-ni:m/	بیایید ببینیم.

28 Beginner's Persian

Let us start.	/bɪ-jvː-jiːd ʃo-ruːʔ ko-niːm/	بیایید شروع کنیم.
Let's go!	/be-ra-viːm/	برویم!
Listen, please.	/lot-fan guːʃ ko-niːd/	لطفاً گوش کنید.
Listen to me.	/be man guːʃ kon/	به من گوش کن.
Look alive!	/zuːd bvːʃ/	زود باش!
Look at it.	/be ʔʌn ne-gvːh kon/	به آن نگاه کن.
Look here!	/ha-vvːs-sat ʔɪn-dʒvː bvː-ʃad/	حواسّت اینجا باشد!
Lots of Luck!	/mo-vaf-faG bvː-ʃiː/	موفّق باشی!
Make it snappy!	/ʔa-dʒa-le kon/	عجله کن!
Make no mistake!	/ʔeʃ-te-bvːh na-kon/	اشتباه نکن!
Make up your mind.	/tas-miː-me xo-dat rvː be-giːr/	تصمیم خودت را بگیر.
Never fear!	/ne-ga-rʌn na-bvːʃ/	نگران نباش!
Never mind!	/biː-xɪ-jvːl/	بی‌خیال!
No lady.	/na-xejr xvː-nom/	نخیر خانم.
No fair!	/mon-se-fvː-ne niːst/	منصفانه نیست!
No way!	/be hiːtʃ vadʒh/	به هیچ وجه!
None of your business.	/be ʃo-mvː mar-buːt niːst/	به شما مربوط نیست.
Not at all.	/ʔa-ba-dan/	ابداً.
Not exactly.	/na daGiː-Gan/	نه دقیقاً.
Not to worry!	/ne-ga-rʌn na-bvːʃ/	نگران نباش!
Nothing doing.	/xa-ba-riː niːst/	خبری نیست.
Nothing to it!	/ʔɪn-ke tʃiː-zi niːst/	اینکه چیزی نیست!
Now you're talking!	/ʔɪn ʃod har-fe he-svːb/	این شد حرف حساب!
Open the door.	/dar rvː bvːz kon/	در را باز کن.
Pardon.	/be-bax-ʃiːd/	ببخشید.
Part it in two.	/nes-faʃ kon/	نصفش کن.
Please!	/xvː-heʃ miː-ko-nam/	خواهش می‌کنم!
Please correct my mistakes. /lot-fan ʔeʃ-te-bvː-hvː-tam rvː tas-hiːh koniːd/		لطفاً اشتباهاتم را تصحیح کنید.
Please explain.	/lot-fan tow-ziːh be-de/	لطفاً توضیح بده.
Please give.	/lot-fan be-de/	لطفاً بده.

Informal Talking

Please repeat.	/lot-fan tek-rɑ:r kon/	لطفاً تکرار کن.
Please show.	/lot-fan ne-ʃɑn be-de/	لطفاً نشان بده.
Please speak more slowly.	/lot-fan ʔɑ:-rɑ:m-tar soh-bat kon/	لطفاً آرامتر صحبت کن.
Please translate.	/lot-fan tar-dʒo-me kon/	لطفاً ترجمه کن.
Please write it down.	/lot-fan ʔɑn rɑ: be-ne-vi:s/	لطفاً آن را بنویس.
Press it down.	/fe-ʃɑ:r be-de/	فشار بده.
Pull the door.	/dar rɑ: be-ke-ʃi:d/	در را بکشید.
Push the door.	/dar rɑ: fe-ʃɑ:r be-da-hi:d/	در را فشار بدهید.
Put yourself in my place.	/xo-dat rɑ: dʒɑ:-je man be-go-zɑ:r/	خودت را جای من بگذار.
Really!	/vɑ:Ge-ʔan/	واقعاً!
Rest yourself.	/xas-te-gɪ-jat rɑ: dar kon/	خستگی‌ات را در کن.
Same here!	/man ham mo-vɑ:-fe-Gam/	من هم موافقم!
She/He just came in.	/ha-mɪn hɑ:-lɑ: vɑ:-red ʃod/	همین حالا وارد شد.
She/He is awfully clever.	/xej-li: ze-raŋ ʔast/	خیلی زرنگ است.
She/He is busy now.	/ʔal-ʔɑn kɑ:r dɑ:-rad/	الان کار دارد.
She/He is done for.	/kɑ:-raʃ zɑ:r ʔast/	کارش زار است.
She/He is made me do it.	/ʔu: madʒ-bu:-ram kard/	او مجبورم کرد.
She/He is my friend.	/du:s-te man ʔast/	دوست من است.
She/He is very tactful.	/ʔu: xej-li: bɑ:-hu:ʃ ʔast/	او خیلی باهوش است.
She/He is very truthful.	/ʔu: xej-li: sɑ:-deG ʔast/	او خیلی صادق است.
She/He is waiting for you.	/mon-ta-ze-re ʃo-mɑ:st/	منتظر شماست.
She/He never lies.	/ʔu: har-gez do-ru:G ne-mi:-gu:-jad/	او هرگز دروغ نمی‌گوید.
Shucks!	/Ga-sam mi:-xo-ram/	قسم می‌خورم!
Shut the window.	/pan-dʒa-re rɑ: be-band/	پنجره را ببند.
Sit down.	/ben-ʃin/	بنشین.
Skip it!	/fa-rɑ:-mu:-ʃaʃ kon/	فراموشش کن!
Snap to it!	/ʔa-dʒa-le kon/	عجله کن!
Stay a little.	/ka-mi: sa-br kon/	کمی صبر کن.
Take care!	/mo-vɑ:-ze-be xo-dat bɑ:ʃ/	مواظب خودت باش!

30 Beginner's Persian

Take it with yourself.	/bʌ: xo-dat be-bar/	با خودت ببر.
Tell me.	/be man be-gu:/	به من بگو.
That belongs to me.	/ʔʌn mʌ:-le man ʔast/	آن مال من است.
That is	/ʔʌn ... ʔast/	آن ... است.
That's bad.	/ʔʌn bad ʔast/	آن بد است.
That's good.	/ʔʌn xu:b ʔast/	آن خوب است.
That's incredible!	/bʌ:-var na-kar-da-ni: ʔast/	باور نکردنی است!
That's just like you.	/do-rost mes-le ʃo-mʌ:st/	درست مثل شماست.
That's of no consequence.	/hi:tʃ na-ti:-dʒe-ʔi: na-dʌ:-rad/	هیچ نتیجه‌ای ندارد.
That's quite of the question.	/ʔas-lan har-faʃ rʌ: na-zan/	اصلاً حرفش را نزن.
That's too heavy.	/xej-li: san-gɪn ʔast/	خیلی سنگین است.
That's too much.	/xej-li: zɪ-jʌ:d ʔast/	خیلی زیاد است.
That's very cheap.	/xej-li: ʔar-zʌn ʔast/	خیلی ارزان است.
That's very expensive.	/xej-li: ge-rʌn ʔast/	خیلی گران است.
That's very well.	/xej-li: xu:b ʔast/	خیلی خوب است.
That sounds good.	/be na-zar xu:b mi:-re-sad/	به نظر خوب می‌رسد.
This is... .	/ʔɪn ... ʔast/	این ... است.
This is mine.	/ʔɪn mʌ:-le man ʔast/	این مال من است.
This gentleman is my friend.	/ʔɪn ʔʌ:-Gʌ: ra-fi:-Ge man ʔast/	این آقا رفیق من است.
This is excellent work.	/ʔɪn kʌ:r ʔʌ:-li: ʔast/	این کار عالی است.
This is my girl friend.	/ʔɪn du:st dox-ta-re man ʔast/	این دوست دختر من است.
This is not mine.	/ʔɪn mʌ:-le man ni:st/	این مال من نیست.
This is yours.	/ʔɪn mʌ:-le ʃo-mʌ:st/	این مال شماست.
This work is full of errors.	/ʔɪn kʌ:r sar tʌ: pʌ: ʔeʃ-te-bʌ:h ʔast/	این کار سرتا پا اشتباه است.
Time drags on.	/za-mʌn kond mi:-go-za-rad/	زمان کند می‌گذرد.
Use your head!	/fek-rat rʌ: be kʌ:r be-jan-dʌ:z/	فکرت را به کار بینداز!
Wait a bit.	/ka-mi: sabr kon/	کمی صبر کن.

Informal Talking

Wait a minute.	/jek da-Gi:-Ge sabr kon/	یک دقیقه صبر کن.
We are friends.	/mv: du:st has-ti:m/	ما دوست هستیم.
We'll see.	/xv:-hi:m di:d/	خواهیم دید.
Well done!	/ʔv:-fa-rɪn/	آفرین!
What a lousy day I've had.	/ʔa-dʒab ru:-ze ba-di: dv:ʃ-tam/	عجب روز بدی داشتم.
What a srudgery!	/tʃe kv:-re ke-sel ko-nan-de-ʔi:/	چه کار کسل کننده‌ای!
What a pity!	/hejf ʃod/	حیف شد!
What about you?	/to tʃe-towr/	تو چطور؟
What's done is done.	/go-zaʃ-te-hv: go-zaʃ-te/	گذشته‌ها گذشته.
Watch it!	/mo-vv:-zeb bv:ʃ/	مواظب باش!
Yes, please.	/ba-le lot-fan/	بله، لطفاً.
Yes sir/ma'am.	/ba-le ʔv:-Gv: (xv:-nom)/	بله آقا (خانم).
You're all abroad.	/kv-me-lan ʔaz mar-ha-le par-ti:/	کاملاً از مرحله پرتی.
You're all wet!	/kv:-me-lan ʔeʃ-te-bv:h mi:-ko-ni:/	کاملاً اشتباه می‌کنی!
You're joking!	/ʃu:-xi: mi:-ko-ni:/	شوخی می‌کنی!
You're right.	/haGG bv: ʃo-mv:st/	حقّ با شماست.
You're very kind.	/ʃo-mv: xej-li: meh-ra-bv:-ni:d/	شما خیلی مهربانید.
You're wrong.	/ʔeʃ-te-bv:h mi:-ko-ni:/	اشتباه می‌کنی.
You can say that again.	/haGG bv: ʃo-mv:st/	حقّ با شماست.
You're a nerve.	/xej-li: ru: dv:-ri:/	خیلی رو داری.
You hear?	/hv:-li:t ʃod/	حالیت شد؟
You must know it.	/bv:-jad ʔɪn rv: be-dv:-ni:/	باید این را بدانی.
You said it!	/do-rost ʔast/	درست است!

1-2
GREETING FAREWELL

All the best.	/beh-ta-rın ʔvː-re-zuː-hvː/	بهترین آرزوها.
Come and see me sometime.	/gvː-hi: be man sar be-zan/	گاهی به من سر بزن.
Don't forget me!	/fa-rvː-muː-ʃam na-kon/	فراموشم نکن!
Don't go away.	/na-ro/	نرو.
Excuse me being late.	/be-baxʃ ke diːr kar-dam/	ببخش که دیر کردم.
Glad to meet you.	/ʔaz mo-lvː-Gvː-te ʃo-mvː xoʃ-vaG-tam/	از ملاقات شما خوش وقتم.
Give him/her my regards.	/sa-lvː-me ma-rvː be ʔuː be-ra-sʌn/	سلام مرا به او برسان.
Good bye.	/xo-dvː-hvː-fez/	خداحافظ.

Good luck!	/mo-vaf-faɢ bɑ:-ʃi:/	!موفق باشی
Good evening.	/ʔasr be-xejr/	عصر بخیر.
Good night.	/ʃab be-xejr/	شب بخیر.
Good noon.	/zohr be-xejr/	ظهر بخیر.
Good morning.	/sobh be-xejr/	صبح بخیر.
Have a good day.	/ru:z xoʃ/	روز خوش.
Have a good trip.	/sa-far be xejr/	سفر به خیر.
Hello/Hi.	/sa-lɑ:m/	سلام.
How are things?	/ʔow-zɑ:ʔ tʃe-towr ʔast/	اوضاع چطور است؟
I've got to go now.	/man dɑ:-ram mi:-ra-vam/	من دارم می‌روم.
It's a pity that I've to go.		
/ʔaz ʔɪn-ke bɑ:-jad be-ra-vam mo-ta-ʔas-se-fam/		متأسّفم، از اینکه باید بروم.
It's too bad that you've to go.	/xej-li: bad ʃod dɑ:-ri:d mi:-ra-vi:d/	
		خیلی بد شد دارید می‌روید.
Nice to see you.	/ʔaz di:-da-nat xoʃ-hɑ:-lam/	از دیدنت خوشحالم.
Pleasant journey!	/sa-far be-xejr/	سفر بخیر.
See you later.	/baʔd mi:-bi:-na-met/	بعد می‌بینمت.
See you tomorrow.	/far-dɑ: mi:-bi:-na-met/	فردا می‌بینمت.
Shall we go?	/be-ra-vi:m/	برویم؟
So long!	/xo-dɑ:-hɑ:-fez/	خداحافظ!
So soon?	/be ʔɪn zu:-di:/	به این زودی؟
What already?	/be ha-mɪn zu:-di:/	به همین زودی؟
When are you off?	/kej rɑ:h mi:-ʔof-ti:/	کی راه می‌افتی؟
We'll meet again.	/do-bɑ:-re ham-di:-gar rɑ: xɑ:-hi:m di:d/	
		دوباره همدیگر را خواهیم دید.
You're welcome.	/xoʃ ʔɑ:-ma-di:d/	خوش آمدید.

1-3
THANKS
CONGRATULATION

Don't mention it. .... /ɢɒ:-bel na-dɒ:-rad/ قابل ندارد.
I can't thank you enough for it. ....
.........../har ɢadr ta-ʃak-kor ko-nam kam ʔast/. هر قدر تشکّر کنم کم است
I congratulate you. .... /tab-ri:k mi:-gu:-jam/. تبریک می‌گویم
I wish you a happy new year. /sɒ:-le now mo-bɒ:-rak/. سال نو مبارک
I wish you joy. /ʔo-mi:d-vɒ:-ram xoʃ be-go-za-rad/. امیدوارم خوش بگذرد
It is very kind of you. .... /xej-li: lotf dɒ:-ri:d/. خیلی لطف دارید
Merry new year's day. ..../now-ru:z mo-bɒ:-rak/. نوروز مبارک
No, thank you. .... /na mo-ta-ʃak-ke-ram/. نه متشکّرم
Thank you. ..../mo-ta-ʃak-ke-ram/. متشکّرم

Thank you all the same. ..../ʔaz har la-hɒ:z se-pɒ:s-go-zɒ:-ram/
از هر لحاظ سپاسگزارم.
Thank you for your attention. ....
...................../ʔaz ta-vadʒ-dʒo-he-tʌn mo-ta-ʃak-ke-ram/ .از توجّهتان متشکّرم
Thank you for your invitation. ....
...................../ʔaz daʔ-va-te-tʌn mo-ta-ʃak-ke-ram/ .از دعوتتان متشکّرم
Thank you for your present. ....
...................../ʔaz ha-dɪ-je-tʌn mo-ta-ʃak-ke-ram/ .از هدیهتان متشکّرم
Thank you for your letter. ....
...................../ʔaz nɒ:-me-tʌn mo-ta-ʃak-ke-ram/ .از نامهتان متشکّرم
You are very kind. ....
...................../xej-li: mo-hab-bat dɒ:-ri:d/ .خیلی محبّت دارید

1-4
APOLOGIES

Excuse me. .... /be-bax-ʃiːd/ .ببخشید
I'm afraid it's broken. .... /mo-ta-ʔas-se-fam ke ʃe-kast/
.متأسّفم که شکست
I'm sorry. .... /mo-ta-ʔas-se-fam/ .متأسّفم
I'm sorry about what happend. ....
.... /dar mo-re-de ʔet-tefː-Gi: ke ʔof-tːd mo-ta-ʔas-se-fam/
.در مورد اتّفاقی که افتاد، متأسّفم
I beg your pardon. .... /be-bax-ʃiːd/ .ببخشید
I'll never do it again. .... /diː-gar tek-rːr ne-miː-ʃa-vad/
.دیگر تکرار نمی‌شود
Sorry. .... /mo-ta-ʔas-se-fam/ .متأسّفم

1-5
ASKING QUESTIONS

Are you?	/dʒed-di:/	جدّی؟
Are you sure?	/mot-ma-ʔen-ni:d/	مطمئنید؟
Could you?	/mi:-ta-vv:-ni:/	می‌توانی؟

Could you help me, please?
................../lot-fan mom-ken ʔast be man ko-mak ko-ni:d/
لطفاً ممکن است به من کمک کنید؟

Does anyone here speak English?
...../ʔın-dʒv: ka-si: hast ke be-ta-vv:-nad ʔeŋ-ge-li:-si: soh-bat ko-nad/
اینجا کسی هست که بتواند انگلیسی صحبت کند؟

Do you hear me?   /se-dv:-je ma-rv: mi:-ʃe-na-vi:/ صدای مرا می‌شنوی؟
Do you know? .... /mi:-dv:-ni:/ می‌دانی؟

Do you know Mr...?	/ʔɑː-ɢɑː-je ... rɑː miː-ʃe-nɑː-siː/	آقای ... را می‌شناسی؟
Do you like art?	/be ho-nar ʔa-lɑː-ɢe dɑː-riː/	به هنر علاقه داری؟
Do you need help?	/ko-mak miː-xɑː-hiː/	کمک می‌خواهی؟
Do you mean that ...?	/man-zuː-rat ʔɪn ʔast ke .../	منظورت این است که ...؟
Do you understand?	/miː-fah-miː/	می‌فهمی؟
Don't you want any?	/tʃiː-ziː ne-miː-xɑː-hiː/	چیزی نمی‌خواهی؟
How?	/tʃe-towr/	چطور؟
How about this one?	/ʔɪn je-kiː tʃe-towr ʔst/	این یکی چطور است؟
How did you find out?	/tʃe-towr fah-miː-diː/	چطور فهمیدی؟
How did you sleep last night?	/diː-ʃab tʃe-towr xɑː-biː-diː/	دیشب چطور خوابیدی؟
How do you open this box?	/ʔɪn dʒaʔ-be rɑː tʃe-towr bɑːz miː-ko-niː/	این جعبه را چطور باز می‌کنی؟
How far?	/dar tʃe fɑː-se-le-ʔiː/	در چه فاصله‌ای؟
How many?	/tʃand tɑː/	چند تا؟
How much?	/tʃe-ɢadr/	چقدر؟
How much does it cost?	/ɢej-ma-taʃ tʃe-ɢadr ʔast/	قیمتش چقدر است؟
Is it correct?	/do-rost ʔast/	درست است؟
Is it true?	/ha-ɢiː-ɢat dɑː-rad/	حقیقت دارد؟
Is Mr ... at home?	/ʔɑː-ɢɑː-je ... xɑː-ne has-tand/	آقای ... خانه هستند؟
May I ask your name?	/mom-ken ʔast ʔes-me-tɑn rɑː be-por-sam/	ممکن است اسمتان را بپرسم؟
Untile when?	/tɑː kej/	تا کی؟
What?	/tʃe/	چه؟
What about?	/rɑː-dʒeʔ be tʃe/	راجع به چه؟
What already?	/tʃe-rɑː be ʔɪn zuː-diː/	چرا به این زودی؟
What are you thinking about?	/be tʃe fekr miː-ko-niː/	به چه فکر می‌کنی؟
What are you waiting for?	/maʔ-ta-le tʃe has-tiː/	معطل چه هستی؟

Informal Talking

What did you ask?	/tʃe por-siː-diː/	چه پرسیدی؟
What did you say?	/tʃe gof-tiː/	چه گفتی؟
What difference does it make?	/tʃe far-Gi miː-ko-nad/	چه فرقی می‌کند؟
What do you call this?	/be ʔɪn tʃe miː-guː-jiːd/	به این چه می‌گویید؟
What do you mean?	/man-zuː-re-tʌn tʃiːst/	منظورتان چیست؟
What do you say?	/tʃe miː-guː-jiː/	چه می‌گویی؟
What do you think of him/her?	/na-za-rat dar-bʌː-re-je ʔuː tʃiːst/	نظرت دربارهٔ او چیست؟
What does it signify?	/ʔɪn ne-ʃʌːn-ga-re tʃiːst/	این نشانگر چیست؟
What else is new?	/tʌː-ze tʃe xa-bar/	تازه چه خبر؟
What for?	/ba-rʌː-je tʃe/	برای چه؟
What goes by?	/tʃe xa-bar ʔast/	چه خبراست؟
What's eating you?	/moʃ-ke-lat tʃiːst/	مشکلت چیست؟
What's that good for?	/ʔɪn ba-rʌː-je tʃe xuːb ʔast/	این برای چه خوب است؟
What's the difference?	/far-Ge-ʃʌn tʃiːst/	فرقشان چیست؟
What's the matter?	/mow-zuːʔ tʃiːst/	موضوع چیست؟
What's the word for "pen" in your language?	/dar za-bʌː-ne ʃo-mʌː be pen tʃe miː-guː-jand/	در زبان شما به "pen" چه می‌گویند؟
What's this?	/ʔɪn tʃiːst/	این چیست؟
What's to be done?	/tʃe kʌːr bʌː-jad kard/	چه کار باید کرد؟
What's up?	/tʃe ʃo-de/	چه شده؟
What is your decision after all?	/be-la-xa-re tas-miː-me-tʌn tʃiːst/	بالاخره تصمیمتان چیست؟
What's your idea?	/na-za-re ʃo-mʌː tʃiːst/	نظر شما چیست؟
What's your occupation?	/ʃoG-le ʃo-mʌː tʃiːst/	شغل شما چیست؟
What's your use?	/ras-me ʃo-mʌː tʃiːst/	رسم شما چیست؟
What news?	/tʃe xa-bar/	چه خبر؟
What now?	/hʌː-lʌː tʃe kʌːr ko-niːm/	حالا چه کار کنیم؟

What of it?	/xu:b ke tʃi:/	خوب که چی؟
What say?	/tʃe gof-ti:/	چه گفتی؟
What shall we do?	/tʃe bɒ:-jad kard/	چه باید کرد؟
What would you like to do?	/du:st dɒ:-ri: tʃe kɒ:r ko-ni:/	دوست داری چه کار کنی؟
Where?	/ko-dʒɒ:/	کجا؟
Where did he/she go?	/ʔu: ko-dʒɒ: raft/	او کجا رفت؟
Where has he/she gone?	/ko-dʒɒ: raf-te ʔast/	کجا رفته است؟
Where were you exactly?	/da-Gi:-Gan ko-dʒɒ: bu:-di:/	دقیقاً کجا بودی؟
Which?	/ko-dɒ:m/	کدام؟
Which one?	/ko-dɒ:m jek/	کدام یک؟
Which one do you prefer?	/ko-dɒ:m jek rɒ: tar-dʒi:h mi:-da-hi:d/	کدام یک را ترجیح می‌دهید؟
Which way?	/ʔaz tʃe rɒ:-hi:/	از چه راهی؟
Who?	/tʃe ka-si:/	چه کسی؟
Who comes?	/tʃe ka-si: mi:-ʔɒ:-jad/	چه کسی می‌آید؟
Who's it?	/ki:st/	کیست؟
Who with?	/bɒ: ki:/	با کی؟
Why?	/tʃe-rɒ:/	چرا؟
Why are you cross with me?	/tʃe-rɒ: ʔaz man nɒ:-rɒ:-ha-ti:/	چرا از من ناراحتی؟
Why don't you answer?	/tʃe-rɒ: dʒa-vɒ:b ne-mi:-da-hi:/	چرا جواب نمی‌دهی؟

1-6
ANSWERS
OPINIONS

Anything you say.	/har tʃe ʃo-mɑ: be-gu:-ji:d/	هر چه شما بگویید.
As you like it.	/bas-te be mej-le ʃo-mɑ:st/	بسته به میل شماست.
Certainly not.	/mo-sal-la-man xejr/	مسلّماً خیر.
Heaven forbid!	/xo-dɑ: na-ko-nad/	خدا نکند!
I agree with you.	/bɑ: ʃo-mɑ: mo-vɑ:-fe-Gam/	با شما موافقم.
I'm afraid not.	/mo-ta-ʔas-se-fɑ:-ne xejr/	متأسفانه خیر.
I'm not certain.	/mot-ma-ʔen ni:s-tam/	مطمئن نیستم.
I'm not clear about that.	/ʔɪn mow-zu:ʔ ba-rɑ:-jam row-ʃan ni:st/	این موضوع برایم روشن نیست.
I couldn't care less.	/ʔas-lan ba-rɑ:-jam mo-hem ni:st/	اصلاً برایم مهم نیست.

44 Beginner's Persian

I'm not sure you're right. ....
.... /mot-ma-ʔen niːs-tam haɢ bvː to bvː-ʃad/
مطمئن نیستم حق با تو باشد.
I don't have it in me. .../ʔaz man bar ne-miː-ʔvː-jad/ از من برنمی‌آید.
I don't know. ..../ne-miː-dvː-nam/. نمی‌دانم.
I don't know what to do. ..../ne-miː-dvː-nam tʃe ko-nam/
نمی‌دانم چه کنم.
I don't like the look of it. .../ʔaz zvː-he-raʃ xo-ʃam ne-miː-ʔvː-jad/
از ظاهرش خوشم نمی‌آید.
I doubt. ..../ʃak dvː-ram/. شک دارم.
I expected as much. ..../ʔen-te-zvː-re biːʃ-ta-riː dvːʃ-tam/
انتظار بیشتری داشتم.
I have no idea. ..../na-za-riː na-dvː-ram/. نظری ندارم.
I have no objection. ..../mo-xvː-le-fa-tiː na-dvː-ram/. مخالفتی ندارم.
I quite agree with you. ....
.... /kvː-me-lan bvː ʃo-mvː mo-vvː-fe-ɢam/. کاملاً با شما موافقم.
I swear to it. ..../ɢa-sam miː-xo-ram/. قسم می‌خورم.
I think so. ..../na-za-re man ham ha-mın ʔast/. نظرمن هم همین است.
I'll see about it. /be ʔʌn re-siː-de-giː miː-ko-nam/. به آن رسیدگی می‌کنم.
I'll tell you later. ..../baʔ-dan xvː-ham goft/. بعداً خواهم گفت.
I wouldn't know. ..../tʃe miː-dvː-nam/. چه می‌دانم.
If you like to. ..../ʔa-gar mo-vvː-feɢ bvː-ʃiː/. اگر موافق باشی.
In my opinion... . .../be ʔa-ɢiː-de-je man/ .....به عقیدهٔ من.
In my opinion you're wrong. /be-na-za-ram ʔeʃ-te-bvːh miː-ko-niːd/
بنظرم اشتباه می‌کنید.
It doesn't appeal to me. ....
............................/tʃan-gi: be del ne-miː-za-nad/. چنگی به دل نمی‌زند.
It's a deal. ..../be-sı-jvːr xuːb ɢa-buːl ʔast/. بسیار خوب، قبول است.
It's almost impossible. ....
..................../ʔın taɢ-riː-ban ɢejr mom-ken ʔast/. این تقریباً غیرممکن است.
It's better ... ./beh-tar ʔast/. .... بهتر است.
It's not so. ..../ʔın-towr niːst/. اینطور نیست.

Informal Talking

Just what I thought.	/do-rost ha-mʌn tʃiː-zi: ke fekr miː-kar-dam/	درست همان چیزی که فکر می‌کردم.
Leave well alone.	/ha-mɪn xuːb ʔast/	همین خوب است.
Let me think it over.	/be-go-zɑːr ka-mi: fekr ko-nam/	بگذار کمی فکر کنم.
maybe	/ʃɑː-jad/	شاید
no	/na/	نه
no one	/hiːtʃ jek/	هیچ یک
No matter.	/mas-ʔa-le-ʔi: niːst/	مسئله‌ای نیست.
None of that!	/diː-gar tek-rɑːr na-ʃa-vad/	دیگر تکرار نشود!
Not at all.	/ʔa-ba-dan/	ابداً.
Not now.	/hɑː-lɑː na/	حالا نه.
Not quite well.	/kɑː-me-lan xuːb niːst/	کاملاً خوب نیست.
Not so.	/ʔɪn-towr na/	اینطور نه.
Nonsense!	/mo-zax-raf ʔast/	مزخرف است!
Of course.	/ʔal-bat-te/	البتّه.
One may say no.	/miː-ta-vʌn goft na/	می‌توان گفت نه.
So far so good.	/tɑː ʔɪn-dʒɑː xuːb buːd/	تا اینجا خوب بود.
So it may be.	/mom-ken ʔast ʔɪn-towr bɑː-ʃad/	ممکن است اینطور باشد.
That's not the way.	/ʔɪn rɑː-haʃ niːst/	این راهش نیست.
That's OK.	/xuːb ʔast/	خوب است.
That tears it!	/Gej-re Gɑː-be-le ta-ham-mol ʔast/	غیر قابل تحمّل است!
That will be the day!	/be-biː-ni: mo taʔ-riːf ko-niːm/	ببینیم و تعریف کنیم!
That will do!	/bas ʔast/	بس است!
too bad	/xej-li: bad/	خیلی بد
very well	/xej-li: xuːb/	خیلی خوب
Well and good.	/mɑː-ne-ʔi: na-dɑː-rad/	مانعی ندارد.
What do I care!	/be man tʃe/	به من چه!
with all my heart	/bɑː ta-mɑː-me vo-dʒuːd/	با تمام وجود
With pleasure.	/bɑː ka-mɑː-le me-jl/	با کمال میل.
Yes.	/ba-le/	بله.
Yes indeed.	/ba-le vɑː-Ge-ʔan/	بله واقعاً.

You're right. .... /haGG bʌ: ʃo-mʌ:st/ حقّ با شماست.
You're doing well. .... /kʌ:-re-tʌn do-rost ʔast/ کارتان درست است.
You're quite wrong. /kʌ:-me-lan dar ʔeʃ-te-bʌ:-hi:d/ کاملاً در اشتباهید.
Your objection don't apply. .... /ʔeʔ-te-rʌ:-ze-tʌn vʌ:-red ni:st/
اعتراضتان وارد نیست.
You said it! .... /mo-vʌ:-fe-Gam/ موافقم!
You should always tell the truth. ....
...../bʌ:-jad ha-mi:-ʃe rʌ:s-taʃ rʌ: be-gu:-ji:d/ باید همیشه راستش را بگویید.

1-7
PHRASES

A1	/ʕɑː-liː/	عالی
above all	/bɑː-lɑː-tar ʔaz ha-me/	بالاتر از همه
according as	/bar ha-sa-be ʔɪn-ke/	بر حسب اینکه
after and well	/ba-ʔd ʔaz ha-me/	بعد از همه
all at once	/be jek bɑː-re/	به یک باره
all night	/ta-mɑː-me ʃab/	تمام شب
almost always	/taɢ-riː-ban ha-miː-ʃe/	تقریباً همیشه
altogether	/ruː-je-ham-raf-te/	روی هم رفته
anywhere else	/har dʒɑː-je diː-gar/	هر جای دیگر
as a matter of fact	/dar ha-giː-gat/	در حقیقت
as clear as mud	/mob-ham/	مبهم
as so	/ba-nɑː-bar-ʔɪn/	بنابراین
at any price	/be har ɢej-mat/	به هر قیمت
at any rate	/be-har-hɑːl/	به هر حال

at choice	/be ʔex-tɪ-jɒ:-re/	به اختیار
at cost	/mɒ:-je be mɒ:-je/	مایه به مایه
at first	/no-xost/	نخست
at last	/sar-ʔan-dʒɒ:m/	سرانجام
at least	/das-te-kam/	دست‌کم
at the outset	/dar ʔɒ:-ɢɒ:z/	در آغاز
at this rate	/dar ʔɪn su:-rat/	در این صورت
at times	/gɒ:h-gɒ:-hi:/	گاهگاهی
ball of fire	/jek pɒ:r-tʃe ʔɒ:-taʃ/	یک پارچه آتش
be upset	/ne-ga-rʌn/	نگران
beat the band	/xej-li: tond/	خیلی تند
by and by	/be-zu:-di:/	به‌زودی
by and large	/ru:-je-ham-raf-te/	روی هم رفته
by any means	/be har nahv/	به هرنحو
by chance	/ʃʌn-si:/	شانسی
by heart	/ʔaz hefz/	از حفظ
by mistake	/be-ʔeʃ-te-bɒ:h/	به‌اشتباه
by no means	/be-hi:tʃ-vadʒh/	به‌هیچ‌وجه
by oneself	/be tan-hɒ:-ji:/	به تنهایی
by the way	/dar-zemn/	درضمن
by turn	/be no-bat/	به نوبت
bye bye	/xo-dɒ:-hɒ:-fez/	خداحافظ
clear record	/hos-ne pi:-ʃi:-ne/	حسن پیشینه
cock of the walk	/pah-la-vɒ:-ne mej-dʌn/	پهلوان میدان
day by day	/ru:z-be-ru:z/	روز به روز
day in	/mo-rat-ta-ban/	مرتّباً
easy as pie	/mes-le ʔɒ:b-xor-dan/	مثل آب خوردن
every so often	/har ka-si:/	هر کسی
everywhere	/ha-me dʒɒ:/	همه جا
face to face	/ru: dar ru:/	رو در رو
first of all	/pi:ʃ ʔaz ha-me/	پیش از همه
first rate	/da-ra-dʒe-jek/	درجه‌یک

Informal Talking

fit as a fiddle	/sɑ:-le mo baʃ-ʃɑ:ʃ/	سالم و بشّاش
fit for a king	/dar dʒa-mʔ mo-nɑ:-seb/	در جمع مناسب
for keeps	/ha-mi:-ʃe-gi:/	همیشگی
for the last time	/ba-rɑ:-je ʔɑ:-xa-rɪn bɑ:r/	برای آخرین بار
from A to Z	/ʔaz ʔav-val tɑ: ʔɑ:-xar/	از اوّل تا آخر
from top to bottom	/ʔaz sar tɑ: pɑ:/	از سر تا پا
gentleman agreement	/ɢo-le mar-dɑ:-ne/	قول مردانه
good as gold	/bi: ɢal-lo-ɢaʃ/	بی غلّ و غش
good time	/ʔow-ɢɑ:-te xoʃ/	اوقات خوش
hale and hearty	/sa-re-hɑ: lo ɢeb-rɑ:ɢ/	سرحال و قبراق
hand over hand	/dast bɑ:-lɑ:-je dast/	دست بالای دست
happy as a calm	/xoʃ-hɑ: lo rɑ:-zi:/	خوشحال و راضی
happy as lark	/xej-li: baʃ-ʃɑ:ʃ/	خیلی بشّاش
hard as nails	/xej-li: saxt/	خیلی سخت
head or tail	/ʃi:r jɑ: xat/	شیر یا خط
high as a kite	/xej-li: bo-land/	خیلی بلند
hot as a hell	/mes-le dʒa-han-nam/	مثل جهنّم
hungry as a bear	/xej-li: go-ros-ne/	خیلی گرسنه
ill at ease	/ne-ga-rʌn (nɑ:-rɑ:-hat)/	نگران (ناراحت)
in a fix	/dar vaz-ʔɪj-ja-te bad/	در وضعیّت بد
in a flash	/be-lɑ:-fɑ:-se-le/	بلافاصله
in a nutshell	/be tow-re xo-lɑ:-se/	به طور خلاصه
in all one's born days	/ha-mi:-ʃe/	همیشه
in bad sorts	/bad ʔax-lɑ:ɢ/	بد اخلاق
in brief	/be tow-re xo-lɑ:-se/	به طور خلاصه
in cool blood	/bi: ʔeh-sɑ:s/	بی احساس
in due course	/be mow-ɢe-ʔe xod/	به موقع خود
in great haste	/xej-li: sa-ri:ʔ/	خیلی سریع
in luck	/xoʃ-bax-tɑ:-ne/	خوشبختانه
in one time	/be-sor-ʔat/	به سرعت
in the air	/ha-me-dʒɑ:/	همه جا
in the hole	/maɢ-ru:z/	مقروض

in the meantime	/dar-zemn/	درضمن
in the nick of time	/do-rost be mow-ɢeʔ/	درست به موقع
in this very moment	/do-rost dar ha-mɪn lah-ze/	درست در همین لحظه
in time	/be-mow-ɢeʔ/	بموقع
in vain	/biː-huː-de/	بیهوده
keyed up	/has-sɑːs va ne-ga-rʌn/	حسّاس و نگران
little by little	/kam-kam/	کم‌کم
mad as hell	/xej-liː ʔa-sa-bɑː-niː/	خیلی عصبانی
more or less	/ka-mo-biːʃ/	کم و بیش
most of all	/bɑː-lɑː-tar ʔaz ha-me/	بالاتر از همه
no doubt	/be-duː-ne ʃakk/	بدون شکّ
not a living soul	/hiːtʃ-kas/	هیچکس
not at all	/ʔa-ba-dan/	ابداً
nowadays	/ʔem-ruː-ze/	امروزه
now and then	/ɢɑːh-hiː/	گاهی
of course	/ʔal-bat-te/	البتّه
on and off	/ɢɑːh-gɑː-hiː/	گاه گاهی
on and on	/mo-rat-ta-ban/	مرتّباً
on purpose	/be-ʔamd/	بعمد
on the contrary	/bar-ʔaks/	برعکس
on the go	/maʃ-ɢuːl/	مشغول
on thin ice	/ruː-je la-be-je tiːɢ/	روی لبۀ تیغ
on time	/be-mow-ɢeʔ/	بموقع
on your own	/be tow-re mos-ta-ɢel/	به طور مستقل
once for all	/ba-rɑː-je ʔɑː-xa-rɪn bɑːr/	برای آخرین بار
once in a blue moon	/be-nod-rat/	بندرت
out of control	/ɢej-re ɢɑː-be-le kon-to-rol/	غیرقابل کنترل
out of order	/xa-rɑːb/	خراب
over and over	/mo-rat-ta-ban/	مرتّباً
quick as a wink	/dar jek tʃeʃm be ham za-dan/	در یک چشم به هم زدن
quiet as a mouse	/pɑː-var-tʃɪn/	پاورچین

Informal Talking

English	Persian	Transcription
right away	بلافاصله	/be-lvː-fvː-se-le/
short cut	میان‌بر	/mɪ-jʌn bor/
side by side	پهلو به پهلو	/pah-luː be pah-luː/
sly as a fox	باهوش (زرنگ)	/bvː-huːʃ (ze-raŋ)/
so far	تاکنون	/tvː-ko-nʊn/
so on	غیره	/Gej-re/
so that	به طوری که	/be towˑ-riː ke/
somehow	به نوعی	/be nowˑ-ʔiː/
sometime	گاهی	/gvː-hiː/
somewhat	تاحدّی	/tvː-had-diː/
somewhere else	یک جای دیگر	/jek dʒvː-je diː-gar/
sooner or later	دیر یا زود	/diːr jvː zuːd/
steamed up	عصبانی	/ʔa-sa-bvː-niː/
strong as an ox	خیلی قوی	/xej-liː Ga-viː/
stubborn as a mule	خیلی کله‌شق	/xej-liː kal-le-ʃaG/
the little people	از ما بهتران	/ʔaz mvː beh-ta-rʌn/
thick as pea soup	خیلی غلیظ	/xej-liː Ga-liːz/
through thick and thin	بین اوقات خوش و بد	/bej-ne ʔo-Gvː-te xo ʃo bad/
time to time	هرچند وقت یکبار	/har tʃand vaGt jek-bvːr/
timely	بموقع	/be-mow-Geʔ/
touch and go	بحرانی (وخیم)	/boh-rvː-niː (va-xiːm)/
under the table	پنهانی	/pen-hvː-niː/
under the weather	مریض	/ma-riːz/
up a tree	در وضعیّت نامناسب	/dar vaz-ʔɪj-ja-te nvː-mo-nvː-seb/
up and down	بالا پایین	/bvː-lv pvː-jɪn/
up front	بی‌ریا (صادق)	/biː-rɪ-jvː (svː-deG)/
upside down	سروته	/sa-ro-tah/
up to date	جدید	/dʒa-diːd/
walk on air	خیلی خوشحال	/xej-liː xoʃ-hvːl/
well to do	آسوده	/ʔvː-suː-de/
white as the driven snow	خیلی سفید	/xej-liː se-fiːd/

wise as an awl	/dɑː-nɑː/	دانا
with a heavy heart	/ɢam-gɪn/	غمگین
with all my heart	/ʔaz sa-miː-me ɢalb/	از صمیم قلبم
within reason	/man-te-ɢiː/	منطقی
without fail	/biː bo-ro bar-gard/	بی بروبرگرد
worse luck	/bad-bax-tɑː-ne/	بدبختانه
Year in, year out	/sɑːl poʃ-te sɑːl/	سال پشت سال

1-8
LANGUAGE

Arabic	عربی	/ʔa-ra-biː/
Chinese	چینی	/tʃiː-niː/
Danish	دانمارکی	/dʌn-mɐːr-kiː/
dictionary	فرهنگ لغت	/far-haŋ-ge loɢat/
Dutch	هلندی	/ho-lan-diː/
English	انگلیسی	/ʔeŋ-ge-liː-siː/
Farsi	فارسی	/fɐːr-siː/
French	فرانسه	/fa-rʌn-se/
German	آلمانی	/ʔɐːl-mɐː-niː/
Greek	یونانی	/juː-nɐː-niː/
Hindi	هندی	/hen-diː/
Italian	ایتالیایی	/ʔiː-tɐː-lɪ-jɐː-jiː/
Japanese	ژاپنی	/ʒɐː-po-niː/
language	زبان	/za-bʌn/

letter	/harf/	حرف
Norwegian	/nor-ve-ʒi:/	نروژی
phrase	/ʔe-bɒː-rat/	عبارت
quick	/tond/	تند
read	/xʌn-dan/	خواندن
repeat	/tek-rɒːr/	تکرار
Russian	/ru:-si:/	روسی
slowly	/ʔɒː-rɒːm-tar/	آرامتر
sound	/se-dɒː/	صدا
Spanish	/ʔes-pɒː-nı-jɒː-ji:/	اسپانیایی
speak	/soh-bat/	صحبت
Swedish	/so-ʔe-di:/	سوئدی
Turkish	/tor-ki:/	ترکی
undrestand	/fah-mi:-dan/	فهمیدن
word	/ka-la-me/	کلمه
write	/ne-veʃ-tan/	نوشتن

Do you speak English? ....
/mi:-ta-vɒː-ni:d ʔeŋ-ge-li:-si: soh-bat ko-ni:d/ می‌توانید انگلیسی صحبت کنید؟
Do you undrestand me? ....
................../man-zu:-ram rɒː mi:-fah-mi:d/ منظورم را می‌فهمید؟
How is this letter(word)written? ....
................./ʔın harf (ka-la-me) tʃe-towr ne-veʃ-te mi:-ʃa-vad/
این حرف (کلمه) چطور نوشته می‌شود؟
How is this word pronounced? ....
/ʔın ka-la-me tʃe-towr ta-laf-foz mi:-ʃa-vad/. این کلمه چطور تلفّظ می‌شود؟
I don't understand you. ....
.............../man-zu:-re-tʌn rɒː ne-mi:-fah-mam/ منظورتان را نمی فهمم.
I speak only English. ..../man fa-ɢat ʔeŋ-ge-li:-si: ba-la-dam/
من فقط انگلیسی بلدم.

Informal Talking

I want to learn to read Farsi. ....
.... /miː-xvː-ham xvːn-da-ne fvːr-si: rvː jvːd be-giː-ram/
می‌خواهم خواندن فارسی را یاد بگیرم.

I want to learn to speak Farsi. ....
.... /miː-xvː-ham fvːr-si: harf za-dan rvː jvːd be-giː-ram/
می‌خواهم فارسی حرف زدن را یاد بگیرم.

I want to learn to write Farsi. ....
.... /miː-xvː-ham ne-veʃ-ta-ne fvːr-si: rvː jvːd be-giː-ram/
می‌خواهم نوشتن فارسی را یاد بگیرم.

Please explain what is written here. ....
.... /lot-fan tow-ziːh da-hiːd ʔɪn-dʒvː tʃe ne-veʃ-te ʔast/
لطفاً توضیح دهید اینجا چه نوشته است.

Please repeat that again. ....
.... /lot-fan do-bvː-re tek-rvːr ko-niːd/ لطفاً دوباره تکرار کنید.

What does this word mean? ....
.... /maʔ-nɪ-je ʔɪn ka-la-me tʃiːst/ معنی این کلمه چیست؟

What is that call in Farsi? ....
/dar fvːr-si: be ʔɪn tʃe miː-guː-jand/؟ در فارسی به این چه می‌گویند؟
What is this letter? .... /ʔɪn ko-dvːm harf ʔast/؟ این کدام حرف است؟

SECTION 2
GENERAL DATA

2-1   NUMBERS

2-2   TIME

2-3   SEASONS/MONTHS

2-4   WATCH

2-5   DIRECTION

2-6   CLIMATE

2-7   AGE

2-8   FAMILY RELATIONSHIPS

2-9   COLORS

2-10 QUALITIES

2-11 EDUCATION

2-12 OCCUPATION

2-1 NUMBERS

CARDINAL .... اصلی /ʔas-li:/

0 zero	....	۰ صفر	/sefr/
1 one	....	۱ یک	/jek/ — YEK
2 two	....	۲ دو	/do/ — DO
3 three	....	۳ سه	/se/ — SAY
4 four	....	۴ چهار	/tʃa-hvːr/ — PANJ
5 five	....	۵ پنج	/pandy/ — PANJ
6 six	....	۶ شش	/ʃeʃ/ — SHESH
7 seven	....	۷ هفت	/haft/ — HAFT
8 eight	....	۸ هشت	/haʃt/ — HASHT
9 nine	....	۹ نه	/noh/
10 ten	....	۱۰ ده	/dah/
11 eleven	....	۱۱ یازده	/jvːz-dah/ — DJAH-

12 twelve	۱۲ دوازده	/da-vː z-dah/
13 thirteen	۱۳ سیزده	/siː z-dah/
14 fourteen	۱۴ چهارده	/tʃa-hvː r-dah/
15 fifteen	۱۵ پانزده	/pvː-nez-dah/
16 sixteen	۱۶ شانزده	/ʃvː-nez-dah/
17 seventeen	۱۷ هفده	/hef-dah/
18 eighteen	۱۸ هیجده	/hiːdʒ-dah/
19 nineteen	۱۹ نوزده	/nuː z-dah/
20 twenty	۲۰ بیست	/biːst/
21 twenty one	۲۱ بیست و یک	/biː s-to-jek/
30 thirty	۳۰ سی	/siː/
32 thirty two	۳۲ سی و دو	/sɪ-jo-do/
40 forty	۴۰ چهل	/tʃe-hel/
43 forty three	۴۳ چهل و سه	/tʃe-he-lo-se/
50 fifty	۵۰ پنجاه	/pan-dʒvː h/
55 fifty five	۵۵ پنجاه و پنج	/pan-dʒvː -ho-pandʒ/
60 sixty	۶۰ شصت	/ʃast/
68 sixty eight	۶۸ شصت و هشت	/ʃas-to-haʃt/
70 seventy	۷۰ هفتاد	/haf-tvː d/
79 seventy nine	۷۹ هفتاد و نه	/haf-tvː -do-noh/
80 eighty	۸۰ هشتاد	/haʃ-tvː d/
90 ninety	۹۰ نود	/na-vad/
100 one hundred	۱۰۰ صد	/sad/
200 two hundred	۲۰۰ دویست	/de-viːst/
205 two hundred and five	۲۰۵ دویست و پنج	/de-viː s-to-pandʒ/
362 three hundred and sixty ۳۶۲ سی صد و شصت و دو		/siː-sa-do-ʃas-to-do/
500 five hundred	۵۰۰ پانصد	/pʌn-sad/
1000 one thousand	۱۰۰۰ هزار	/he-zvː r/
5000 five thousand	۵۰۰۰ پنج هزار	/pandʒ he-zvː r/
7041 seven thousand and forty one ۷۰۴۱ هفت هزار و چهل و یک /haft-he-zvː-ro-tʃe-he-lo-jek/		

10 000 ten thousand ..../dah he-zɑ:r/ ۱۰۰۰۰ دههزار
100 000 one hundred thousand ..../jek-sad he-zɑ:r/
۱۰۰۰۰۰ یکصد هزار
600 000 six hundred thousand /ʃeʃ-sad he-zɑ:r/ ششصدهزار ۶۰۰۰۰۰
1 000 000 one million ..../jek mi:l-jon/ یک میلیون ۱۰۰۰۰۰۰
1 462 853 one million, four hundred and sixty two thousand, eight hundred and fifty three ....
/jek mi:l-jo-no tʃa-hɑ:r-sa-do ʃas-to do-he-zɑ:-ro haʃt sa-do pan-dʒɑ:-ho-se/
۱۴۶۲۸۵۳ یک میلیون و چهار صدو شصت و دو هزارو هشتصدو پنجاه و سه

ORDINAL ..../tar-ti:-bi:/ ترتیبی

1st first	........................../ʔav-val (jek-kom)/	اوّل (یکّم)
2nd second	................................/dov-vom/	دوّم
3rd third	..../sev-vom/	سوّم
4th fourth	................................/tʃa-hɑ:-rom/	چهارم
5th fifth	..../pan-dʒom/	پنجم
6th sixth	..../ʃeʃ-ʃom/	ششم
7th seventh	..../haf-tom/	هفتم
8th eighth	..../haʃ-tom/	هشتم
9th ninth	..../no-hom/	نهم
10th tenth	..../da-hom/	دهم
11th eleventh	................................../jɑ:z-da-hom/	یازدهم
12th twelfth	................................./da-vvɑ:z-da-hom/	دوازدهم
13th thirteenth	...................................../si:z-da-hom/	سیزدهم
14th fourteenth	........................./tʃa-hɑ:r-da-hom/	چهاردهم
15th fifteenth	....................................../pɑ:-nez-da-hom/	پانزدهم
16th sixteenth	..../ʃɑ:-nez-da-hom/	شانزدهم
17th seventeenth	.................................../hef-da-hom/	هفدهم
18th eighteenth	.................................../hi:dʒ-da-hom/	هیجدهم
19th nineteenth	...................................../nu:z-da-hom/	نوزدهم

20th twentieth .... بیستم /biːs-tom/
21st twenty-first .... بیست‌ویکم /biːs-to-jek-kom/
30th thirtieth .... سی‌ام /siː-ʔom/
32nd thirty-second .... سی‌ودوّم /sɪ-jo-dov-vom/
40th fortieth .... چهلم /tʃe-he-lom/
43rd forty-third .... چهل‌وسوّم /tʃe-he-lo-sev-vom/
50th fiftieth .... پنجاهم /pan-dʒː-hom/
60th sixtieth .... شصتم /ʃas-tom/
70th seventieth .... هفتادم /haf-tvː-dom/
80th eightieth .... هشتادم /haʃ-tvː-dom/
90th ninetieth .... نودم /na-va-dom/
100th one hundredth .... صدم /sa-dom/
121st one hundred twenty-first .... /sa-do-biːs-to-jek-kom/
صدوبیست‌ویکم
200th two hundredth .... دویستم /de-viːs-tom/
1000th one thousandth .... هزارم /he-zvː-rom/
1 000 000 one millionth .... یک میلیونیم /jek miːl-jo-nɪ-jom/

VULGAR FRACTIONS .... کسر متعارفی /kas-re mo-ta-ʔvː-ra-fiː/

$\frac{1}{8}$ one eighth .... یک هشتم /jek-haʃ-tom/

$\frac{1}{4}$ one quarter .... یک چهارم /jek-tʃa-hvː-rom/

$\frac{1}{3}$ one third .... یک سوّم /jek-sev-vom/

$\frac{1}{2}$ one half .... یک دوّم (نیم) /jek-dov-vom (niːm)/

$\frac{3}{4}$ three quarters .... سه‌چهارم /se-tʃa-hvː-rom/

$\frac{5}{7}$ five sevenths .... پنج هفتم /pandʒ-haf-tom/

$5\frac{2}{9}$ five and two ninths .... /pan-dʒo-do-no-hom/ پنج‌ودونهم ۵‌$\frac{۲}{۹}$

$13\frac{3}{4}$ thirteen and three quarters ....
.... /siːz-da-ho-se-tʃa-hvː-rom/ سیزده و سه‌چهارم ۱۳$\frac{۳}{۴}$

DECIMAL FRACTIONS .... /kas-re ʔaʔ-ʃvː-riː/ کسر اعشاری

0.136 (nought) point one three six .... /sa-do-sɪ-jo-ʃeʃ-he-zvː-rom/
(صدوسی‌وشش هزارم)۰/۱۳۶
0.25 (nought) point two five .... /biːs-to-pandʒ-sa-dom/
(بیست‌وپنج صدم)۰/۲۵
0.5 (nought) point five .... /niːm/ (نیم)۰/۵
0.33 (nought) point three three .... /sɪ-jo-se-sa-dom/
(سی‌وسه صدم) ۰/۳۳
5.5 five point five .... /pandʒ ʔo niːm/ پنج و نیم ۵/۵
17.75 (seventeen point seven five) ....
.... /hef-da-ho-haf-tvː-do-pandʒ-sa-dom/ هفده‌وهفتادوپنج‌صدم ۱۷/۷۵
6 (a half dozen) .... /dʒɪn/ (جین) ۶
12 (one dozen) .... /do-dʒɪn/ (دوجین) ۱۲
-10 minus ten .... /man-fɪ-je dah/ منفی ده -۱۰
+25 plus twenty five .../mos-ba-te biːs to pandʒ/ مثبت بیست‌وپنج ۲۵+
+ adding .... /dʒamʔ/ جمع +
3+2=5 Three and two are five. ...../se ʔo do miː-ʃa-vad pandʒ/
سه و دو می‌شود پنج. ۵=۲+۳
- subtraction .... /taf-riːG/ تفریق -
3-2=1 Three take away two are one. ....
.... /se men-hvː-je do miː-ʃa-vad jek/ سه منهای دو می‌شود یک. ۱=۲-۳
× multiplication .... /zarb/ ضرب ×
3×2=6 Three multiply by two are six. ....
...... /se zarb dar do miː-ʃa-vad ʃeʃ/ سه ضرب در دو می‌شود شش. ۶=۲×۳

تقسیم /taG-si:m/ : division

6:2=3 Six divide by two are three.

۳=۲:۶ شش تقسیم بر دو می‌شود سه. /ʃeʃ taG-si:m bar do mi:-ʃa-va-d se/.

٪ (درصد) /dar-sad/ .... % (percent)

۲۵٪ (بیست و پنج درصد) /bi:s to pandʒ dar-sad/ 25% (twenty five percent)

یکبار /jek-bɑ:r/ .... once
دوبار /do bɑ:r/ .... twice
سه‌بار /se bɑ:r/ .... three times
بیست‌بار /bi:st bɑ:r/ .... twenty times

General Data 65

2-2
TIME

WEEK	/haf-te/	هفته
Saturday	/ʃam-be/	شنبه
Sunday	/jek-ʃam-be/	یکشنبه
Monday	/do-ʃam-be/	دوشنبه
Tuesday	/se-ʃam-be/	سه‌شنبه
Wednesday	/tʃa-hɑ:r-ʃam-be/	چهارشنبه
Thursday	/pandʒ-ʃam-be/	پنجشنبه
Friday	/dʒom-ʔe/	جمعه
by day	/ru:-zɑ:-ne/	روزانه
brithday	/ru:-ze ta-val-lod/	روز تولّد
century	/ɢarn/	قرن
day	/ru:z/	روز

66 Beginner's Persian

day after day	/ha-me ruː-ze/	همه‌روزه
day by day	/har ruːz/	هر روز
day long	/jek ruː-ze/	یک روزه
evening	/ʔasr/	عصر
every other day	/jek ruːz dar mɪ-jʌn/	یک روز در میان
eternal	/ha-mi:-ʃe-gi:/	همیشگی
forever	/ba-rʌ:-je ha-mi:-ʃe/	برای همیشه
from now on	/ʔaz hʌ:-lʌ: be ba-ʔd/	از حالا به بعد
future	/ʔʌ:-jan-de/	آینده
holiday	/taʔ-ti:l/	تعطیل
How long?	/tʌ: tʃe vaGt?/	تا چه وقت؟
How often?	/tʃand vaGt be tʃand vaGt/	چند وقت به چند وقت؟
in a fortnight	/zar-fe do haf-te/	ظرف دو هفته
in time	/be-mow-Geʔ/	به‌موقع
just then	/dar ʔɪn hen-gʌːm/	در این هنگام
last	/go-zaʃ-te/	گذشته
last month	/mʌː-he go-zaʃ-te/	ماه گذشته
last night	/di:-ʃab/	دیشب
last year	/pʌːr-sʌːl/	پارسال
month	/mʌːh/	ماه
morning	/sobh/	صبح
midday	/niːm-ruːz/	نیم‌روز
midnight	/niːm-ʃab/	نیم‌شب
new year	/sʌː-le no/	سال نو
next month	/mʌː-he ʔʌ:-jan-de/	ماه آینده
next year	/sʌː-le ʔʌ:-jan-de/	سال آینده
night long	/ta-mʌː-me ʃab/	تمام شب
nightly	/ʃa-bʌː-ne/	شبانه
now	/hʌ:-lʌ:/	حالا
old	/Ga-diːm/	قدیم
past	/go-zaʃ-te/	گذشته
present	/hʌːl/	حال

General Data 67

season	فصل	/fasl/
soon	زود	/zu:d/
sooner or later	دیر یا زود	/di:r jʌ zu:d/
sunrise	طلوع	/to-luːʔ/
sunset	غروب	/ɢo-ru:b/
the day after tomorrow	پس فردا	/pas far-dʌː/
the day before yesterday	پریروز	/pa-ri:-ru:z/
the night after tomorrow	پس فردا شب	/pas far-dʌː ʃab/
the night before last	پریشب	/pa-ri:-ʃab/
the other day	چند روز پیش	/tʃand ru:z piːʃ/
the year before last	پیرارسال	/pɪ-jʌːr-sʌːl/
then	بعداً	/baʔ-dan/
this day week	یک هفته از امروز	/jek haf-te ʔaz ʔem-ru:z/
till then	تا آن وقت	/tʌː ʔʌn vaɢt/
today	امروز	/ʔem-ru:z/ — EM ROOZ
tomorrow	فردا	/far-dʌː/ — FAR DAH
tomorrow night	فردا شب	/far-dʌː ʃab/ — FAR DAH SH-
tomorrow week	هشت روز دیگر	/haʃt ru:-ze di:-gar/
tonight	امشب	/ʔem-ʃab/ — EM SHAB
toward evening	نزدیکیهای عصر	/naz-di:-ki:-hʌː-je ʔasr/
toward midnight	نزدیکیهای شب	/naz-di:-ki:-hʌː-je ʃab/
toward noon	نزدیکیهای ظهر	/naz-di:-ki:-hʌː-je zohr/
up to now	تا حالا	/tʌː hʌː-lʌː/
week	هفته	/haf-te/
weekend	آخر هفته	/ʔʌː-xa-re haf-te/
year	سال	/sʌːl/
yesterday	دیروز	/di:-ru:z/ — DEE ROOZ

Come at about six o´clock.   /he-du:-de sʌː-ʔa-te ʃeʃ bɪ-jʌː/
حدود ساعت شش بیا.
I waited a couple of hours.   /man do sʌː-ʔat mon-ta-zer ʃo-dam/
من دو ساعت منتظر شدم.

It's late already.	/di:r ʃo-de ʔast/	دیر شده است.
It's still early.	/ha-nu:z zu:d ʔast/	هنوز زود است.
She was there before 8 o'clock.	/ʔu: Gabl ʔaz sʌ:-ʔa-te haʃt ʔʌn-dʒʌ: bu:d/	او قبل از ساعت ۸ آنجا بود.
Today is Monday.	/ʔem-ru:z do-ʃam-be ʔast/	امروز دوشنبه است.
Today is Tir 12th.	/ʔem-ru:z da-vʌ:z-da-ho-me ti:r ʔast/	امروز دوازدهم تیر است.
What day?	/tʃe ru:-zi:/	چه روزی؟
What day is today?	/ʔem-ru: tʃe ru:-zi: ʔast/	امروز چه روزی است؟
What is the data today?	/ʔem-ru:z tʃan-dom ʔast/	امروز چندم است؟
What time?	/tʃe mow-Geʔ/	چه موقع؟
When?	/tʃe mow-Geʔ/	چه موقع؟
When are you off?	/kej mi:-xʌ:-hi: be-ra-vi:/	کی می‌خواهی بروی؟
When can I see you?	/kej mi:-ta-vʌ:-nam be-bi:-na-mat/	کی می‌توانم ببینمت؟
When did you arrive here?	/to kej ʔɪn-dʒʌ: re-si:-di:/	تو کی اینجا رسیدی؟
When exactly?	/da-Gi:-Gan tʃe mow-Geʔ/	دقیقاً چه موقع؟
Will you be tomorrow?	/far-dʌ: has-ti:/	فردا هستی؟

2-3
SEASONS
MONTHS

Spring .... /ba-hɑ:r/ بهار

21 March - 20 April(31 days) ..../far-var-dɪn/	فروردین (۳۱ روز)
21 April - 21 May(31 days) ....../ʔor-di:-be-heʃt/	اردیبهشت (۳۱ روز)
22 May - 21 June(31 days) ..../xor-dɑ:d/	خرداد (۳۱ روز)

Summer .... /tɑ:-bes-tʌn/ تابستان

22 June - 22 July(31 days) ..../ti:r/	تیر (۳۱ روز)
23 July - 22 August(31 days) ..../mor-dɑ:d/	مرداد (۳۱ روز)

23 August - 22 September(31 days) /ʃah-ri:-var/ شهریور (۳۱ روز)

Autumn .... /pʌ:-ji:z/ پاییز

23 September - 22 October(30 days) .... /mehr/ مهر (۳۰ روز)
23 October - 21 November(30 days) .... /ʔʌ:-bʌn/ آبان (۳۰ روز)
22 November - 21 December(30 days) ...... /ʔʌ:-zar/ آذر (۳۰ روز)

Winter .... /ze-mes-tʌn/ زمستان

22 December - 20 January(30 days) .... /dej/ دی (۳۰ روز)
21 January - 19 February(30 days) .... /bah-man/ بهمن (۳۰ روز)
20 February - 20 March(29 days) .... /ʔes-fand/ اسفند (۲۹ روز)

2-4
WATCH

a.m	/Gab ʔaz zohr/	قبل از ظهر
p.m	/baʔd ʔaz zohr/	بعد از ظهر
hour	/sv:-ʔat/	ساعت
half an hour	/ni:m sv:-ʔat/	نیم ساعت
hourly	/sv:-ʔat be sv:-ʔat/	ساعت به ساعت
minute	/da-Gi:-Ge/	دقیقه
second	/sv:-nɪ-je/	ثانیه
1:00 one o'clock	/sv:-ʔa-te jek/	ساعت ۱
2:00 two o'clock	/sv:-ʔa-te do/	ساعت ۲
3:00 three o'clock	/sv:-ʔa-te se/	ساعت ۳
4:00 four o'clock	/sv:-ʔa-te tʃv:-hv:r/	ساعت ۴
5:00 five o'clock	/sv:-ʔa-te pandʒ/	ساعت ۵
18:00 eighteen o'clock	/sv:-ʔa-te hi:dʒ-dah/	ساعت ۱۸
19:00 nineteen o'clock	/sv:-ʔa-te nu:z-dah/	ساعت ۱۹

20:00 twenty o'clock	/sɑ:-ʔa-te bi:st/	۲۰ ساعت
1:05 five past one	/je-ko-pandʒ-da-ɢi:-ɢe/	۱ و ۵ دقیقه
2:10 ten past two	/do-ʔo-dah-da-ɢi:-ɢe/	۲ و ۱۰ دقیقه
3:15 a quarter past three	/se-ʔo-robʔ/	۳ و ربع
4:20 twenty past four	/tʃa-hʋ:-ro-bi:st-da-ɢi:-ɢe/	۴ و ۲۰ دقیقه
5:25 twenty five past five	/pan-dʒo-bi:s-to-pandʒ-da-ɢi:-ɢe/	۵ و ۲۵ دقیقه
6:30 half past six	/ʃe-ʃo-ni:m/	۶ و نیم

7:35 thirty five past seven (twenty five to eight) ....
............/haf-to-sɪ-jo-pandʒ-da-ɢi:-ɢe (bi:s-to-pandʒ-da-ɢi:-ɢe-be-haʃt)/
۷ و ۳۵ دقیقه (۲۵ دقیقه به ۸)

8:40 forty past eight (twenty to nine) ....
...........................//haʃ-to-tʃe-hel-da-ɢi:-ɢe (bi:st-da-ɢi:-ɢe-be-noh)/
۸ و ۴۰ دقیقه (۲۰ دقیقه به ۹)

21:45 forty five past twenty one (quarter to twenty two) ....
.............../bi:s-to-je-ko-tʃe-he-lo-pandʒ-da-ɢi:-ɢe (jek-robʔ-be-bi:s-to-do/
۲۱ و ۴۵ دقیقه (یک ربع به ۲۲)

22:50 fifty past twenty two (ten to twenty three)...................
.............../bi:s-to-do-ʔo-pan-dʒʋ:h-da-ɢi:-ɢe (dah-da-ɢi:-ɢe-be-bi:s-to-se)/
۲۲ و ۵۰ دقیقه (۱۰ دقیقه به ۲۳)

23:55 fifty five past twenty three (five to twenty four) ....
/bi:s-to-se-vo-pan-dʒʋ:-ho-pandʒ-da-ɢi:-ɢe (pandʒ-daɢi:-ɢe-be-bi:s-to-tʃʋ:-hʋ:r)/
۲۳ و ۵۵ دقیقه(۵ دقیقه به ۲۴)

24:00 (midnight)	/bi:s-to-tʃʋ:hʋ:r(nes-fe ʃab)/	۲۴ (نصف شب)
At 9:00 sharp.	/do-rost sɑ:-ʔa-te noh/	درست ساعت ۹.
Ten minutes from now.	/dah da-ɢi:-ɢe-je di:-gar/	ده دقیقه دیگر.

How about 1:30?	/je ko ni:m tʃe-towr ʔast/	۱:۳۰ چطور است؟
Is 8:00 OK?	/haʃt xu:b ʔast/	هشت خوب است؟
It's 1:00 o'clock.	/sɑ:-ʔat jek ʔast/	ساعت ۱ است.
It's just 8 o'clock.	/sɑ:-ʔat do-rost haʃt ʔast/	ساعت درست ۸ است.

Tell me the time, please. /lot-fan sv:-ʔat rv: be-gu:/ لطفاً ساعت را بگو.
What time do the shops open (close)? ....
/kej ma-ɢv:-ze-hv: bv:z (bas-te) mi:-ʃa-vand/ کی مغازه‌ها باز(بسته) می‌شوند؟
What is your explanation for being late? ....
.... /ʔel-la-te di:r ʔv:-ma-da-nat tʃi:st/ علّت دیر آمدنت چیست؟
What time is it? .... /sv:-ʔat tʃand ʔast/ ساعت چند است؟
What time is it by your watch? ....
.... /sv:-ʔa-te ʃo-mv: tʃand ʔast/ ساعت شما چند است؟
When are you at home? .... /kej man-zel has-ti:/ کی منزل هستی؟
When can I see you? .... /kej mi:-ta-vv:-nam be-bi:-na-mat/
کی می‌توانم ببینمت؟
When does the movie start? .... /fi:lm kej ʃo-ru:ʔ mi:-ʃa-vad/
فیلم کی شروع می‌شود؟
Will you be in tomorrow? .... /far-dv: has-ti:/ فردا هستی؟

General Data 75

2-5
DIRECTIONS

back	پشت	/poʃt/
down	پایین	/pɒ:ʔɪn/
east	شرق	/ʃarG/
eastern	شرقی	/ʃar-Gi:/
eastward	به سمت شرق	/be sam-te ʃarG/
front	جلو	/dʒe-low/
left	چپ	/tʃap/
north	شمال	/ʃo-mɒ:l/
northeast	شمال شرق	/ʃo-mɒ:-le ʃarG/
northeastern	شمال شرقی	/ʃo-mɒ:-le ʃar-Gi:/
northern	شمالی	/ʃo-mɒ:-li:/
northerhly	از سمت شمال	/ʔaz sam-te ʃo-mɒ:l/
northward	سوی شمال	/su:-je ʃo-mɒ:l/
northwest	شمال غرب	/ʃo-mɒ:-le Garb/

northwestern	/ʃo-mɒ:-le ɢar-bi:/	شمال غربی
on the east	/ʔaz sam-te ʃarɢ/	از سمت شرق
on the west	/ʔaz sam-te ɢarb/	از سمت غرب
right	/rɒ:st/	راست
side	/ka-nɒ:r/	کنار
south	/dʒu:-nu:b/	جنوب
southeast	/dʒu:-nu:-be ʃarɢ/	جنوب شرق
south eastern	/dʒu:-nu:-be ʃar-ɢi:/	جنوب شرقی
southerly	/ʔaz sam-te dʒu:-nu:b/	از سمت جنوب
southern	/dʒu:-nu:-bi:/	جنوبی
southward	/be sam-te dʒu:-nu:b/	به سمت جنوب
southwest	/dʒu:-nu:-be ɢarb/	جنوب غرب
southwestern	/dʒu:-nu:-be ɢar-bi:/	جنوب غربی
up	/bɒ:-lɒ:/	بالا
west	/ɢarb/	غرب
western	/ɢar-bi:/	غربی
westward	/be sam-te ɢarb/	به سمت غرب

# 2 - 6
CLIMATE

a sun beam	/par-to-ve ʔɒːf-tɒːb/	پرتو آفتاب
Beautiful day!	/ruː-ze xuː-bi: ʔast/	روز خوبی است!
Do you have such a weather in Tabriz?	/ʃo-mɒː tʃe-nin ha-vɒː-ʔi: dar tab-riːz dɒː-riːd/	شما چنین هوایی در تبریز دارید؟
fierce storm	/tuː-fɒː-ne ʃa-di:d/	توفان شدید
harash weather	/ha-vɒː-je nɒː-mat-buːʔ/	هوای نامطبوع
How cold is it!	/tʃe-Gadr sard ʔast/	چقدر سرد است!
How is the weather?	/ha-vɒː tʃe-towr ʔast/	هوا چطور است؟
I'm afraid it will rain today.	/miː-tar-sam ʔem-ruːz bɒː-rɒn be-bɒː-rad/	می‌ترسم امروز باران ببارد.
I'm extremely hot.	/xej-liː gar-mam ʔast/	خیلی گرمم است.
I heard thunder.	/man sa-dɒː-je raʔd ʃe-niː-dam/	من صدای رعد شنیدم.

78 Beginner's Persian

I hope it will clear off soon. ....
.............................../ʔo-miːd-vʌː-ram be-zuː-di: haː-vʌː sʌːf ʃa-vad/
امیدوارم بهزودی هوا صاف شود.
I feel cold. ..../sar-dam ʔast/. سردم است.
I prefer cold(hot) weather. ....
......................../man haː-vʌː-je sard (garm) rʌː tar-dʒiːh miː-da-ham/
من هوای سرد (گرم) را ترجیح میدهم.
It's hailing. ..../dʌː-rad ta-garg miː-bʌː-rad/. دارد تگرگ میبارد.
It's raining hard. /bʌː-rʌn be ʃed-dat miː-bʌː-rad/. باران بهشدّت میبارد.
stars ..../se-tʌː-re-gʌn/ ستارگان
the moon ..../mʌːh/ ماه
the sun ..../xor-ʃiːd/ خورشید
The sun is rising. ..../xor-ʃiːd dʌː-rad to-luːʔ miː-ko-nad/
خورشید دارد طلوع میکند.
The sun is setting. ..../xor-ʃiːd dʌː-rad ɢo-ruːb miː-ko-nad/
خورشید دارد غروب میکند.
The weather grew colder. ..../haː-vʌː sard-tar ʃod/. هوا سردتر شد.
The weather is awfully cold. ..../haː-vʌː bad dʒuː-riː sard ʔast/
هوا بدجوری سرد است.
The weather is cleaning off. ..../haː-vʌː dʌː-rad sʌːf miː-ʃa-vad/
هوا دارد صاف میشود.
The weather is fine. ..../haː-vʌː xuːb ʔast/. هوا خوب است.
The weather is red hot. . /havʌː xej-liː garm ʔast/. هوا خیلی گرم است.
The weather is very bad. ... /havʌː xej-liː bad ʔast/. هوا خیلی بد است.
The weather is warm today. ....
........................../havʌː ʔem-ruːz garm ʔast/. هوا امروز گرم است.
There's a lightning. ..../raʔ do barɢ ʔast/. رعدوبرق است.
There's a rainbow. ..../ʔʌn-dʒʌː raŋ-gin-ka-mʌn hast/
آنجا رنگینکمان هست.
It hails. ..../ta-garg miː-bʌː-rad/. تگرگ میبارد.
It has been raining all day. ....
................./ta-mʌː-me ruːz bʌː-rʌn bʌː-riːd/. تمام روز باران بارید.

It's a fine night.	/ʃa-be ɢa-ʃan-gi: ʔast/	شب قشنگی است.
It's a nice day.	/ru:-ze xu:-bi: ʔast/	روز خوبی است.
It's awful windy.	/bɒ:-de ʃa-di:-di: mi:-va-zad/	باد شدیدی می‌وزد.
It's below zero.	/ha-vɒ: zi:-re sefr ʔast/	هوا زیر صفر است.
It's cloudy.	/ha-vɒ: ʔab-ri: ʔast/	هوا ابری است.
It's dense fog.	/me-he ɢa-li:-zi: ʔast/	مه غلیظی است.
It's dry.	/ha-vɒ: xoʃk ʔast/	هوا خشک است.
It's dust.	/ha-vɒ: gar-do-xɒ:k ʔast/	هوا گرد و خاک است.
It's foggy.	/ha-vɒ: meh ʔast/	هوا مه است.
It's freezing.	/jax-ban-dʌn ʔast/	یخبندان است.
It's going to rain.	/mi:-xɒ:-had bɒ:-rʌn be-bɒ:-rad/	می‌خواهد باران ببارد.
It's mild.	/ha-vɒ: mo-lɒ:-jem ʔast/	هوا ملایم است.
It's moonlight.	/mah-tɒ:b ʔast/	مهتاب است.
It's raining.	/bɒ:-rʌn mi:-ʔɒ:-jad/	باران می‌آید.
It's slippy outside.	/bi:-run li:z ʔast/	بیرون لیز است.
It's snowing.	/barf mi:-bɒ:-rad/	برف می‌بارد.
It's stormy.	/ha-vɒ: tu:-fɒ:-ni: ʔast/	هوا طوفانی است.
It's very hard to walk.	/rɒ:h raf-tan xej-li: moʃ-kel ʔast/	راه رفتن خیلی مشکل است.
It's very misty.	/xej-li: ʃar-dʒi: ʔast/	خیلی شرجی است.
It may clear off tomorrow.	/mom-ken ʔast far-dɒ: ha-vɒ: sɒ:f ʃa-vad/	ممکن است فردا هوا صاف شود.
It rained during the night.	/ta-mɒ:-me ʃab bɒ:-rʌn bɒ:-ri:d/	تمام شب باران بارید.
It snowed last night.	/di:-ʃab barf bɒ:-ri:d/	دیشب برف بارید.
It will probably rain.	/ʔeh-te-mɒ:-lan bɒ:-rʌn xɒ-had bɒ:-ri:d/	احتمالاً باران خواهد بارید.
Look, it's raining.	/ne-gɒ:h kon bɒ:-rʌn mi:-bɒ:-rad/	نگاه کن باران می‌بارد.
Such a rain!	/tʃe bɒ:-rɒ:-ni:/	چه بارانی!
We've a very sever winter.	/ze-mes-tɒ:-ne sax-ti: dɒ:-ri:m/	زمستان سختی داریم.

What a heavenly day!	/tʃe ruː-ze ziː-bɑː-jiː/	!چه روز زیبایی
What a storm!	/tʃe tuː-fɑː-niː/	!چه طوفانی
What's the weather like in spiring in Zanjan?	/ha-vɑː-je ba-hɑːr dar zan-dʒɑn tʃe-towr ʔast/	هوای بهار در زنجان چطور است؟
Will it clear off?	/ha-vɑː sɑːf xɑː-had ʃod/	هوا صاف خواهد شد؟

2-7

AGE

age	/sen/	سن
aged six	/ʃeʃ sɑː-le/	شش ساله
at five years old	/dar pan-dʒ sɑː-le-giː/	در پنج‌سالگی
at the age of nine	/dar noh sɑː-le-giː/	در ۹ سالگی

He/She is at least sixty. ....
............../ʔuː had-de-ʔa-ɢal ʃast sɑːl dɑː-rad/. او حدّاقل شصت سال دارد.
He/She is ten years old. ..../ʔuː dah sɑːl dɑː-rad/. او ده سال دارد.
How old are you? ..../tʃand sɑːl dɑː-riː/ ؟ چند سال داری
I'm only eighteen. ..../man fa-ɢat hiːdʒ-dah sɑːl dɑː-ram/
من فقط هیجده سال دارم.
I'm twenty two years old. ..../man biːs to do sɑː-le has-tam/
من بیست‌ودو ساله هستم.
I shall soon be thirty. ..../be-zuː-diː siː sɑː-le xɑː-ham buːd/
به‌زودی سی ساله خواهم بود.

My birthday is seventh January. ....
.... /ru:-ze ta-val-lo-de man haf-to-me ʒʌn-vɪ-je ʔast/
روز تولّد من هفتم ژانویه است.
the old .... /pi:-rʌn/ پیران
Today is my birthday. .... /ʔem-ru: ru:-ze ta-val-lo-de man ʔast/
امروز روز تولّد من است.
under age .... /xord-sʌ:l/ خردسال
We are the same age. .... /mʌ ham-sen-no-sʌ:l has-ti:m/
ما همسن و سال هستیم.
When is your birthday? .... /ru:-ze ta-val-lo-de ʃo-mʌ kej ʔast/
روز تولّد شما کی است؟
You look old. .... /ʃo-mʌ pi:r-tar ne-ʃʌn mi:-da-hi:d/
شما پیرتر نشان می‌دهید.
You look younger. .... /ʃo-mʌ dʒa-vʌn-tar ne-ʃʌn mi:-da-hi:d/
شما جوانتر نشان می‌دهید.

2-8 FAMILY RELATIONSHIPS

aunt	/ʔam-me (xɑ:-le)/	عمّه (خاله)
baby	/batʃ-tʃe/	بچّه
bear	/ta-val-lod/	تولّد
boy	/pe-sar/	پسر
boy friend	/du:st pe-sar/	دوست پسر
brother	/ba-rɑ:-dar/	برادر
brother-in-law	/ba-rɑ:-dar zan (ba-rɑ:-dar ʃow-har)/	برادر زن (برادر شوهر)
child	/far-zand/	فرزند
chum	/du:s-te sa-mi:-mi:/	دوست صمیمی
comrade	/ra-fi:G/	رفیق

cousin	/ʔa-mu: zɑ:de (ʔam-me zɑ:-de)(xɑ:-le zɑ:-de)(dɑ:-ji: zɑ:-de)/	عموزاده (عمّه‌زاده)(خاله‌زاده)(دایی‌زاده)
daughter	/far-zan-de dox-tar/	فرزند دختر
death	/marg/	مرگ
divorce	/ta-lɑːɢ/	طلاق
father	/pe-dar/	پدر
father-in-law	/pe-dar-zan (pe-dar-ʃow-har)/	پدرزن (پدرشوهر)
female	/mo-ʔan-nas/	مؤنّث
foe	/doʃ-man/	دشمن
foster mother	/mɑ:-da-re ʃi:-ri:/	مادر شیری
friend	/du:st/	دوست
girl	/dox-tar/	دختر
girlfriend	/du:st dox-tar/	دوست دختر
godfather	/pe-dar-xʌn-de/	پدرخوانده
godmother	/mɑ:-dar-xʌn-de/	مادرخوانده
grandchild	/na-ve/	نوه
granddaughter	/na-ve-je dox-ta-ri:/	نوهٔ دختری
grandfather	/pe-dar bo-zorg/	پدربزرگ
grandmother	/mɑ:-dar bo-zorg/	مادربزرگ
grandson	/na-ve-je pe-sa-ri:/	نوهٔ پسری
great-granddaughter	/na-ti:-dʒe-je dox-tar/	نتیجهٔ دختر
great-grandfather	/dʒad-de pe-da-ri:/	جدّ پدری
great-grandmother	/dʒad-de mɑ:-da-ri:/	جدّ مادری
great-grandson	/na-ti:-dʒe-je pe-sar/	نتیجهٔ پسر
husband	/ʃow-har/	شوهر
lad	/pe-sar-batʃ-tʃe (now-dʒa-vʌn)/	پسر بچّه (نوجوان)
male	/mo-zak-kar/	مذکّر
man	/mard/	مرد
marriage	/ʔez-de-vɑ:dʒ/	ازدواج
maternal aunt	/xɑ:-le/	خاله
maternal uncle	/dɑ:-ji:/	دایی
mother	/mɑ:-dar/	مادر

mother-in-law	/mɒ:-dar-zan (mɒ:-dar-ʃow-har)/	مادرزن (مادرشوهر)
neighbor	/ham-sɒ:-je/	همسایه
nephew	/pe-sar xɒ:-har (pe-sar ba-rɒ:-dar)/	پسرخواهر (پسربرادر)
niece	/dox-tar xɒ:-har (dox-tar ba-rɒ:-dar)/	دخترخواهر (دختربرادر)
puberty	/bo-lu:G/	بلوغ
relative	/xi:-ʃɒ:-vand/	خویشاوند
sister	/xɒ:-har/	خواهر
sister-in-law	/xɒ:-har zan (xɒ:-har ʃow-har)/	خواهرزن (خواهرشوهر)
son	/pe-sar/	پسر
spouse	/ham-sar/	همسر
stepdaughter	/nɒ: ba-rɒ:-da-ri:/	نابرادری
stepdaughter	/nɒ: dox-ta-ri:/	نادختری
stepfather	/nɒ: pe-da-ri:/	ناپدری
stepmother	/nɒ: mɒ:-da-ri:/	نامادری
stepson	/nɒ: pe-sa-ri:/	ناپسری
uncle	/ʔa-mu:/	عمو
wife	/ham-sar/	زن
woman	/zan/	زن
young	/dʒa-vʌn/	جوان
youth	/dʒa-vɒ:-ni:/	جوانی

Have you got any childern?	/ʃo-mɒ: batʃ-tʃe dɒ:-ri:d/	شما بچّه دارید؟
I'm married.	/man mo-ta-ʔah-hel has-tam/	من متأهل هستم.
I'm single.	/man mo-dʒar-rad has-tam/	من مجرّد هستم.
I have one child.	/man jek batʃ-tʃe dɒ:-ram/	من یک بچّه دارم.
Shapur is Mani's brother.	/ʃɒ:-pu:r ba-rɒ:-da-re mɒ:-ni: ʔast/	شاپور برادر مانی است.
This is my father.	/ʔɪn pe-da-re man ʔast/	این پدر من است.

2-9 COLORS

azure	/lɒː-dʒe-var-diː/	لاجوردی
beige	/beʒ/	بژ
black	/sɪ-jɒːh/	سیاه
blond	/zar-de xor-mɒː-ʔiː/	زرد خرمایی
blue	/ʔɒː-biː/	آبی
brown	/gah-ve-ʔiː/	قهوه‌ای
burnt ochre	/zar-de suːx-te/	زرد سوخته
canary yellow	/zar-de ɢa-nɒː-riː/	زرد قناری
chestnut	/ba-luː-tiː/	بلوطی
dark	/tiː-re/	تیره
dark carmine	/ɢer-me-ze dʒe-ga-rɪ-je tiː-re/	قرمز جگری تیره
dark orange	/nɒː-ren-dʒɪ-je tiː-re/	نارنجی تیره
dull brown	/ɢah-ve-ʔɪ-je siːr/	قهوه‌ای سیر
emerald	/zo-mor-ro-diː/	زمرّدی

gray	/xvː-kes-ta-riː/	خاکستری
green	/sabz/	سبز SABZ
gold ochre	/zar-de ta-lvː-jiː/	زرد طلایی
golden	/ta-lvː-jiː/	طلایی
honey	/ʔa-sa-liː/	عسلی
jasper	/jaʃ-miː/	یشمی
khaky	/xvː-kiː/	خاکی
lemon	/liː-muː-jiː/	لیمویی
light	/row-ʃan/	روشن
light blue	/ʔvː-bɪ-je row-ʃan/	آبی روشن
light cobalt blue	/ʔvː-se-mvː-nɪ-je row-ʃan/	آسمانی روشن
light orange	/nvː-ren-dʒɪ-je row-ʃan/	نارنجی روشن
milky	/ʃiː-riː/	شیری
moss green	/sab-ze Guːr-bvː-Ge-ʔiː/	سبز قورباغه‌ای
olive	/zej-tuː-niː/	زیتونی
one-colour	/tak-raŋ/	تک‌رنگ
opaline	/ʃiː-rɪ-je mvːt/	شیری مات
orange	/nvː-ren-dʒiː/	نارنجی
peach	/zar-de huː-luː-ʔiː/	زرد هلویی
peacock blue	/ʔvː-bɪ-je tvː-vuː-siː/	آبی طاووسی
peanut	/no-xo-diː/	نخودی
pearl	/sa-da-fiː/	صدفی
pink	/suː-ra-tiː/	صورتی
ponceau	/sor-xe ʔvː-ta-ʃiː/	سرخ آتشی
prussian blue	/ʔvː-bɪ-je tond/	آبی تند
purple	/ʔar-Ga-vvː-niː/	ارغوانی
red	/Ger-mez/	قرمز GAIR MEZ
ruby	/jvː-Guː-tiː/	یاقوتی
rufous	/nvː-ren-dʒɪ-je siːr/	نارنجی سیر
rusty	/ʔvː-dʒo-riː/	آجری
sap green	/sab-ze row-ʃan/	سبز روشن
scarlet	/Ger-me-ze max-ma-liː/	قرمز مخملی

sepia	/Gah-ve-ʔɪ-je sorx/	قهوه‌ای سرخ
silver	/noG-re-ʔi:/	نقره‌ای
tan	/bo-ron-ze/	برنزه
true blue	/ʔv:-bɪ-je xv:-les/	آبی خالص
turquoise	/fi:-ru:-ze-ʔi:/	فیروزه‌ای
violet	/ba-naʃʃ/	بنفش
white	/se-fi:d/ SE FEED	سفید
yellow	/zard/ ZARD	زرد

She was dressed in white. /ʔu: se-fi:d pu:-ʃi:-de ʔast/ او سفید پوشیده است.

She wore a green dress. /ʔu: le-bv:-se sab-zi: pu:-ʃi:d/ او لباس سبزی پوشید.

That's a bright yellow dress. /ʔʌn le-bv:s zar-de row-ʃan ʔast/ آن لباس زرد روشن است.

The sea is blue. /dar-jv: ʔv:-bi: raŋ ʔast/ دریا آبی رنگ است.

What color do you like? /tʃe raŋ-gi: rv: du:st dv:-ri:d/ چه رنگی را دوست دارید؟

2-10
QUALITIES

bad	/bad/	بد
cool	/xo-nak/	خنک
beautiful	/xoʃ-gel/	خوشگل
big	/bo-zorg/	بزرگ
cheap	/ʔar-zʌn/	ارزان
cold	/sard/	سرد
dull	/Gam-gɪn/	غمگین
excellent	/ʔv:-li:/	عالی
expensive	/ge-rʌn/	گران
fair	/xu:b/	خوب
good	/xu:b/	خوب
handsome	/xoʃ-ʔan-dʌ:m/	خوش‌اندام
heavy	/saŋ-gɪn/	سنگین
high	/bo-land/	بلند

hot	داغ	/dɑ:G/
interesting	جالب	/dʒɑ:-leb/
light	سبک	/sa-bok/
long	دراز	/de-rɑ:z/
low	پایین	/pɑ:-jɪn/
middle	میانه	/mɪ-jɑ:-ne/
narrow	باریک	/bɑ:-ri:k/
new	تازه	/tɑ:-ze/
nice	نازنین	/nɑ:-za-nɪn/
old	پیر (کهنه)	/pi:r (koh-ne)/
quick	سریع	/sa-ri:ʔ/
short	کوتاه	/ku:-tɑ:h/
slow	آهسته	/ʔɑ:-hes-te/
small	کوچک	/ku:-tʃak/
strong	قوی	/Ga-vi:/
tall	بلند	/bo-land/
thick	کلفت	/ko-loft/
thin	نازک	/nɑ:-zok/
ugly	زشت	/zeʃt/
uninteresting	ناجالب	/nɑ:-dʒɑ:-leb/
young	جوان	/dʒa-vʌn/
weak	ضعیف	/za-ʔi:f/
warm	گرم	/garm/
wide	پهن	/pahn/

I'm taller than you.	من بلندتر از شما هستم.	/man bo-lan-tar ʔaz ʃo-mɑ: has-tam/
It's interesting.	جالب است.	/dʒɑ:-leb ʔast/
She/he is young.	او جوان است.	/ʔu: dʒa-vʌn ʔast/
The weather is hot.	هوا گرم است.	/ha-vɑ: garm ʔast/

These stockings are long. ..../ʔin dʒuː-rɑːb-hɑː boland hastand/
این جورابها بلند هستند.
This book is better than that one. ....
..../ʔin ketɑːb behtar ʔaz ʔɑn jeki ʔast/ این کتاب بهتر از آن یکی است.
This one is good. ..../ʔin jeki xuːb ʔast/ این یکی خوب است.
This shirt is loose. /ʔin piː-rɑː-han goʃɑːd ʔast/ این پیراهن گشاد است.

2 - 11
EDUCATION

academician	/ʔoz-ve far-haŋ-ges-tʌn/	عضو فرهنگستان
boarding school	/mad-ra-se-je ʃa-bʌː-ne ruː-ziː/	مدرسهٔ شبانه روزی
college	/kʌː-ledʒ/	کالج
dean	/ra-ʔiː-se dʌː-neʃ-ka-de/	رئیس دانشکده
degree	/rot-be-je tah-si-liː/	رتبهٔ تحصیلی
education	/tah-siː-lʌːt/	تحصیلات
educational institute	/mo-ʔas-se-se-je ʔʌː-muː-ze-ʃiː/	مؤسسه آموزشی
elementary education	/tah-si-lʌː-te ʔeb-te-dʌː-jiː/	تحصیلات ابتدایی
elementary school	/da-bes-tʌn/	دبستان
exam	/ʔem-te-hʌn/	امتحان
examination period	/dow-re-je ʔem-te-hʌː-nʌːt/	دورهٔ امتحانات
examinations	/ʔem-te-hʌː-nʌːt/	امتحانات
faculty	/dʌː-neʃ-ka-de/	دانشکده
final examinations	/ʔem-te-hʌː-nʌː-te na-hʌː-jiː/	امتحانات نهایی

96 Beginner's Persian

guidance school /mad-ra-se-je rɑ:h-no-mɑ:-ji:/ مدرسهٔ راهنمایی
headmaster /mo-di:r/ مدیر
higher education /tah-si:-lɑ:-te ʔɑ:-li:/ تحصیلات عالی
institute /mo-ʔas-se-se/ مؤسّسه
institution of higher education /dɑ:-neʃ-sa-rɑ:-je ʔɑ:-li:/ دانشسرای عالی
lecture /so-xan-rɑ:-ni:/ سخنرانی
lesson /dars/ درس
post-graduate /bɑ:-lɑ:-je li:-sɑ:ns/ بالای لیسانس
professor /ʔos-tɑ:d/ استاد
pupil /dɑ:-neʃ-ʔɑ:-mu:z (dɑ:-neʃ-dʒu:)/ دانش‌آموز (دانشجو)
rector /ra-ʔi:-se dɑ:-neʃ-gɑ:h/ رئیس دانشگاه
research institute /mo-ʔas-se-se-je tah-Gi:-Gɑ:-ti:/ مؤسّسهٔ تحقیقاتی
scholarship /bu:r-se tah-si:-li:/ بورس تحصیلی
school /mad-ra-se/ مدرسه
school-leaving certificate
/go-vɑ:-hi:-nɑ:-me-je pɑ:-jɑ:-ne tah-si:-lɑ:-te mo-ta-vas-se-te/
گواهینامهٔ پایان تحصیلات متوسّطه
secondary education /tah-si:-lɑ:-te mo-ta-vas-se-te/ تحصیلات متوسّطه
secondary school /da-bi:-res-tʌn/ دبیرستان
secondary special education
/tah-si:-lɑ:-te ʔex-te-sɑ:-si:-je mo-ta-vas-se-te/ تحصیلات اختصاصی متوسّطه
student /dɑ:-neʃ-ʔɑ:-mu:z (dɑ:-neʃ-dʒu:)/ دانش‌آموز (دانشجو)
study assistance /ko-mak ha-zi:-ne-je tah-si:-li:/ کمک هزینهٔ تحصیلی
teacher /mo-ʔal-lem/ معلّم
technical school /ho-na-res-tʌn/ هنرستان
term /term/ ترم
text-book /ke-tɑ:-be dar-si:/ کتاب درسی
thesis /pɑ:-jʌn-nɑ:-me/ پایان‌نامه
under-graduate student /dɑ:-neʃ-dʒu:-je li:-sɑ:ns/ دانشجوی لیسانس
university /dɑ:-neʃ-gɑ:h/ دانشگاه
vacation /taʔ-ti:-lɑ:t/ تعطیلات

How long are the summer holidays? ....
تعطیلات تابستانی چقدر است؟ /taʔ-tiː-lvː-te tvː-bes-tvː-ni: tʃe-Gadr ʔast/ ....
How many years does the school course last? ....
................/dow-re-je tah-siː-lvːt dar mad-ra-se tʃand svːl ʔast/
دورهٔ تحصیلات در مدرسه چند سال است؟
I'm interested in linguistics. ....
/man be za-bʌn-ʃe-nvː-si: ʔa-lvː-Ge-man-dam/ .من به زبان‌شناسی علاقه‌مندم
I'm studying at Tehran university. ....
..................../man dar dvː-neʃ-gvː-he teh-rʌn tah-siː1 miː-ko-nam/
من در دانشگاه تهران تحصیل می‌کنم.
I'm a post-graduate student. ....
.........................../man dvː-neʃ-dʒuː-je fow-Ge liː-svːns has-tam/
من دانشجوی فوق‌لیسانس هستم.
I'm studying art. ..../man ho-nar miː-xvː-nam/. .من هنر می‌خوانم
What faculties are at your university? ....
................/dar dvː-neʃ-gvː-he ʃo-mvː tʃe dvː-neʃ-ka-de-hvː-ji: ʔast/
در دانشگاه شما چه دانشکده‌هایی هست؟
What is the subject of your graduation thesis? ....
/mow-zuː-ʔe pvː-jʌn-nvː-me-je ʃo-mvː tʃiːst/. موضوع پایان‌نامهٔ شما چیست؟
When do the examinations begin? ....
........./ʔem-te-hvː-nvːt kej ʃo-ruːʔ miː-ʃa-vad/ امتحانات کی شروع می‌شود؟
When does the academic year begin? ....
.. /svː-le tah-siː-liː kej ʃo-ruːʔ miː-ʃa-vad/ سال تحصیلی کی شروع می‌شود؟
Which course are you in? ..../reʃ-te-je ʃo-mvː tʃiːst/
رشتهٔ شما چیست؟
Which course do you like? ....
................/ko-dvːm reʃ-te rv du:st dvː-riːd/ کدام رشته را دوست دارید؟
Which faculty are you in? ....
.............../dar ko-dvːm dvː-neʃ-ka-de has-tiːd/ در کدام دانشکده هستید؟

2-12
OCCUPATIONS

architect	طرّاح معمار	/tar-rɑ:-he meʔ-mɑ:r/
actor/actress	هنرپیشه	/ho-nar-pi:-ʃe/
artist	هنرمند	/ho-nar-mand/
carpenter	نجّار	/nadʒ-dʒɑ:r/
chemist	شیمیدان	/ʃi:-mi:-dɑn/
cook	آشپز	/ʔɑ:ʃ-paz/
correspondent	خبرنگار	/xa-bar-ne-gɑ:r/
dock-worker	کارگر بندر	/kɑ:r-ga-re ban-dar/
doctor	پزشک	/pe-zeʃk/
driver	راننده	/rɑ:-nan-de/
economist	اقتصاددان	/ʔeG-te-sɑ:d-dɑn/
editor	سردبیر	/sar-da-bi:r/
electrician	برق‌کار	/barg-kɑ:r/
engineer	مهندس	/mo-han-des/

farmer	/ke-ʃɑ:-varz/	کشاورز
film director	/kɑ:r-gar-dɑ:-ne si:-ne-mɑ:/	کارگردان سینما
goldsmith	/zar-gar/	زرگر
hairdresser	/ʔɑ:-rɑ:-jeʃ-gar/	آرایشگر
journalist	/ru:z-nɑ:-me ne-gɑ:r/	روزنامه‌نگار
lawyer	/va-ki:l/	وکیل
mason	/ban-nɑ:/	بنّا
mechanic	/me-kɑ:-ni:k/	مکانیک
merchant	/bɑ:-zar-gʌn/	بازرگان
miner	/maʔ-dan-tʃi:/	معدنچی
musician	/mu:-se-ɢi:-dʌn/	موسیقیدان
office worker	/kɑ:r-mand/	کارمند
painter	/naɢ-ɢɑ:ʃ/	نقّاش
part-timer	/kɑ:r-ga-re ni:-me vaɢt/	کارگر نیمه‌وقت
physicist	/fi:-zi:k-dʌn/	فیزیکدان
pilot	/xa-la-bʌn/	خلبان
scientist	/dɑ:-neʃ-mand/	دانشمند
seller	/fo-ru:-ʃan-de/	فروشنده
shop assistant	/fo-ru:-ʃan-de/	فروشنده
student	/dɑ:-neʃ-dʒu:/	دانشجو
tailor	/xaj-jɑ:t/	خیّاط
teacher	/mo-ʔal-lem/	معلّم
typist	/mɑ:-ʃin ne-vi:s/	ماشین‌نویس
waiter/waitress	/pi:ʃ-xed-mat/	پیشخدمت
worker	/kɑ:r-gar/	کارگر

Fill out this form. /ʔɪn form rɑ: por ko-ni:d/ این فرم را پر کنید.
Have you had any experience? /tadʒ-ro-be-je ɢab-li: dɑ:-ri:d/
تجربهٔ قبلی دارید؟
Have you got yourself a job? /xo-dat kɑ:r pej-dɑ: kar-di:/
خودت کار پیدا کردی؟

General Data 101

I'm a student.	/man dɒ:-neʃ-dʒu: has-tam/	من دانشجو هستم.
I'm an engineer.	/man mo-han-des has-tam/	من مهندس هستم.
I want to apply for a job.	/mi:-xɒ:-ham ta-ɢɒ:-zɒ:-je kɒ:r be-ko-nam/	می‌خواهم تقاضای کار بکنم.
I work in a factory.	/man dar kɒ:r-xɒ:-ne kɒ:r mi:-ko-nam/	من در کارخانه کار می‌کنم.
I work in a Ministary.	/man dar ve-zɒ:-rat-xɒ:-ne kɒ:r mi:-ko-nam/	من در وزارتخانه کار می‌کنم.
I work in a refinary.	/man dar pɒ:-lɒ:-jeʃ-gɒ:h kɒ:r mi:-ko-nam/	من در پالایشگاه کار می‌کنم.
I work in an office.	/man dar ʔe-dɒ:-re kɒ:r mi:-ko-nam/	من در اداره کار می‌کنم.
What are your terms?	/ʃa-rɒ:-je-te-tʌn tʃi:st/	شرایطتان چیست؟
What is your occupation?	/ʃoɢ-le ʃo-mɒ: tʃi:st/	شغل شما چیست؟
What is your present job?	/ʃoɢ-le feʔ-lɪ-je ʃo-mɒ: tʃi:st/	شغل فعلی شما چیست؟
Where do you work?	/ʃo-mɒ: ko-dʒɒ: kɒ:r mi:-ko-ni:d/	شما کجا کار می‌کنید؟

SECTION 3
ARRIVAL/DEPARTURE

3-1 CUSTOMS

3-2 AIRPORT

3-3 AIRPORT LOUDSPEAKER

3-4 FLIGHT IDIOMS

3-5 INSIDE A PLANE

3-6 TRAVELLING BY RAIL

3-7 TRAVELLING BY CAR

3-8 GARAGE

3-9 TRAVELLING BY SHIP

3-1
CUSTOMS

aliens' officer	/mas-ʔuː-le ʔat-bvː-ʔe xvː-re-dʒiː/	مسئول اتباع خارجی
border	/marz/	مرز
business trip	/mo-svː-fe-ra-te kvːriː/	مسافرت کاری
customs	/gom-rok/	گمرک
customs declaration	/ʔez-hvːr-nvː-me-je gom-ro-kiː/	اظهارنامهٔ گمرکی
customs insepector	/bvːz-ra-se gom-rok/	بازرس گمرک
customs regulation	/mo-ɢar-ra-rvː-te gom-ro-kiː/	مقرّرات گمرکی
customs restrictions	/mah-duː-dɪj-jat-hvː-jeʻ gom-ro-kiː/	محدودیّتهای گمرکی
document	/sa-nad/	سند
duties	/ʔa-vvː-rez/	عوارض
entry visa	/ra-vvː-diː-de voː-ruːd/	روادید ورود
exit visa	/ra-vvː-diː-de xo-ruːdʒ/	روادید خروج
extension of a visa	/tam-diː-de ra-vvː-diːd/	تمدید روادید
foreign currency	/ʔar-ze xvː-re-dʒiː/	ارز خارجی

number of passport	/ʃo-mɑː-re-je go-zar-nɑː-me/	شمارهٔ گذرنامه
stamp	/mohr/	مُهر
passport	/go-zar-nɑː-me/	گذرنامه
passport control	/kon-to-ro-le go-zar-nɑː-me/	کنترل گذرنامه
period of stay	/mod-da-te ʔe-ɢɑː-mat/	مدّت اقامت
profession	/her-fe/	حرفه
purpose of the trip	/ha-daf ʔaz mo-sɑː-fe-rat/	هدف از مسافرت
residence permit	/ʔe-dʒɑː-ze-je ʔe-ɢɑː-mat/	اجازهٔ اقامت
tourist trip	/sa-fa-re tuː-riːs-tiː/	سفر توریستی
travel documents	/ma-dɑː-re-ke sa-far/	مدارک سفر
trip	/mo-sɑː-fe-rat/	مسافرت
visa	/ra-ʌʌ-diːd/	روادید
transit visa	/ra-ʌʌ-diː-de te-rʌn-ziːt/	روادید ترانزیت

Are you alone?	/tan-hɑː has-tiːd/	تنها هستید؟
Are you married?	/mo-ta-ʔa-hel has-tiːd/	متأهل هستید؟
Are you together?	/bɑː ham has-tiːd/	با هم هستید؟
Fill out this form.	/ʔɪn form rɑː por ko-niːd/	این فرم را پر کنید.
Have you been in this country before?		
	/ɢab-lan dar ʔɪn keʃ-var buː-de-ʔiːd/	قبلاً در این کشور بوده‌اید؟
Here's my passport.		
/be-far-mɑː-ʔiːd, ʔɪn ham go-zar-nɑː-me-je man/		بفرمایید، این هم گذرنامهٔ من.
Here are my things.	/ʔɪn va-sɑː-je-le man ʔast/	این وسایل من است.
Here's my declaration form.		
	/ʔɪn ʔez-hɑːr-nɑː-me-je man ʔast/	این اظهارنامهٔ من است.
How many are you?	/tʃand na-far has-tiːd/	چند نفر هستید؟
How old are you?	/tʃand sɑːl dɑː-riːd/	چند سال دارید؟
I'm twenty five years old.		
	/man biːs to pandʒ sɑː-le has-tam/	من بیست و پنج ساله هستم.

Arrival/Departure

I was born in Nice, France. ....
.... /man dar ni:-se fa-rʌn-se mo-ta-val-led ʃo-de-ʔam/
من در نیس فرانسه متولّد شده‌ام.
Is this all yours? .../ʔɪn-hvː va-svː-je-le ʃo-mvːst/ اینها وسایل شماست؟
My first name is ... ./ʔes-me man ... ʔast/ اسم من ... است.
My last name is ... ./ʔes-me fvː-mi:-le man ... ʔast/
اسم فامیل من ... است.
Please show me your passport. ....
/lot-fan go-zar-nvː-me-tʌn rʌ ne-ʃʌn da-hi:d/. لطفاً گذرنامه‌تان را نشان دهید.
Please show me your visa. ....
.../lot-fan ra-vvː-di:-de-tʌn rʌ ne-ʃʌn da-hi:d/ لطفاً روادیدتان را نشان دهید.
Shall I open my suitcase? ..../tʃa-ma-dvː-nam rʌ bvːz ko-nam/
چمدانم را باز کنم؟
This's my bag. ..../ʔɪn sʌ-ke man ʔast/. این ساک من است.
The permit to stay, please. ..../ʔe-dʒvː-ze-je ʔe-ɢvː-mat lot-fan/
اجازهٔ اقامت، لطفاً.
The visa, please. ..../ra-vvː-di:d lot-fan/. روادید، لطفاً.
This passport isn't valid. ....
............/ʔeʔ-te-bvː-re ʔɪn go-zar-nvː-me ta-mvːm ʃo-de ʔast/
اعتبار این گذرنامه تمام شده است.
What's your name? ..../ʔes-me ʃo-mvː tʃiːst/؟ اسم شما چیست
What's your nationality? /mel-lɪ-ja-te ʃo-mvː tʃiːst/؟ ملّیت شما چیست
What's your occupation? ..../ʃoɢ-le ʃo-mvː tʃiːst/؟ شغل شما چیست
Where are you coming from? ..../ʔaz ko-dʒvː mi:-ʔvː-jid/
از کجا می‌آیید؟
Where are you from? ..../ʔah-le ko-dʒvː-ʔi:d/؟ اهل کجایید
Where do you wish to go? ..../ko-dʒvː mi:-xvː-hi:d be-ra-vi:d/
کجا می‌خواهید بروید؟
Where's the customs control? ../kon-to-ro-le gom-ro-ki ko-dʒvːst/
کنترل گمرکی کجاست؟
Where were you born? ...../ma-hal-le ta-val-lo-de-tʌn/؟ محلّ تولّدتان
Your passport, please. ..../go-zar-nvː-me lot-fan/ گذرنامه لطفاً

3-2
AIRPORT

arrival	/vɒː-re-dɪn/	واردين
baggage retrieval	/dar-jvː-fte bvːr/	دريافت بار
bookshop	/ke-tvːb fo-ruː-ʃiː/	كتابفروشى
change	/tab-diː-le puːl/	تبديل پول
entrance	/voruː-diː/	ورودى
exit	/xo-ruːdʒ/	خروج
fire alarm	/zan-ge xa-ta-re ha-riːɢ/	زنگ خطر حريق
fire station	/ʔiːst-gvː-he ʔvː-taʃ-ne-ʃvː-niː/	ايستگاه آتش‌نشانى
first aid	/ko-mak-hvː-je ʔav-va-lɪ-je/	كمكهاى اوّليه
flights	/be ta-ra-fe ha-vvː-pej-mvː/	به طرف هواپيما
gentlemen's toilet	/dast-ʃuː-ʔɪ-je mar-dvː-ne/	دستشويى مردانه
gift shop	/ma-ɢvː-ze-je sow-ɢvːt/	مغازهٔ سوغات
hotel reservation	/za-xiː-re-je dʒvː dar ho-tel/	ذخيرهٔ جا در هتل
information	/ʔet-te-lvː-ʔvːt/	اطلاعات

ladies restroom	/ʔo-tʌ:-Ge ʔes-te-rʌ:-ha-te bʌ:-nu:-vʌn/	اتاق استراحت بانوان
ladies toilet	/dast ʃu:-ʔi-je za-nʌ:-ne/	دستشویی زنانه
luggage claim	/dar-jʌ:f-te bʌ:r/	دریافت بار
no admittance	/vo-ru:d mam-nu:ʔ/	ورود ممنوع
passport check	/kon-to-ro-le go-zar-nʌ:-me/	کنترل گذرنامه
police	/po-li:s/	پلیس
private	/xo-su:-si:/	خصوصی
restroom	/ʔo-tʌ:-Ge ʔes-te-rʌ:-hat/	اطاق استراحت
restaurant	/Ga-zʌ:-xo-ri:/	غذاخوری
snack	/ʔaG-zi-je-je sa-bok/	اغذیهٔ سبک
subway	/met-ro/	مترو
tax-free shop	/ma-Gʌ:-ze-je be-du:-ne mʌ:-li-jʌ:t/	مغازهٔ بدون مالیات
transit lounge	/sʌ:-lo-ne te-rʌn-zi:t/	سالن ترانزیت
to bus	/be ta-ra-fe ʔo-tu:-bu:s/	به طرف اتوبوس
to taxi	/be ta-ra-fe tʌ:k-si:/	به طرف تاکسی
to telephone	/be ta-ra-fe te-le-fon/	به طرف تلفن
waiting room	/sʌ:-lo-ne ʔen-te-zʌ:r/	سالن انتظار
way out	/rʌ:-he xo-ru:dʒ/	راه خروج

This's my ticket.	/ʔin be-li:-te man ʔast/	این بلیط من است.
Where am I to check in?	/be ko-dʒʌ: bʌ:-jad mo-rʌ:-dʒe-ʔe ko-nam/	به کجا باید مراجعه کنم؟
On your left No.5.	/be ta-ra-fe tʃap, ʃo-mʌ:-re-je pandʒ/	به طرف چپ، شمارهٔ پنج.
Are these your luggage?	/ʔin-hʌ: ʔa-sʌ:-se ʃo-mʌ:st/	اینها اثاث شماست؟
Yes, they are.	/ba-le ha-min-towr ʔast/	بله، همینطور است.
I'll only check this one.	/man fa-Gat ha-min je-ki: rʌ: tah-vi:l mi:-da-ham/	من فقط همین یکی را تحویل می‌دهم.

The other one to be shipped unaccompanied. ....
.................../diː-ga-ri: be suː-ra-te bvː-re Gej-re ham-rvːh ʔast/
دیگری به صورت بار غیر همراه است.
Are you going to Shiraz? ..../ʃo-mvː be ʃiː-rvːz miː-ra-viːd/
شما به شیراز می‌روید؟
No, I'll have a short break in Hamadan. ....
......../xejr, man ta-vaG-Go-fe kuː-tvː-hi: dar ha-me-dʌn xvː-ham dvːʃt/
خیر، من توقف کوتاهی در همدان خواهم داشت.
Please, check my luggage for Abadan. ....
...../lot-fan bvː-re ma-rvː mos-ta-Giː-man be ʔvː-bvː-dʌn haml ko-niːd/
لطفاً، بار مرا مستقیماً به آبادان حمل کنید.
Please, let me have a window seat. ....
.........../lot-fan san-da-lɪ-je ka-nvː-re pan-dʒa-re be man be-da-hiːd/
لطفاً، صندلی کنار پنجره به من بدهید.
Please, let me have an aisle seat. ....
.........../lot-fan san-da-lɪ-je mo-dʒvː-ve-re rvːh-ro be man be-da-hiːd/
لطفاً، صندلی مجاور راهرو به من بدهید.
Is the flight on schedule? ....
/par-vvːz be mo-GeʔʔPan-dʒvːm xvː-had ʃod/
پرواز به موقع انجام خواهد شد؟
I'm afraid, there's a 15 minute delay. ....
......................../mo-ta-ʔas-se-fvː-ne, jek robʔ ta-xiːr xvː-had dvːʃt/
متأسفانه، یک ربع تأخیر خواهد داشت.
Do I've enough time to do shopping? ....
.........../ba-rvː-je xa-riːd vaG-te kvː-fi: dvː-ram/
برای خرید وقت کافی دارم؟
No, you've a little time. ..../na ʃo-mvː vaG-te ka-mi: dvː-riːd/
نه شما وقت کمی دارید.
Is here anyone who speaks English? ....
...................../ʔɪn-dʒvː ka-si: hast ke ʔeŋ-ge-liː-si: soh-bat ko-nad/
اینجا کسی هست که انگلیسی صحبت کند؟
Yes, Sir/Ma'am. We can speak English. ....
/ba-le ʔvː-Gvː (xvː-nom) mvː miː-ta-vvː-niːm ʔeŋ-ge-liː-si: soh-bat ko-niːm/
بله، آقا(خانم) ما می‌توانیم انگلیسی صحبت کنیم.

Have you an agent for the French line? ....
.... /ba-rɒ:-je xat-te fa-rʌn-se ʃoʔ-be dɒ:-ri:d/ ؟برای خطّ فرانسه شعبه دارید
Yes, this is the place. /ba-le ha-mɪn ma-hal ʔast/ بله، همین محل است
When will the next flight of the French line leave for Paris? ..
.... /par-vɒ:-ze baʔ-dɪ-je ma-si:-re fa-rʌn-se be mag-sa-de pɒ:-ri:s kej
ha-re-kat mi:-ko-nad/؟پرواز بعدی مسیر فرانسه به مقصد پاریس کی حرکت می‌کند
Next saturday at 8 p.m. ....
..................../ʃam-be-je ʔɒ:-jan-de sɒ:-ʔa-te haʃ-te baʔd ʔaz zohr/
شنبهٔ آینده ساعت ۸ بعدازظهر.
What's the fare for first class? ....
........../ke-rɒ:-je da-ra-dʒe jek tʃe-ɢadr ʔast/ ؟کرایه درجه یک چقدر است
When's it due at Paris? ....
../tʃe mow-ɢeʔ be pɒ:-ri:s xɒ:-had re-si:d/ ؟چه موقع به پاریس خواهد رسید
5 hours after its departure. ....
............../pandʒ sɒ:-ʔat ba-ʔd ʔaz ha-re-ka-taʃ/. ۵ ساعت بعد از حرکتش
Give me a first class ticket to Tabriz. ....
.................../jek be-li:-te da-ra-dʒe jek ba-rɒ:-je tab-ri:z be-da-hi:d/
یک بلیط درجه یک برای تبریز بدهید.
This is your ticket. ..../ʔɪn be-li:-te ʃo-mɒ:st/ این بلیط شماست
Where can I change my money? ....
...................../ko-dʒɒ: mi:-ta-vɒ:-nam pu:-lam rɒ: tab-di:l ko-nam/
کجا می‌توانم پولم را تبدیل کنم؟
How much is a dollar worth by rial? ....
........................./ʔar-ze-ʃe jek do-lɒ:r be rɪ-jɒ:l tʃe-ɢadr ʔast/
ارزش یک دلار به ریال چقدر است؟
Where's the ticket office? ....
.............../daf-ta-re fo-ru:-ʃe be-li:t ko-dʒɒ:st/ ؟دفتر فروش بلیط کجاست
Where's the toilet? ..../dast-ʃu:-ʔi: ko-dʒɒ:st/ ؟دستشویی کجاست
Where's the waiting hall? ....
...................../sɒ:-lo-ne ʔen-te-zɒ:r ko-dʒɒ:st/ ؟سالن انتظار کجاست

Arrival/Departure 113

Is there a place to drink water? ....
................./ʔın-dʒv: ma-hal-li: ba-rv:-je nu:-ʃi:-da-ne ʔv:b hast/
اینجا محلّی برای نوشیدن آب هست؟
Is there a restaurant near by? ....
.........../ʔın naz-di:-ki:-hv: Ga-zv:-xo-ri: hast/ این نزدیکیها غذاخوری هست؟
I want a one-way air ticket to Roma. ....
/jek be-li:-te jek-sa-re be rom mi:-xv:-ham/ یک بلیط یکسره به رم می‌خواهم.
With which airline do you want to fly and when? ....
/bv: ko-dv:m xat-te ha-vv:-ʔi: va tʃe ru:-zi: mv:-je-li:d par-vv:z ko-ni:d/
با کدام خطّ هوایی و چه روزی مایلید پرواز کنید؟
With first available flight and on Homa. ....
..................../bv: ʔav-va-lın par-vv:-ze xat-te ha-vv:-ʔı-je ho-mv:/
با اوّلین پرواز خطّ هوایی هما.
We need two seats. ....
................../mv: do san-da-li: mi:-xv:-hi:m/ ما دو صندلی می‌خواهیم.
Please, book me two tickets on the plane for Berlin. ....
............./lot-fan do be-lit ba-rv:-je man be ber-lın re-zerv ko-ni:d/
لطفاً، دو بلیط برای من به برلین رزرو کنید.
My luggage is lost. ....
..../ʔas-bv:-be sa-fa-re man gom ʃo-de ʔast/ اسباب سفر من گم شده است.
I want to fly to Stockholm on Thursday, the first. ./mi:-xv:-ham
bv: ʔv-va-lın par-vv:-ze ru:-ze pandʒ-ʃan-be be ʔes-tok-holm be-ra-vam/
می‌خواهم با اوّلین پرواز روز پنجشنبه به استکهلم بروم.
Let me see what's available. ....
............/ʔe-dʒv:-ze be-da-hi:d be-bi:-nam ko-dv:m jek maG-du:r ʔast/
اجازه بدهید ببینم کدام یک مقدور است.
I'd prefer a morning flight. ....
.........................../man par-vv:-ze sobh rv: tar-dʒi:h mi:-da-ham/
من پرواز صبح را ترجیح می‌دهم.
What time do I have to be at the airport? ....
......................../tʃe mow-Geʔ bv:-jad dar fo-ru:d-gv:h bv:-ʃam/
چه موقع باید در فرودگاه باشم؟

Check in time is 9:15. ...../za-mɑː-ne kon-to-rol no ho rob? ʔast/
زمان کنترل ۹:۱۵ است.
I'd like to make a reservation to Oslo next Sunday. ....
/mɑː-je-lam jek-ʃan-be-je ʔɑː-jan-de ba-rɑː-je ʔos-lo be-liːt re-zerv ko-nam/
مایلم یکشنبهٔ آینده برای اسلو بلیط رزرو کنم.
I'll need an economy ticket. ....
.... /man jek be-liːte ʔar-zɑn-ɢej-mat miː-xɑː-ham/
من یک بلیط ارزان‌قیمت می‌خواهم.
I'd like to travel with first class. ....
/mɑː-je-lam bɑː da-ra-dʒe jek par-vɑːz ko-nam/. مایلم با درجه یک پرواز کنم.
You've to be there two hours before departure time. ....
.... /ʃo-mɑː bɑː-jad do sɑː-ʔat ɢabl ʔaz par-vɑːz ʔɑn-dʒɑː bɑː-ʃiːd/
شما باید دو ساعت قبل از پرواز آنجا باشید.

3-3
AIRPORT
LOUDSPEAKER

Attention, please. .... /lot-fan ta-vadʒ-dʒoh ko-niːd/. لطفاً توجّه کنید.
All passengers holding a ticket for Homa flight 182 to London, please go to...
/kol-lɪ-je mo-sæ-fe-ræ-ni: ke dæ-ræ-je be-liː-te ho-mæ baː-ræ-je par-vvː-ze
sa do haʃ-tæd ʔo do be maG-sa-de lan-dan has-tand lot-fan be...
mo-ræ-dʒe-ʔe ko-nand/ ....
کلّیه مسافرانی که دارای بلیط هما برای پرواز ۱۸۲ به مقصد لندن هستند لطفاً بـ ...
مراجعه کنند.
Boarding gate No.8 ... /xo-ruː-dʒɪ-je ʃo-mæ-re haʃt/ ۸ خروجی شماره
Customs department ..../bax-ʃe gom-rok/ بخش گمرک
Departure gate No.2 .... /xo-ruː-dʒɪ-je ʃo-mæ-re do/ ۲ خروجی شماره
Hall No.5 ..../sæ-lo-ne ʃo-mæ-re pandʒ/ ۵ سالن شماره

Information counter	/bɑː-dʒe-je ʔet-te-lɑː-ʔɑːt/	باجهٔ اطّلاعات
Insurance desk	/bɑː-dʒe-je biː-me/	باجهٔ بیمه
Main entrance	/dar-be ʔas-lɪ-je vo-ruːd/	درب اصلی ورود
Passport check	/kon-to-ro-le go-zar-nɑː-me/	کنترل گذرنامه
Transit lounge	/sɑː-lo-ne te-rʌn-ziːt/	سالن ترانزیت
VIP lounge	/sɑː-lo-ne ʔaʃ-xɑː-se mo-hem/	سالن اشخاص مهم

3-4 FLIGHT IDIOMS

airborne	هوابرد	/ha-vɒː-bord/
aircraft	هواپیما	/ha-vɒː-pej-mɒː/
airline	خط هوایی	/xat-te ha-vɒː-ʔiː/
aisle seat	صندلی کنار راهرو	/san-da-lɪ-je ka-nɒː-re rɒːh-ro/
altitude	ارتفاع	/ʔer-te-fɒːʔ/
arrival	ورود	/vo-ruːd/
boarding	سوار شدن	/sa-vɒːr ʃo-dan/
boarding pass	کارت ورود به هواپیما	/kɒːr-te vo-ruːd be ha-vɒː-pej-mɒː/
captain	کاپیتان	/kɒː-piː-tʌn/
course	مسیر	/ma-siːr/
crew	خدمه	/xa-da-me/

destination	/maɢ-sad/	مقصد
departure	/ha-re-kat/	حرکت
departure gate	/dar-be ha-re-kat/	درب حرکت
emergency exit	/xo-ru:-dʒe ʔez-te-rʌ:-ri:/	خروج اضطراری
emergency landing	/fo-ru:-de ʔez-te-rʌ:-ri:/	فرود اضطراری
flight number	/ʃo-mʌ:-re-je par-vʌ:z/	شمارهٔ پرواز
flight time	/mod-da-te par-vʌ:z/	مدّت پرواز
gate pass	/kʌ:r-te ʔo-bu:r/	کارت عبور
headphone	/gu:-ʃi:/	گوشی
host	/meh-mʌn-dʌ:r/	مهماندار
hostess	/xʌ:-no-me meh-mʌn-dʌ:r/	خانم مهماندار
landing	/fo-ru:d/	فرود
life vest	/dʒe-li:-ɢe-je ne-dʒʌ:t/	جلیقهٔ نجات
luggage	/bʌ:-re sa-far (ʔa-sʌ:s)/	بار سفر (اثاث)
luggage tag	/ʔe-ti:-ke-te tʃa-ma-dʌn/	اتیکت چمدان
pilot	/xa-la-bʌn/	خلبان
reservation	/za-xi:-re-je dʒʌ:/	ذخیرهٔ جا
route	/xat-te sejr/	خط سیر
runway	/bʌ:nd/	باند
safety	/ʔi:-me-ni:/	ایمنی
schedules	/za-mʌn ban-di:/	زمان‌بندی
seat belt	/ka-mar band/	کمربند
side window	/pan-dʒa-re-je ba-ɢal/	پنجرهٔ بغل
stewardess	/xʌ:-no-me meh-mʌn-dʌ:r/	خانم مهماندار
suitcase	/tʃa-ma-dʌn/	چمدان
take off	/bo-land ʃo-dan/	بلند شدن
touch down	/fo-ru:d/	فرود
visibility	/mej-dʌ:-ne di:d/	میدان دید
window seat	/san-da-lı-je ka-nʌ:-re pan-dʒa-re/	صندلی کنار پنجره

3-5 INSIDE A PLANE

Where is 4-F please? ....
................../san-da-lı-je tʃa-hv:r ʔef ko-dʒv:st/ ؟صندلی ۴ - اف کجاست
2nd row on your right. ....
..................../ra-di:-fe dov-vom sam-te rv:st/. ردیف دوّم، سمت راست
The aisle seat. ...../san-da-lı-je ka-nv:-re rv:h-row/. صندلی کنار راهرو
The middle seat. ..../san-da-lı-je va-sa-ti:/. صندلی وسطی
The window seat. ../san-da-lı-je ka-nv:-re pan-dʒa-re/. صندلی کنار پنجره
Let me direct you to your seat. ....
..................../ʔe-dʒv:-ze da-hi:d san-da-lı-je-tʌn rv: ne-ʃʌn da-ham/
اجازه دهید صندلی‌تان را نشان دهم.

On behalf of captain ... and crew, ...
.........../ʔaz ta-ra-fe kʌː-piː-tʌn ... va xa-da-me/ از طرف کاپیتان ... و خدمه
I welcome you aboard the Tehran to London. ....
/voruːde ʃo-mʌː rʌ be par-vʌː-ze teh-rʌn lan-dan xo-ʃʌː-mad miː-guː-jam/
ورود شما را به پرواز تهران - لندن خوشامد می‌گویم.
Our estimated flight time to London is 6 hours. ....
..../mod-da-te par-vʌː-ze mʌː be lan-dan tax-miː-nan ʃeʃ sʌː-ʔat ʔast/
مدّت پرواز ما به لندن تخمیناً ۶ ساعت است.
We will be flying at altitude of 30 000 feet. ....
........../mʌː dar ʔer-te-fʌː-ʔe si: he-zʌːr pʌː-ʔi: par-vʌːz xʌː-hiːm kard/
ما در ارتفاع ۳۰۰۰۰ پایی پرواز خواهیم کرد.
You're now requested to fasten your seat belts; ....
../ʔaz ʃo-mʌː ta-Gʌː-zʌː miː-ʃa-vad ka-mar-band-hʌː-je-tʌn rʌ be-ban-diːd/
از شما تقاضا می‌شود کمربندهایتان را ببندید؛
and observe the no smoking sign. ....
......./va be ʔa-lʌː-ma-te siː-gʌːr na-ke-ʃiːd ta-vadʒ-dʒoh far-mʌː-ʔiːd/
و به علامت ٔ سیگار نکشید ٔ توجّه فرمایید.
A glass of water, please. ./jek liː-vʌn ʔʌːb lot-fan/ یک لیوان آب، لطفاً.
A cup of tea, please. /jek fen-dʒʌn tʃʌːj lot-fan/. یک فنجان چای، لطفاً.
A cup of coffee, please. ..../jek fen-dʒʌn Gah-ve lot-fan/
یک فنجان قهوه، لطفاً.
A newspaper, please. ....../jek ruːz-nʌː-me lot-fan/. یک روزنامه، لطفاً.
A magazine, please. ..../jek ma-dʒal-le lot-fan/. یک مجلّه، لطفاً.
A blanket, please. ..../jek pa-tu: lot-fan/. یک پتو، لطفاً.
A pillow, please. ..../jek bʌː-leʃ lot-fan/. یک بالش، لطفاً.
A tablet for airsick, please. ./jek Gor-se zed-de ta-hav-voʔ lot-fan/
یک قرص ضدّ تهوّع، لطفاً.
A tablet for headache, please. /jek Gors ba-rʌː-je sar-dard lot-fan/
یک قرص برای سردرد، لطفاً.

3-6
TRAVELLING BY RAIL

arrival	/voːruːd/	ورود
carriage	/vːgon/	واگن
compartment	/kuːpe/	کوپه
corridor	/rɑːhro/	راهرو
dining-car	/vːgone ɢazɑːxoriː/	واگن غذاخوری
emergency brake	/tormoze ʔezterɑːriː/	ترمز اضطراری
luggage van	/vːgone bɑːr/	واگن بار
luggage department	/ɢesmate bɑːr/	قسمت بار
luggage-tag	/bar tʃasbe bɑːr/	برچسب بار
passenger	/mosɑːfer/	مسافر
platform	/sakkuː/	سکّو

Beginner's Persian

porter	/bɒ:r-bar/	باربر
railway	/rɒ:h-ʔɒ:-han/	راه‌آهن
station	/ʔi:s-gɒ:h/	ایستگاه
station-master	/ra-ʔi:-se ʔi:s-gɒ:h/	رئیس ایستگاه
stop	/ʔi:st/	ایست
suitcase	/tʃa-ma-dʌn/	چمدان
ticket	/be-li:t/	بلیط
return ticket	/be-li:-te bar-gaʃt/	بلیط برگشت
timetable	/bar-nɒ:-me-je Ga-tɒ:r/	برنامهٔ قطار
track	/ma-si:r/	مسیر
electric train	/Ga-tɒ:-re bar-Gi:/	قطار برقی
express train	/Ga-tɒ:-re ʔeks-pe-res/	قطار اکسپرس
fast train	/Ga-tɒ:-re sa-ri:-ʔol-sejr/	قطار سریع السیر
transfer	/taʔ-vi:-ze Ga-tɒ:r/	تعویض قطار
tunnel	/tu:-nel/	تونل
luggage collection point	/ma-hal-le dar-jɒ:f-te bɒ:r/	محلّ دریافت بار
luggage delivery point	/ma-hal-le tah-vi:-le bɒ:r/	محل تحویل بار
to the trains	/be ta-ra-fe Ga-tɒ:r/	به طرف قطار
platform No. ...	/sak-ku:-je ʃo-mɒ:-re/	سکّوی شماره ...
station of destination	/ʔi:s-gɒ:-he maG-sad/	ایستگاه مقصد
time of departure	/za-mɒ:-ne ha-re-kat/	زمان حرکت

A first-class ticket to ... please.
........./lot-fan jek be-li:-te da-ra-dʒe jek be maG-sa-de ... be-da-hi:d/
لطفاً یک بلیط درجه یک به مقصد ... بدهید.
Be careful with this suitcases, please.
.../lot-fan mo-vɒ:-ze-be ʔin tʃa-ma-dʌn bɒ:-ʃi:d/
لطفاً مواظب این چمدان باشید...
Bring me a glass of tea.
/jek ʔes-te-kʌn tʃɒ:j ba-rɒ:-jam bi-jɒ:-va-ri:d/
یک استکان چای برایم بیاورید.
Here is my luggage. ..../ʔin bɒ:-re man ʔast/.
این بار من است.

Here is my luggage receipt. .... /ʔɪn Gab-ze bv̈:-re man ʔast/
این قبض بار من است.
How long does the trip to ... take? ....
...../Ga-tv̈:r tʃand sv̈:-ʔa-te tv̈: ... mi:-ra-vad/ ؟می‌رود ... تا ساعته چند قطار
How much does a first-class ticket to Tehran cost? ....
........../Gej-ma-te be-li:-te da-ra-dʒe jek tv̈: teh-rʌn tʃe-Gadr ʔast/
قیمت بلیط درجه یک تا تهران چقدر است؟
I'd like to change to another compartment. ....
................/man mi:-xv̈:-ham be ku:-pe-je di:-ga-ri: be-ra-vam/
من می‌خواهم به کوپهٔ دیگری بروم.
Is this the train for Tabriz? ....
....................../ʔɪn Ga-tv̈:-re tab-ri:z ʔast/ ؟است تبریز قطار این
Please bring me a magazine. ....
......./lot-fan ba-rʌ:-jam ma-dʒal-le bɪ-jv̈:-va-ri:d/ لطفاً برایم مجلّه بیاورید.
Please bring me an extra blanket. ....
................./lot-fan be man jek pa-tu:-je ʔe-zʌ:-fi: be-da-hi:d/
لطفاً به من یک پتوی اضافی بدهید.
Please, give me my things. .. /lot-fan va-sʌ:-je-lam rʌ: be-da-hi:d/
لطفاً وسایلم را بدهید.
Please show me my seat. ....
.../lot-fan san-da-li:-je ma-rʌ: ne-ʃʌn da-hi:d/ لطفاً صندلی مرا نشان دهید.
Take these suitcases to the train No. ....
........./ʔɪn tʃa-ma-dʌn-hʌ: rʌ: be Ga-tv̈:-re ʃo-mv̈:-re ... be-ba-ri:d/
این چمدانها را به قطار شماره ... ببرید.
Wake me up an hour before we arrive at ... .
........../jek sʌ:-ʔat pi:ʃ ʔaz re-si:-dan be ... bi:-dʌ:-ram ko-ni:d/
یک ساعت پیش از رسیدن به ... بیدارم کنید.
What's the name of this station? ....
..................../ʔes-me ʔɪn ʔi:s-gʌ:h tʃi:st/ ؟چیست ایستگاه این این اسم
What platform does train No. ... leave from? ....
..../Ga-tv̈:-re ʃo-mv̈:-re ... ʔaz ko-dʌ:m sak-ku: ha-re-kat mi:-ko-nad/
قطار شماره ... از کدام سکّو حرکت می‌کند؟
What time does train No. ... arrive? ....
./Ga-tv̈:-re ʃo-mv̈:-re ... kej vv̈:-red mi:-ʃa-vad/ ؟می‌شود وارد کی ... شماره قطار

What time does train No. ... leave? ....
................../Ga-tv:-re ʃo-mv:-re ... kej ha-re-kat mi:-ko-nad/
قطار شماره ... کی حرکت می‌کند؟

What trains are there to Tehran? ....
/ko-dv:m Ga-tv:r-hv: be teh-rʌn mi:-ra-vand/ کدام قطارها به تهران می‌روند؟

We have missed the train. ....
............./mv: ʔaz Ga-tv:r dʒv: mʌn-de-ʔi:m/ ما از قطار جا مانده‌ایم.

When does the train arrive at ... ? ....
......./Ga-tv:r tʃe mo-Geʔ be ... mi:-re-sad/؟ قطار چه موقع به ... می‌رسد

Where is the attendant? ....
...................../maʔ-mu:-re Ga-tv:r ko-dʒv:st/ مأمور قطار کجاست؟

Where is the booking-office? ....../gi:-ʃe ko-dʒv:st/؟ گیشه کجاست

Where is the carriage No. ...? ....
................./vv:-go-ne ʃo-mv:-re ... ko-dʒv:st/ واگن شماره ... کجاست؟

Where is the dining-car? ....
.............../vv:-go-ne Ga-zv:-xo-ri: ko-dʒv:st/ واگن غذاخوری کجاست؟

Where is the timetable? ....
...................../bar-nv:-me-je Ga-tv:r ko-dʒv:st/ برنامهٔ قطار کجاست؟

Where is this train from? ....
.........../ʔɪn Ga-tv:r ʔaz ko-dʒv: mi:- ʔv:-jad/ این قطار از کجا می‌آید؟

Where is this train going? ....
.........../ʔɪn Ga-tv:r be ko-dʒv: mi:-ra-vad/؟ این قطار به کجا می‌رود

3-7
TRAVELLING BY CAR

accelerator	/pe-dɒ:-le gɒ:z/	پدال گاز
battery	/bɒ:t-ri:/	باطری
body	/ba-da-ne/	بدنه
brake	/tor-moz/	ترمز
bumper	/se-par/	سپر
carburettor	/kɒ:r-be-rɒ:-towr/	کاربراتور
chassis	/ʃɒ:-si:/	شاسی
clutch	/ke-lɒ:tʃ/	کلاچ
crankshaft	/mi:l laŋ/	میل لنگ
driver	/rɒ:-nan-de/	راننده
engine	/mo-towr/	موتور
exhaust	/ʔeg-zoz/	اگزوز

fan belt	/tas-me par-vː-ne/	تسمه پروانه
fuel	/suːxt/	سوخت
garage	/gvː-rvːʒ/	گاراژ
gas station	/pom-pe ben-zɪn/	پمپ بنزین
gear-box	/dʒaʔ-be dan-de/	جعبه دنده
gear-lever	/das-te dan-de/	دسته دنده
hammer	/tʃak-koʃ/	چکّش
hand brake	/tor-moz das-tiː/	ترمزدستی
headlights	/tʃe-rvːɢ-hvː-je dʒe-low/	چراغهای جلو
horn	/buːɢ/	بوق
ignition	/ʔes-tvːrt/	استارت
jack	/dʒak/	جک
lorry	/kvː-mɪ-jon/	کامیون
motor	/mo-towr/	موتور
oil	/ro-ɢan/	روغن
oil pump	/pom-pe ro-ɢan/	پمپ روغن
petrol	/ben-zɪn/	بنزین
petrol tube	/ʃe-laŋ-ge ben-zɪn/	شلنگ بنزین
pliers	/ʔan-bor/	انبر
pump	/pomp/	پمپ
radiator	/rvː-dɪ-jvː-towr/	رادیاتور
repair	/taʔ-miːr/	تعمیر
road sign	/ʔa-lvː-ʔe-me dʒvːd-de-ʔiː/	علائم جادّه‌ای
safety belt	/ka-mar-ban-de ʔiː-me-niː/	کمربند ایمنی
screwdriver	/piːtʃ guːʃ-tiː/	پیچ‌گوشتی
spanner	/ʔvː-tʃvːr/	آچار
spare parts	/ɢa-te-ʔvː-te ja-da-kiː/	قطعات یدکی
spark plug	/ʃamʔ/	شمع
speed	/sor-ʔat/	سرعت
speed limit	/had-de-ʔak-sa-re sor-ʔat/	حدّاکثر سرعت
speedometer	/kiː-lo-metr ʃo-mvːr/	کیلومترشمار
starter	/ʔes-tvːr-ter/	استارتر
stop-light	/tʃe-rvːɢ tor-moz/	چراغ ترمز
tank	/bvːk/	باک

Arrival/Departure 127

tool	/ʔab-zɒ:r ɒ:-lɒ:t/	ابزارآلات
tow-rope	/si:-me bok-sel/	سیم بکسل
traffic lights	/tʃe-rɒ:-Ge rɒ:h-ne-mɒ:-ʔi:/	چراغ راهنمایی
trailer	/te-rej-ler/	تریلر
tyre	/tɒ:-jer/	تایر
tyre pressure	/bɒ:-de lɒ:s-ti:k/	باد لاستیک
van	/vɒ:-net/	وانت
warning sign	/ʔa-lɒ:-ma-te xa-tar/	علامت خطر
water	/ʔɒ:b/	آب
wheel	/tʃarx/	چرخ
windscreen	/ʃi:-ʃe-je dʒe-low/	شیشهٔ جلو

Are we driving in the right direction? ....
.... /mɒ: rɒ:h rɒ: do-rost mi:-ra-vi:m/ ما راه را درست می‌رویم؟
Fill the tank, please. /lot-fan bɒ:k rɒ: por ko-ni:d/ لطفاً باک را پر کنید.
Here is my driving licence. ....
.... /ʔin go-vɒ:-hi:-nɒ:-me-je man ʔast/ این گواهینامهٔ من است.
How do I get to Urumieh? ....
.... /tʃe-towr mi:-ta-vɒ:-nam be ʔu:-ru:-mɪj-je be-ra-vam/ چطور می‌توانم به ارومیّه بروم؟
How far is to the nearest town? ....
.... /tɒ: naz-di:k-ta-rɪn ʃahr tʃand ki:-lo-metr rɒ:h ʔast/ تا نزدیکترین شهر چند کیلومتر راه است؟
How long will the journey to Yazd take? ....
.... /tɒ: jazd tʃand sɒ:-ʔat rɒ:h ʔast/ تا یزد چند ساعت راه است؟
How many kilometers are to Rasht? ....
.... /tɒ: raʃt tʃand ki:-lo-metr ʔast/ تا رشت چند کیلومتر است؟
how much do I owe you? .... /tʃe-Gadr bɒ:-jad par-dɒ:xt ko-nam/ چقدر باید پرداخت کنم؟
I've run out of petrol. .... /man ben-zɪn ta-mɒ:m kar-de-ʔam/ من بنزین تمام کردم

I need to fill the radiator. ....
.... /man bv:-jad rv:-dı-jv:-towr rv: por ko-nam/ من باید رادیاتور را پر کنم.
I want 4 litres of petrol. .. /man tʃa-hv:r li:tr ben-zın mi:-xv:-ham/
من ۴ لیتر بنزین می‌خواهم.
I want some oil. ..... /ka-mi: ro-Gan mi:-xv:-ham/ کمی روغن می‌خواهم.
What direction should I go in? ....
.... /ʔaz ko-dv:m ta-raf bv:-jad be-ra-vam/ از کدام طرف باید بروم؟
What's the shorter way to Sari? ....
.... /ku:-tv:h-ta-rın ma-si:r be sv:-ri: ko-dv:m ʔast/
کوتاه‌ترین مسیر به ساری کدام است؟
please give me a road-map. ....
.... /lot-fan jek naG-ʃe-je dʒv:d-de be man be-da-hi:d/
لطفاً یک نقشهٔ جادّه به من بدهید.
Please wash the car. ....
.... /lot-fan mv:-ʃın rv: be-ʃu:-ʔi:d/ لطفاً ماشین را بشویید.
Where can we camp for the night? ....
.................../ʃab rv: ko-dʒv: mi:-ta-vv:-ni:m ʔot-rv:G koni:m/
شب را کجا می‌توانیم اتراق کنیم؟
Where can we park our car?................................
.... /ko-dʒv: mi:-ta-vv:-ni:m mv:-ʃın rv: pv:rk ko-ni:m/
کجا می‌توانیم ماشین را پارک کنیم؟
Where is the nearest gas station? ....
.. /naz-di:k-ta-rın pom-pe ben-zın ko-dʒv:st/ نزدیک‌ترین پمپ‌بنزین کجاست؟

Arrival/Departure 129

3 - 8
GARAGE

Could you please help me? ....
/lot-fan mi:-ʃa-vad be man ko-mak ko-ni:d/ لطفاً می‌شود به من کمک کنید؟
Could you please repair the brakes? ....
............../lot-fan mi:-ʃa-vad tor-moz-hv: rv: taʔ-mi:r ko-ni:d/
لطفاً می‌شود ترمزها را تعمیر کنید؟
Could you please repair the carburettor? ....
.............../lot-fan mi:-ʃa-vad kv:r-be-rv:-towr rv: taʔ-mi:r ko-ni:d/
لطفاً می‌شود کاربراتور را تعمیر کنید؟
Could you please repair the clutch? ....
................./lot-fan mi:-ʃa-vad ke-lv:tʃ rv: taʔ-mi:r ko-ni:d/
لطفاً می‌شود کلاچ را تعمیر کنید؟
Could you please repair the engine? ....
................/lot-fan mi:-ʃa-vad mo-towr rv: taʔ-mi:r ko-ni:d/
لطفاً می‌شود موتور را تعمیر کنید؟

Could you please repair the speedometer? ....
........../lot-fan mi:-ʃa-vad ki:-lo-metr ʃo-mv:r rv: taʔ-mi:r ko-ni:d/
لطفاً می‌شود کیلومترشمار را تعمیر کنید؟
Could you please tow away my car? ....
.............../lot-fan mi:-ʃa-vad mv:-ʃi:-ne ma-rv: bok-sel ko-ni:d/
لطفاً می‌شود ماشین مرا بکسل کنید؟
How much do I owe you for repairs? ....
............./tʃe-ɢadr ʔaz bv:-ba-te taʔ-mi:r bv:-jab be-par-dv:-zam/
چقدر از بابت تعمیر باید بپردازم؟
I have a puncture. ....
................/tv:-je-re ʔo-to-mo-bi:-le man pan-tʃar ʃo-de ʔast/
تایر اتومبیل من پنچر شده.
I have a spare wheel. ..../man zv:-pv:s dv:-ram/. من زاپاس دارم
It will take 2 hours to repair your car. ....
............./taʔ-mi:-re mv:-ʃi:-ne ʃo-mv: do sv:-ʔat tu:l mi:-ke-ʃad/
تعمیر ماشین شما ۲ ساعت طول می‌کشد.
Please change the fan-belt. ....
/lot-fan tas-me par-vv:-ne rv: ʔa-vaz ko-ni:d/. لطفاً تسمه پروانه را عوض کنید
Please change the headlight. ....
/lot-fan tʃe-rv:-ɢe dʒe-low rv: ʔa-vaz ko-ni:d/. لطفاً چراغ جلو را عوض کنید
Please change the wheel. ....../lot-fan tʃarx rv: ʔa-vaz ko-ni:d/
لطفاً چرخ را عوض کنید.
Please check the ignition system. ....
................/lot-fan si:s-te-me ʔes-tv:rt rv: kon-to-rol ko-ni:d/
لطفاً سیستم استارت را کنترل کنید.
Please check the lubricating system. ....
............./lot-fan si:s-te-me ro-ɢan-kv:-ri: rv: kon-to-rol ko-ni:d/
لطفاً سیستم روغنکاری را کنترل کنید.
Please check the tyre pressure. ....
/lot-fan bv:-de tʃarx-hv: rv: kon-to-rol ko-ni:d/. لطفاً باد چرخها را کنترل کنید
Please get the carburettor cleaned. ....
.../lot-fan kv:r-be-rv:-towr rv: ta-mi:z ko-ni:d/. لطفاً کاربراتور را تمیز کنید
Please get the spark plugs cleaned. ....
............./lot-fan ʃam-hv: rv: ta-mi:z ko-ni:d/. لطفاً شمع‌ها را تمیز کنید

Arrival/Departure 131

Please give me the jack. ..../lot-fan dʒak rvː beːde/. لطفاً جک را بده.
Please give me the spanner. ..../lot-fan ʔvː-tʃvːr rvː beːde/
لطفاً آچار را بده.
Please press the accelerator. /lot-fan gvːz be-da-hiːd/.لطفاً گاز بدهید.
Please press the brake pedal. ....
./lot-fan peː-dvː-le tor-moz rvː fe-ʃvːr da-hiːd/. لطفاً پدال ترمز را فشار دهید.
Please pump up this tyre. ....
................./lot-fan tʃarx rvː bvːd be-za-niːd/. لطفاً چرخ را باد بزنید.
Please release the brake pedal. ....
................./lot-fan tor-moz rvː vel ko-niːd/. لطفاً ترمز را ول کنید.
Please switch on the headlights. ....
....../lot-fan tʃe-rvːɢ-hvː rvː row-ʃan ko-niːd/. لطفاً چراغها را روشن کنید.
Please switch on the starter. ..../lot-fan ʔes-tvːrt be-za-niːd/
لطفاً استارت بزنید.
Please switch off the headlights. ....
..../lot-fan tʃe-rvːɢ-hvː rvː xvː-muːʃ ko-niːd/. لطفاً چراغها را خاموش کنید.
Somthing is wrong with the cooling system. ....
,............/siːs-te-me xo-nak ko-nan-de ʔiː-rvːd pej-dvː kar-de ʔast/
سیستم خنک کننده ایراد پیدا کرده است.
Somthing is wrong with the oil pump. ....
......................./pom-pe ro-ɢan ʔiː-rvːd pej-dvː karde ʔast/
پمپ روغن ایراد پیدا کرده است.
Somthing is wrong with the petrol feed. ....
............./siːs-te-me ben-zɪn ra-svː-ni: ʔiː-rvːd pej-dvː kar-de ʔast/
سیستم بنزین رسانی ایراد پیدا کرده است.
Somthing is wrong with the hand-brake. ....
.... /tor-moz das-ti: ʔiː-rvːd pej-dvː kar-de ʔast/
ترمز دستی ایراد پیدا کرده است.
Somthing is wrong with the stop-lights. ....
................/tʃe-rvːɢ-hvː-je tor-moz ʔiː-rvːd pej-dvː kar-de ʔast/
چراغهای ترمز ایراد پیدا کرده است.
The engine cuts out. ..../mo-towr xvː-muːʃ ʃo-de ʔast/
موتور خاموش شده است.

The engine is out of order. ....
.... /mo-towr kv:r ne-mi:-ko-nad/ .موتور کار نمی‌کند
The engine won't start. ....
.... /mo-towr ?es-tv:rt ne-mi:-za-nad/ .موتور استارت نمی‌زند
The gear-box doesn't work. ....
.... /dʒa?-be dan-de ?eʃ-kv:l dv:-rad/ .جعبه دنده اشکال دارد
We have had an accident. ....
.... /mv: ta-sv:-dof kar-de-?i:m/ .ما تصادف کرده‌ایم
Where can I get the car repaired? ....
.... /ko-dʒv: mi:-ta-vv:-nam mv:-ʃın rv: ta?-mi:r ko-nam/
کجا می‌توانم ماشین را تعمیر کنم؟

3-9 TRAVELLING BY SHIP

anchor	/lɑŋ-gar/	لنگر
boat	/ɢɒ:-jeɢ/	قایق
bows	/si:-ne-je kaʃ-ti:/	سینهٔ کشتی
bridge	/pol/	پل
cabin	/kɒ:-bɪn/	کابین
captain	/nɒ:-xo-dɒ: (kɒ:-pi:-tʌn)/	ناخدا (کاپیتان)
coast	/sɒ:-hel/	ساحل
crew	/xa-da-me/	خدمه
deck	/ʔar-ʃe/	عرشه
deck-chair	/san-da-lɪ-je rɒ:-ha-ti:/	صندلی راحتی
hand-rails	/das-gi:-re-hɒ:/	دستگیره‌ها
harbour	/ban-dar/	بندر
island	/dʒa-zi:-re/	جزیره

life-belt	/ka-mar-ban-de ʔi:-me-ni:/	کمربند ایمنی
life-boat	/ɢʌ:-je-ɢe ne-dʒɑ:t/	قایق نجات
life-buoy	/hal-ɢe-je ne-dʒɑ:t/	حلقهٔ نجات
lighthouse	/tʃe-rɑ:-ɢe dar-jɑ:-ʔi:/	چراغ دریائی
mate	/mo-ʔɑ:-ve-ne kɑ:-pi:-tɑn/	معاون کاپیتان
passenger	/mo-sɑ:-fer/	مسافر
pilot	/rɑ:h-ne-mɑ:-je kaʃ-ti:/	راهنمای کشتی
port	/ban-dar/	بندر
promenade deck	/ʔes-te-rɑ:-hat-ɢɑ:-he ru:-je ʔar-ʃe/	استراحتگاه روی عرشه
quay	/ʔes-ke-le/	اسکله
sailor	/ma-la-vɑn/	ملوان
sea	/dar-jɑ:/	دریا
seasikness	/dar-jɑ: za-de-gi:/	دریازدگی
ship	/kaʃ-ti:/	کشتی
side	/pah-lu:/	پهلو
starboard	/sam-te rɑ:-st kaʃ-ti:/	سمت راست کشتی
stern	/ɢes-ma-te ʔa-ɢa-be kaʃ-ti:/	قسمت عقب کشتی
storm	/tu:-fɑn/	توفان
sun deck	/ma-hal-le ʔɑ:f-tɑ:b ge-ref-tan/	محلّ آفتاب گرفتن
tossing	/te-kɑ:-ne kaʃ-ti:/	تکان کشتی
wave	/mowdʒ/	موج
wind	/bɑ:d/	باد

I don't feel well. ..../man hɑ:-lam bad ʔast/. من حالم بد است.
I feel seasick. ..... /man dar-jɑ: za-de ʃo-de-ʔam/ من دریا زده شده‌ام.
I've got a ticket for a first class cabin. ....
............./be-li:-te , man ba-rɑ:-je kɑ:-bi:-ne da-ra-dʒe jek ʔast/
بلیط من برای کابین درجه یک است.
I'd like to send a radiotelegram. ....
................/mi:-xɑ:-ham jek rɑ:-dɪ-jo te-leg-rɑ:m be-fe-res-tam/
می‌خواهم یک رادیوتلگرام بفرستم.

Arrival/Departure

How long does the voyage take? ....
........../sa-far tʃand ru:z tu:l mi:-ke-ʃad/ ‎سفر چند روز طول می‌کشد؟‎
What's this port called? ..../ʔes-me ʔın ban-dar tʃi:st/
‎اسم این بندر چیست؟‎
When are we sailing? ./kej ha-re-kat mi:-ko-ni:m/ ‎کی حرکت می‌کنیم؟‎
When does the ship sail for Baku? ....
................../kaʃ-ti: tʃe mow-Ge? vː-re-de bvː-ku: mi:-ʃa-vad/
‎کشتی چه موقع وارد باکو می‌شود؟‎
Where can I play ping-pong? ....
........................./ko-dʒvː mi:-ta-vʌn pıŋ-poŋ bvː-zi: kard/
‎کجا می‌توان پینگ‌پونگ بازی کرد؟‎
Where is my cabin? ..../kvː-bi:-ne man ko-dʒvːst/ ‎کابین من کجاست؟‎
Where is the restaurant? ./Ga-zvː-xo-ri: ko-dʒvːst/ ‎غذاخوری کجاست؟‎

SECTION 4

IN TOWN

- 4-1 TAXI
- 4-2 TOWN (SIGN, ADDRESS, ...)
- 4-3 BUS
- 4-4 HOTEL
- 4-5 BANK/MONEY
- 4-6 POST
- 4-7 TELEPHONE
- 4-8 RESTAURANT (MENU, ...)
- 4-9 MUSEUM
- 4-10 FACTORY

4-1
TAXI

taxi	/tɒ:k-si:/	تاکسی
airport	/fo-ru:d-gɒ:h/	فرودگاه
bus terminal	/ter-mi:-nɒ:-le ʔo-tu:-bu:s/	ترمینال اتوبوس
Homa hotel	/ho-tel ho-mɒ:/	هتل هما
art museum	/mu:-ze-je ho-na-ri:/	موزهٔ هنری
bazaar	/bɒ:-zɒ:r/	بازار
city center	/mar-ka-ze ʃahr/	مرکز شهر
Ferdowsi street	/xɪ-jɒ:-bɒ:-ne fer-dow-si:/	خیابان فردوسی
fun-fair	/ʃah-re bɒ:-zi:/	شهربازی
nearest hospital	/naz-di:k-ta-rɪn bi:-mɒ:-res-tʌn/	نزدیکترین بیمارستان
nearest library	/naz-di:k-ta-rɪn ke-tɒ:b-xɒ:-ne/	نزدیکترین کتابخانه
nearest police station	/naz-di:k-ta-rɪn ka-lʌn-ta-ri:/	نزدیکترین کلانتری
nearest post office	/naz-di:k-ta-rɪn ʔe-dɒ:-re-je post/	نزدیکترین ادارهٔ پست

park .... /pɒ:rk/ پارک
railroad station .... /ʔi:s-gɒ:-he ɢɑ-tɒ:r/ ایستگاه قطار
Swedish Embassy .... /se-fɒ:-ra-te so-ʔed/ سفارت سوئد
town hall .... /tɒ:-lɒ:-re ʃahr/ تالار شهر
zoo .... /bɒ:-ɢe vahʃ/ باغ وحش

How much further is it? .... /tʃe-ɢadr di:-gar mʌn-de ʔast/
چقدر دیگر مانده است؟
How much is my fare? .... /ke-rɒ:-je man tʃe-ɢadr mi:-ʃa-vad/
کرایه من چقدر می‌شود؟
I want to try to catch a 8:00 flight. ....
.... /mi:-xɒ:-ham be par-vɒ:-ze sɒ:-ʔa-te haʃt be-ra-sam/
می‌خواهم به پرواز ساعت ۸ برسم.
Please hurry, I'm late. ....
.... /lot-fan tond-tar be-rɒ:-ni:d man di:-ram ʃo-de ʔast/
لطفاً تندتر برانید، من دیرم شده‌است
Please, let me off at second crossroads. ....
.... /lot-fan dar tʃa-hɒ:r-rɒ:-he dov-vom pi-jɒ:-de-ʔam ko-ni:d/
لطفاً در چهارراه دوّم پیاده‌ام کنید.
Please stop around the corner. ....
.... /lot-fan ʔʌn gu:-ʃe ne-gah dɒ:-ri:d/ لطفاً آن گوشه نگه دارید.
Please take me to... /lot-fan ma-rɒ: be ... be-ba-ri:d/ لطفاً مرا به ... ببرید.
Stop here, please. /lot-fan ʔin-dʒɒ: ne-gah dɒ:-ri:d/ لطفاً اینجا نگه دارید.
Wait for me, please. /lot-fan mon-ta-ze-ram bɒ:-ʃi:d/ لطفاً منتظرم باشید.

4-2
TOWN
(SIGN, ADDRESSE, ...)

sign	تابلو	/tɒ:b-lo/
airport	فرودگاه	/fo-ru:d-gɒ:h/
alley	کوچه	/ku:-tʃe/
attention	توجّه	/ta-vadʒ-dʒoh/
bakery	نانوایی	/nʌn-vɒ:-ʔi:/
bank	بانک	/bɒ:nk/
barber	آرایشگاه	/ʔɒ:-rɒ:-jeʃ-gɒ:h/
bell	زنگ	/zaŋ/
block	بلوک	/bu:-lu:k/
bookshop	کتابفروشی	/ke-tɒ:b-fo-ru:-ʃi:/
boulevard	بلوار	/bol-vɒ:r/
bridge	پل	/pol/
bus stop	ایستگاه اتوبوس	/ʔi:s-gɒ:-he ʔo-tu:-bu:s/

carpet shop	/farʃ fo-ruː-ʃiː/	فرش‌فروشی
cinema	/siː-ne-mɑː/	سینما
Closed!	/bas-te ʔast/	بسته است!
confectionery	/ɢan-nɑː-diː/	قنادی
crooked road	/dʒɑːd-de-je por piː-tʃo-xam/	جادّهٔ پرپیچ و خم
crossroads	/tʃa-hɑːr-rɑːh/	چهارراه
curve	/piːtʃ/	پیچ
dentist	/dan-dɑn-pe-zeʃk/	دندان‌پزشک
doctor	/pe-zeʃk/	پزشک
downtown	/pɑː-ʔiː-ne ʃahr/	پایین شهر
Drive slowly!	/ʔɑː-hes-te be-rɑː-niːd/	آهسته برانید!
dry cleaner	/xoʃk-ʃuː-ʔiː/	خشک‌شویی
embankment	/xɪ-jɑː-bɑː-ne sɑː-he-liː/	خیابان ساحلی
entrance	/vo-ruː-diː/	ورودی
exit	/xo-ruː-dʒi/	خروجی
fire station	/ʔɑː-taʃ-ne-ʃɑː-niː/	آتش‌نشانی
for men	/mar-dɑː-ne/	مردانه
for rent	/ba-rɑː-je ʔe-dʒɑː-re/	برای اجاره
for sale	/ba-rɑː-je fo-ruːʃ/	برای فروش
for women	/za-nɑː-ne/	زنانه
full stop	/ta-vaɢ-ɢo-fe kɑː-mel/	توقف کامل
grocery	/xɑːr-bɑːr fo-ruː-ʃiː/	خواربارفروشی
high way	/bo-zorg-rɑːh/	بزرگراه
hospital	/biː-mɑː-res-tɑn/	بیمارستان
hotel	/ho-tel/	هتل
Information	/ʔet-te-lɑː-ʔɑːt/	اطّلاعات
jewelery	/dʒa-vɑː-her fo-ruː-ʃiː/	جواهرفروشی
Keep right.	/ʔaz sam-te rɑːst be-rɑː-niːd/	از سمت راست برانید.
lane	/kuː-tʃe/	کوچه
laundry	/le-bɑːs ʃuː-ʔiː/	لباس‌شویی
lavatory	/tuː-ɑː-let/	توالت
minibus	/mi-niː-buːs/	مینی‌بوس
Ministry of Agriculture	/ve-zɑː-ra-te ke-ʃɑː-var-ziː/	وزارت کشاورزی

Ministry of Culture and Art ....
.... /ve-zɑ:-ra-te ʔer-ʃɑ:d/ وزارت ارشاد
Ministry of Education ..... /ve-zɑ:-ra-te ʔɑ:-mu:-zeʃ va par-va-reʃ/
وزارت آموزش و پرورش
Ministry of Energy ....
.... /ve-zɑ:-ra-te ni:-ru:/ وزارت نیرو
Ministry of Foreign Affairs ....
.................../ve-zɑ:-ra-te ʔe-mu:-re xɑ:-re-dʒe/ وزارت امور خارجه
Ministry of Health .... /ve-zɑ:-ra-te beh-dɑ:ʃt/ وزارت بهداشت
Ministry of Heavy Industries ..../ve-zɑ:-ra-te sa-nɑ:-jeʔ san-gɪn/
وزارت صنایع سنگین
Ministry of Higher Education ....
.... /ve-zɑ:-ra-te ʔɑ:-mu:-ze-ʃe ʔɑ:-li:/ وزارت آموزش عالی
Ministry of Industries ..../ve-zɑ:-ra-te sa-nɑ:-jeʔ/ وزارت صنایع
Ministry of Interior .... /ve-zɑ:-ra-te keʃ-var/ وزارت کشور
Ministry of Labour .... /ve-zɑ:-ra-te kɑ:r/ وزارت کار
Ministry of P.T.T ..../ve-zɑ:-ra-te pos to tel-ge-rɑ: fo te-le-fon/
وزارت پست و تلگراف و تلفن
Ministry of Defence .... /ve-zɑ:-ra-te de-fɑ:ʔ/ وزارت دفاع
money exchange ..../sar-rɑ:-fi:/ صرّافی
newspaper kiosk .... /kɪ-ju:s-ke ru:z-nɑ:-me/ کیوسک روزنامه
No admittance! ..../vo-ru:d mam-nu:ʔ/ ورود ممنوع!
No parking! ..../pɑ:rk kar-dan mam-nu:ʔ/ پارک کردن ممنوع!
No passing zone! ./mo-hav-va-te seb-ɢat mam-nu:ʔ/ محوطه سبقت ممنوع!
No right turn! ...../gar-deʃ be rɑ:st mam-nu:ʔ/ گردش به راست ممنوع!
No U turn! .... /dor za-dan mam-nu:ʔ/ دور زدن ممنوع!
north side ..../ʃo-mɑ:-le ʃahr/ شمال شهر
office block .... /modʒ-ta-meʔ ʔe-dɑ:-ri:/ مجتمع اداری
one way street ..../xɪ-jɑ:-bɑ:-ne jek-ta-ra-fe/ خیابان یکطرفه
open .... /bɑ:z/ باز
park .... /pɑ:rk/ پارک
pavement ..../pɪ-jɑ:-de-ro/ پیاده رو
pharmacy .... /dɑ:-ru:-xɑ:-ne/ داروخانه
post box .... /san-du:-ɢe post/ صندوق پست

post office	/ʔe-dɒ:-re-je post/	ادارهٔ پست
police station	/ʔe-dɒ:-re-je po-li:s/	اداره پلیس
private	/xo-su:-si:/	خصوصی
public health	/beh-dɒ:-ri:/	بهداری
Pull.	/be-ke-ʃi:d/	بکشید.
Push.	/fe-ʃɒ:r da-hi:d/	فشار دهید.
Push the bell.	/zaŋ be-za-ni:d/	زنگ بزنید.
residential area	/man-ta-ɢe-je mas-ku:-ni:/	منطقهٔ مسکونی
restaurant	/ɢa-zɒ:-xo-ri:/	غذاخوری
rush hours	/sɒ:-ʔɒ:-te te-rɒ:-fi:-ke saŋ-gɪn/	ساعات ترافیک سنگین
shoes shop	/kaf-fɒ:-ʃi:/	کفاشی
Silence!	/su:-ku:t/	سکوت!
Slow down!	/sor-ʔat rɒ: kam ko-ni:d/	سرعت را کم کنید!
south side	/dʒu:-nu:-be ʃahr/	جنوب شهر
speed	/sor-ʔat/	سرعت
square	/mej-dʌn/	میدان
stationer	/ne-veʃt ʔaf-zɒ:r fo-ru:ʃ/	نوشت‌افزار فروش
stop	/ʔi:s-gɒ:h/	ایستگاه
Stop!	/ʔist/	ایست!
street	/xɪ-jɒ:-bʌn/	خیابان
super market	/su:-per mɒ:r-ket/	سوپرمارکت
the main road into town	/xɪ-jɒ:-bɒ:-ne ʔas-lɪ-je ʃahr/	خیابان اصلی شهر
town center	/mar-ka-ze ʃahr/	مرکز شهر
traffic lights	/tʃe-rɒ:-ɢe rɒ:h-ne-mɒ:/	چراغ راهنما
uneven road	/dʃɒ:d-de-je nɒ:-ham-vɒ:r/	جادّهٔ ناهموار
Will reopen.	/mo-dʒad-da-dan bɒ:z xɒ:-had ʃod/	مجدّداً باز خواهد شد.

As does quarter.	/ha-mɪn ba-ɢal/	همین بغل.
At the beginning of the block.	/dar ʔɒ:-ɢɒ:-ze bu:-lu:k/	در آغاز بلوک.
At the end of the next block.	/dar pɒ:-jɒ:-ne bo-lu:-ke baʔ-di:/	در پایان بلوک بعدی.

Between N and M streets. .... /bej-ne xɪ-jvː-bʌn-hvː-je N va M / بین خیابانهای N و M.
Can you tell me where main street is? ....
.............../miː-ta-vvː-niːd be-guː-ʔiːd xɪ-jvː-bvː-ne ʔas-li: ko-dʒvːst/
می‌توانید بگویید خیابان اصلی کجاست؟
Cross the road. ..../ʔʌn ta-ra-fe xɪ-jvː-bʌn/. آن طرف خیابان.
Do you know this district? .... /ʔɪn man-ta-Ge rvː miː-ʃe-nvː-siːd/
این منطقه را می‌شناسید؟
Drive with caution. ....
............./bvː ʔeh-tɪ-jvːt rvː-nan-de-gi: ko-niːd/. با احتیاط رانندگی کنید.
Go down street. ... /be-ra-viːd pvː-ʔiː-ne xɪ-jvː-bʌn/. بروید پایین خیابان.
Go straight on. ..../mos-ta-Giːm be-ra-viːd/. مستقیم بروید.
Go up street. ...... /be-ra-viːd bvː-lvː-je xɪ-jvː-bʌn/. بروید بالای خیابان.
I'm a foreigner. ..../man jek xvː-re-dʒi: has-tam/. من یک خارجی هستم.
I'm looking for Mansoor street. ....
.... /man don-bvː-le xɪ-jvː-bvː-ne man-suːr miː-gar-dam/
من دنبال خیابان منصور می‌گردم.
I'm looking for number 31. ....
.... /man don-bvː-le ʃo-mvː-re-je sɪ jo jek miː-gar-dam/
من دنبال شمارهٔ سی و یک می‌گردم.
I'm looking for Abrasan square. ....
............./man don-bvː-le tʃa-hvːr-rvː-he ʔvːb-ra-sʌn miː-gar-dam/
من دنبال چهار راه آبرسان می‌گردم.
I've lost my way. ..../man rvː-ham rvː gom kar-de-ʔam/
من راهم را گم کرده‌ام.
In the middle of the next block. ....
................../dar va-sa-te bo-luː-ke baʔ-diː/
در وسط بلوک بعدی.
Is it far? ..../duːr ʔast/? دور است؟
Is it far from here? ..../ʔaz ʔɪn-dʒvː duːr ʔast/? از اینجا دور است؟
Is it too far to walk? /ne-miː-ʃe pɪ-jvː-de be-ra-vam/? نمیشه پیاده بروم؟
It's an hour's ride. ..../sa-vvː-re jek svː-ʔat rvːh ʔast/
سواره، یک ساعت راه است.
It's only a five minute walk. .... /fa-Gat pandʒ da-Giː-Ge rvːh ʔast/
فقط پنج دقیقه راه است.

It's quite far.	/xej-li: du:r ʔast/	خیلی دور است.
Just before ...	/na-re-si:-de be/	نرسیده به ....
Just past.	/do-rost baʔ-di:/	درست بعدی.
Keep to your left.	/ʔaz sam-te tʃap be-ra-vi:d/	از سمت چپ بروید.
Not very far.	/zi-jv:d du:r ni:st/	زیاد دور نیست.
On Avesta street.	/dar xi-jv:-bv:-ne ʔa-ves-tv:/	در خیابان اوستا.
On the corner.	/dar nabʃ/	در نبش.
On the corner of B and C street.	/dar nab-ʃe xi-jv:-bʌn-hv:-je B va C/	در نبش خیابانهای B و C.
On the other side.	/dar ta-ra-fe di:-gar/	در طرف دیگر.
On this side.	/dar ʔin ta-raf/	در این طرف.
Opposite side.	/sam-te mo-Gv:-bel/	سمت مقابل.
Please draw me a plan of the way. /lot-fan ma-si:r rv: ba-rv:-jam be-ke-ʃi:d/		لطفاً مسیر را برایم بکشید.
Please point.	/lot-fan ne-ʃʌn da-hi:d/	لطفاً نشان دهید.
Please show me on the map. /lot-fan ʔaz ru:-je naG-ʃe ne-ʃʌn da-hi:d/		لطفاً از روی نقشه نشان دهید.
Please write down the address. /lot-fan ʔv:d-res rv: be-ne-vi:-si:d/		لطفاً آدرس را بنویسید.
Should I take a bus? /bv:-jad ʔo-tu:-bu:s sa-vv:r ʃa-vam/		باید اتوبوس سوار شوم؟
The police have blocked the road. /po-li:s dʒv:d-de rv: bas-te ʔast/		پلیس جادّه را بسته است.
Turn to the left.	/be ta-ra-fe tʃap be-pi:-tʃi:d/	به طرف چپ بپیچید.
Turn to the right.	/be ta-ra-fe rv:st be-pi:-tʃi:d/	به طرف راست بپیچید.
We went into the town center. /mv: be mar-ka-ze ʃahr raf-ti:m/		ما به مرکز شهر رفتیم.
What direction should I go in? /ʔaz ko-dv:m ma-si:r bv:-jad be-ra-vam/		از کدام مسیر باید بروم؟
How does it take on foot? /pi-jv:-de tʃe-Gadr rv:h ʔast/		پیاده چقدر راه است؟
What's that building?	/ʔʌn sv:x-te-mʌn tʃi:st/	آن ساختمان چیست؟
What's that sign?	/ʔʌn ʔa-lv:-ma-te tʃi:st/	آن علامت چیست؟

In Town

What's the name of this street? ..../ʔes-me ʔin xɪ-jvː-bʌn tʃiːst/
اسم این خیابان چیست؟

What's the name of this town? ..../ʔes-me ʔin ʃahr tʃiːst/
اسم این شهر چیست؟

What street is this? . /ʔɪn tʃe xɪ-jvː-bvː-ni: ʔast/ این چه خیابانی است؟

Where does this street lead on? ....
........./ʔɪn xɪ-jvː-bʌn be ko-dʒvː miː-re-sad/ این خیابان به کجا می رسد؟

Where is the airport? ...... /fo-ruːd-gvːh ko-dʒvːst/ فرودگاه کجاست؟

Where is the city center? /mar-ka-ze ʃahr ko-dʒvːst/ مرکز شهر کجاست؟

Which direction do I've to go? ....
........../ʔaz ko-dvːm ta-raf bvː-jad be-ra-vam/ از کدام طرف باید بروم؟

Which is the way to A street? ....
.... /xɪ-jvː-bvː-ne A ko-dvːm ta-raf ʔast/ خیابان A کدام طرف است؟

Which is the way to Germany Embassy? ....
.............../ʔaz tʃe ma-siː-riː be se-fvː-ra-te ʔvːl-mʌn be-ra-vam/
از چه مسیری به سفارت آلمان بروم؟

You are better take a taxi. ... /beh-tar ʔast bvː tvːk-si: be-ra-viːd/
بهتر است با تاکسی بروید.

4-3
BUS

fare .... /Gej-ma-te be-li:t/ قیمت بلیط
bus stop .... /ʔi:s-gʏ:-he ʔo-tu:-bu:s/ ایستگاه اتوبوس
route .... /ma-si:-re ha-re-kat/ مسیر حرکت
the nearest stop .... /naz-di:k-ta-rın ʔi:s-gʏ:h/ نزدیکترین ایستگاه
the next stop .... /ʔi:s-gʏ:-he baʔ-di:/ ایستگاه بعدی
ticket .... /be-li:t/ بلیط

How many stops to Vanak Square are? ....
/tʏ: mej-dʏ:-ne va-nak tʃand ʔi:s-gʏ:h ʔast/ تا میدان ونک چند ایستگاه است؟
Please hand on my ticket. ....
.... /lot-fan be-li:-te ma-rʏ: be-gi:-ri:d/. لطفاً بلیط مرا بگیرید
Please let me know when to get off. ....
........../lot-fan be man be-gu:-ʔi: tʃe mo-Geʔ pi-jʏ:-de ʃa-vam/
لطفاً به من بگویید چه موقع پیاده شوم.
This is your stop. ...... /ʔın ʔi:s-gʏ:-he ʃo-mʏ:st/ این ایستگاه شماست

What bus go to Tajrish? ....
/ko-dɑ:m ʔo-tu:-bu:s be tadʒ-ri:ʃ mi:-ra-vad/ کدام اتوبوس به تجریش می‌رود؟
What is this stop called? .... /ʔes-me ʔɪn ʔi:s-gɑ:h tʃi:st/
اسم این ایستگاه چیست؟
What is the next stop? .... /ʔi:s-gɑ:-he baʔ-di: ko-dɑ:m ʔast/
ایستگاه بعدی کدام است؟
When will the bus come? ....
................../ʔo-tu:-bu:s kej mi:-re-sad/ اتوبوس کی می‌رسد؟
Where is the nearest Bus stop? ....
................./naz-di:k-ta-rɪn ʔi:s-gɑ:-he ʔo-tu:-bu:s ko-dʒɑ:st/
نزدیکترین ایستگاه اتوبوس کجاست؟
You have taken the wrong bus. ....
............../ʃo-mɑ: ʔo-tu:-bu:s rɑ: ʔeʃ-te-bɑ:-hi: sa-vɑ:r ʃo-de-ʔi:d/
شما اتوبوس را اشتباهی سوار شده‌اید.
You have to get off at the next stop. ....
.............../ʃo-mɑ: bɑ:-jad dar ʔi:s-gɑ:-he baʔ-di: pɪ-jɑ:-de ʃa-vi:d/
شما باید در ایستگاه بعدی پیاده شوید.
You have to get off at the second stop. ....
............/ʃo-mɑ: bɑ:-jad dar ʔi:s-gɑ:-he dov-vom pɪ-jɑ:-de ʃa-vi:d/
شما باید در ایستگاه دوّم پیاده شوید.
You have to take bus number 105. ....
... /ʃo-mɑ: bɑ:-jad bɑ: ʔo-tu:-bu:-se ʃo-mɑ:-re sa do pandʒ be-ra-vi:d/
شما باید با اتوبوس شماره ۱۰۵ بروید.

4-4
HOTEL

bath	/ham-mʌːm/	حمّام
bed-linen	/ma-lʌːfe/	ملافه
doorman	/dar-bʌn/	دربان
floor	/ta-ba-ɢe/	طبقه
front room	/ʔo-tʌː-ɢe dʒe-low/	اتاق جلو
furnished room	/ʔo-tʌː-ɢe mob-le/	اتاق مبله
hot and cold water	/ʔʌː-be gar mo sard/	آب گرم و سرد
hotel manager	/mo-di:-rIj-ja-te ho-tel/	مدیریّت هتل
information desk	/mi:-ze ʔet-te-lʌː-ʔʌːt/	میز اطّلاعات
key	/ki:-li:d/	کلید
lift	/ʔʌː-sʌn-sor/	آسانسور
pillow	/bʌː-leʃ/	بالش
rent	/ʔe-dʒʌː-re/	اجاره
service bureau	/daf-ta-re xa-da-mʌːt/	دفتر خدمات
shower	/duːʃ/	دوش
side room	/ʔo-tʌː-ɢe ke-nʌː-re/	اتاق کناره

152 Beginner's Persian

single room .... /ʔo-tɑ:-Ge jek na-fa-re/ اتاق یک‌نفره
toilet .... /dast-ʃu:-ʔi:/ دستشویی
top floor .... /ta-ba-Ge ʔɑ:-xar/ طبقه آخر
towel .... /ho-le/ حوله
unfurnished room .... /ʔo-tɑ:-Ge Gej-re mob-le/ اتاق غیرمبله
window .... /pan-dʒa-re/ پنجره

At what time dinner/lunch is served? ....
.... /tʃe sɑ:-ʔa-ti: nɑ:-hɑ:r (ʃɑ:m) dɑ:-de mi:-ʃa-vad/
چه ساعتی ناهار (شام) داده می‌شود؟
Do you have a better room? /ʔo-tɑ:-Ge beh-ta-ri: dɑ:-ri:d/ اتاق بهتری دارید؟
Do you have a cheaper room? ... /ʔo-tɑ:-Ge ʔar-zɑn-tar dɑ:-ri:d/
اتاق ارزانتر دارید؟
Do you know a good hotel? .... /ho-te-le xu:b mi:-ʃe-nɑ:-si:d/
هتل خوب می‌شناسید؟
Do you want the rent in advance? ....
.... /ke-rɑ:-je rɑ: pi:ʃ mi:-xɑ:-hi:d/ کرایه را پیش می‌خواهید؟
Did anyone ask for me? .... /ka-si: so-rɑ:-Ge ma-rɑ: ge-reft/
کسی سراغ مرا گرفت؟
Have I any letter? .... /ba-rɑ:-je man nɑ:-me-ʔi: ʔɑ:-ma-de ʔast/
برای من نامه‌ای آمده است؟
Have I any message? ....
.... /ba-rɑ:-je man pej-Gɑ:-mi: re-si:-de ʔast/ برای من پیغامی رسیده است؟
Have you a directory of the town? ....
.... /rɑ:h-ne-mɑ:-je ʃahr rɑ: dɑ:-ri:d/ راهنمای شهر را دارید؟
Have you a map of the town? ....
.... /nɑG-ʃe-je ʃahr rɑ: dɑ:-ri:d/ نقشهٔ شهر را دارید؟
Have you any vacant room? /ʔo-tɑ:-Ge xɑ:-li: dɑ:-ri:d/ اتاق خالی دارید؟
How long will you be staying? ..... /tʃe mod-dat xɑ:-hi:d mɑ:nd/
چه مدت خواهید ماند؟
How much a day is the room? ....
.... /ke-rɑ:-je ʔo-tɑ:G ru:-zi: tʃand ʔast/ کرایه اتاق روزی چند است؟

In Town

I'll take this room for three days. ....
................../man ʔo-tʌ:G rʌ: ba-rʌ:-je se ru:z mi:-xʌ:-ham/
من اتاق را برای سه روز می‌خواهم.

Is my bill ready? .... /su:-rat-he-sʌ:-bam hʌ:-zer ʔast/
صورتحسابم حاضر است؟

Is the city center far from here? ....
...../mar-ka-ze ʃahr ʔaz ʔɪn-dʒʌ: du:r ʔast/ است؟ دور اینجا از شهر مرکز

Is the rent paid in advance? ....
......../ke-rʌ:-je ʔav-val par-dʌ:xt mi:-ʃa-vad/ می‌شود؟ پرداخت اول کرایه

May I have a look at it? ..../mom-ken ʔast ne-gʌ:-hi: be-ko-nam/
ممکن است نگاهی بکنم؟

May I speak to the manager? ....
/mom-ken ʔast bʌ: mo-di:r soh-bat ko-nam/ کنم؟ صحبت مدیر با است ممکن

Please bring me an extra blanket ....
./lot-fan jek pa-tu:-je ʔe-zʌ:-fi: bɪ-jʌ:-va-ri:d/ بیاورید اضافی پتوی یک لطفاً

Till what time is the hotel open? .... /hotel tʌ: kej bʌ:z ʔast/
هتل تا کی باز است؟

What do you charge for the meals? ....
.................../Gej-ma-te Gazʌ: tʃe-Gadr ʔast/ است؟ چقدر غذا قیمت

What have you got for the dinner? ....
...................../ba-rʌ:-je ʃʌ:m tʃe dʌ:-ri:d/ دارید؟ چه شام برای

What's the rent? ..../ke-rʌ:-je tʃe-Gadr ʔast/ است؟ چقدر کرایه

What time is breakfast? ....
....../sʌ:-ʔa-te tʃand sob-hʌ:-ne mi:-da-hi:d/ می‌دهید؟ صبحانه چند ساعت

Where can I make a telephone call? ....
/ʔaz ko-dʒʌ: mi:-ta-vʌ:-nam te-le-fon be-za-nam/ بزنم؟ تلفن می‌توانم کجا از

Where's the nearest hotel? ....
/naz-di:k-ta-rɪn mo-sʌ:-fer-xʌ:-ne ko-dʒʌ:st/ کجاست؟ مسافرخانه نزدیکترین

Where's the toilet? ..../dast-ʃu:-ʔi: ko-dʒʌ:st/ کجاست؟ دستشویی

Which floor is my room? ....
....../ʔo-tʌ:Ge man ta-ba-Ge-je tʃan-dom ʔast/ است؟ چندم طبقهٔ از من اتاق

Give me my bill please. /lot-fan su:-rat-he-sʌ:-be ma-rʌ: be-da-hi:d/
لطفاً صورتحساب مرا بدهید.

Here's the room. ..../be-far-mʌ:-ʔi:d ʔo-tʌ:-Ge-tʌn/. اتاقتان بفرمایید

I'm expecting a phone call from Paris. ....
................/man mon-ta-ze-re te-le-fo-ni: ʔaz pɒː-riːs has-tam/
من منتظر تلفنی از پاریس هستم.
I want a single room. ....
........./jek ʔo-tɒː-Ge jek na-fa-re miː-xɒː-ham/ .یک اتاق یک نفره می‌خواهم
No vacancies. .... /dʒɒː-je xɒː-liː niːst/ .جای خالی نیست
Please, change the bed sheets. ....
........./lot-fan ma-lɒː-fe-hɒː rɒː ʔa-vaz ko-niːd/ .لطفاً ملافه‌ها را عوض کنید
Please wake me up at eight o'clock in the morning. ....
.... /lot-fan sɒː-ʔa-te haʃ-te sobh ma-rɒː biː-dɒːr ko-niːd/
لطفاً ساعت هشت صبح مرا بیدار کنید.
The key to room No. 8, please. ....
/lot-fan ke-liː-de ʔo-tɒː-Ge haʃt rɒː be-da-hiːd/ .لطفاً کلید اتاق ۸ را بدهید
There's a mistake in the bill. ....
....................../dar ʔin suː-rat-he-sɒːb ʔeʃ-te-bɒːh-i: ʃo-de ʔast/
در این صورتحساب اشتباهی شده است.
This is the only room vacant. . /ʔin tan-hɒː ʔo-tɒː-Ge xɒː-li: ʔast/
این تنها اتاق خالی است.
We want a room with a double bed. ....
.... /mɒː ʔo-tɒː-Giː bɒː tax-te do-na-fa-re miː-xɒː-hiːm/
ما اطاقی با تخت دونفره می‌خواهیم.

4-5 BANK MONEY

bill	/ʔes-ke-nɒ:s/	اسکناس
change	/pu:-le xord/	پول خرد
coin	/sek-ke/	سکّه
commission	/kɒ:r-mozd/	کارمزد
currency	/ʔarz, pu:-le rɒ:-jedʒ/	ارز، پول رایج
Dollar	/do-lɒ:r/	دلار
Franc	/fe-rɒ:nk/	فرانک
Mark	/mɒ:rk/	مارک
Pound	/pond/	پوند
Rial	/rɪ-jɒ:l/	ریال
traveller's cheque	/tʃe-ke mo-sɒ:-fe-ra-ti:/	چک مسافرتی

1 Rial coin	/sek-ke-je jek rɪ-jvː-liː/	سکّهٔ ۱ ریالی
2 Rials coin	/sek-ke-je do rɪ-jvː-liː/	سکّهٔ ۲ ریالی
5 Rials coin	/sek-ke-je pandʒ rɪj-vː-liː/	سکّهٔ ۵ ریالی
10 Rials coin	/sek-ke-je dah rɪ-jvː-liː/	سکّهٔ ۱۰ ریالی
20 Rials coin	/sek-ke-je biːst rɪ-jvː-liː/	سکّهٔ ۲۰ ریالی
50 Rials coin	/sek-ke-je pan-dʒvːh rɪ-jvː-liː/	سکّهٔ ۵۰ ریالی
100 Rials coin	/sek-ke-je sad rɪ-jvː-liː/	سکّهٔ ۱۰۰ ریالی
250 Rials coin	/sek-ke-je diː-viːs to pan-dʒvːh rɪ-jvː-liː/	سکّهٔ ۲۵۰ ریالی
100 Rials bill	/ʔes-ke-nvː-se sad rɪ-jvː-liː/	اسکناس ۱۰۰ ریالی
200 Rials bill	/ʔes-ke-nvː-se diː-viːst rɪ-jvː-liː/	اسکناس ۲۰۰ ریالی
500 Rials bill	/ʔes-ke-nvː-se pʌn-sad rɪ-jvː-liː/	اسکناس ۵۰۰ ریالی
1000 Rials bill	/ʔes-ke-nvː-se he-zvːr rɪ-jvː-liː/	اسکناس ۱۰۰۰ ریالی
2000 Rials bill	/ʔes-ke-nvː-se do he-zvːr rɪ-jvː-liː/	اسکناس ۲۰۰۰ ریالی
5000 Rials bill	/ʔes-ke-nvː-se pandʒ hezvːr rɪ-jvː-liː/	اسکناس ۵۰۰۰ ریالی
10 000 Rials bill	/ʔes-ke-nvː-se dah he-zvːr rɪ-jvː-liː/	اسکناس ۱۰ ۰۰۰ ریالی
first name	/nvːm/	نام
last name	/nvː-me xvː-ne-vvː-de-giː/	نام خانوادگی
date of birth	/tvː-riː-xe ta-val-lod/	تاریخ تولّد
place of birth	/ma-hal-le ta-val-lod/	محلّ تولّد
nationality	/mel-lɪj-jat/	ملّیّت
occupation	/ʃoɢl/	شغل
age	/sen/	سن
address	/ne-ʃvː-niː/	نشانی
date	/tvː-riːx/	تاریخ
signature	/ʔem-zvː/	امضا

A new cheque book, please. ....
.... /lot-fan jek das-te tʃek be-da-hiːd/ لطفاً یک دسته چک بدهید.
Can I change my traveller's cheques? ....
.... /miː-ta-vvː-nam tʃe-ke mo-svː-fe-ra-tiː rv be puːl tab-diːl ko-nam/
می‌توانم چک مسافرتی را به پول تبدیل کنم؟

In Town

Could I change these Dollars for rials? ....
.........../mom-ken ʔast ʔın do-lɑ:r-hɑ: rɑ: be rı-jɑ:l tab-di:l ko-ni:d/
ممکن است این دلارها را به ریال تبدیل کنید؟

Could you change these for me, please? ....
................./mom-ken ʔast ʔın rɑ: ba-rɑ:-jam tab-di:l ko-ni:d/
ممکن است این را برایم تبدیل کنید؟

Could you give me some change? ....
.................../ʔem-kʌn dɑ:-rad ka-mi: pu:l xord ko-ni:d/
امکان دارد کمی پول خرد کنید؟

Could you tell me my balance? ....
.................../mom-ken ʔast mo-dʒu:-dı-jam rɑ: be-gu:-ʔi:d/
ممکن است موجودیم را بگویید؟

I want to cash this cheque. ....
.........../mi:-xɑ:-ham tʃek rɑ: naɢd ko-nam/
می‌خواهم چک را نقد کنم.

I want to change money. ....
.........../mi:-xɑ:-ham pu:l tab-di:l ko-nam/
می‌خواهم پول تبدیل کنم.

I want to send money. ....
.........../mi:-xɑ:-ham pu:l bef-res-tam/
می‌خواهم پول بفرستم.

I'd like to know how to send money to Sweden. ....
/mɑ:-je-lam be-dɑ:-nam tʃe-towr mi:-ta-vʌn be so-ʔed pu:l fe-res-tɑ:d/
مایلم بدانم که چطور می‌توان به سوئد پول فرستاد.

I'd like to know the exchange rent for Dollar. ....
................/mɑ:-je-lam ner-xe tab-di:-le do-lɑ:r rɑ: be-dɑ:-nam/
مایلم نرخ تبدیل دلار را بدانم.

I'd like to open a savings account. ....
................/mɑ:-je-lam jek he-sɑ:-be pas ʔan-dɑ:z bɑ:z ko-nam/
مایلم یک حساب پس‌انداز باز کنم.

I'd like to open an account. ....
.............../mɑ:-je-lam he-sɑ:-bi: bɑ:z ko-nam/
مایلم حسابی باز کنم.

How do you want in? ....
........./tʃe noʔ ʔes-ke-nɑ:-si: mi:-xɑ:-hi:d/
چه نوع اسکناسی می‌خواهید؟

Please take your currency exchange receipt. ....
................/lot-fan ra-si:-de tab-di:-le ʔarz rɑ: bar-dɑ:-ri:d/
لطفاً رسید تبدیل ارز را بردارید.

What's the exchange rate? ....
................./ner-xe tab-di:l tʃe-Gadr ʔast/ نرخ تبدیل چقدر است؟
When's the bank open/close? ....
................./bv:nk kej bv:z (bas-te) ʔast/ بانک کی باز (بسته) است؟
Where can change money? ....
......./ko-dʒʌ: mi:-ta-vʌn ʔarz tab-di:l kard/ کجا می‌توان ارز تبدیل کرد؟
Where's the nearest bank? ....
.............../naz-di:k-ta-rın bv:nk ko-dʒʌ:st/ نزدیکترین بانک کجاست؟
Will you please fill out this form? ....
../mom-ken ʔast ʔın form rʌ: por ko-ni:d/ ممکن است این فرم را پر کنید؟
Would you cash this traveler check, please? ....
/lot-fan mom-ken ʔast ʔın tʃe-ke mo-sv:-fe-ra-ti: rʌ: par-dʌ:xt ko-ni:d
لطفاً ممکن است این چک مسافرتی را پرداخت کنید؟

4-6
POST

airmail	پست هوایی	/pos-te ha-vɑː-ʔiː/
envelope	پاکت نامه	/pɑː-ka-te nɑː-me/
express	فوری	/fow-riː/
general delivery	پست عادی	/pos-te ʔɑː-diː/
money-order	حوالهٔ پولی	/ha-vɑː-le-je puː-liː/
parcel	بستهٔ پستی	/bas-te-je pos-tiː/
postage	پول تمبر	/puː-le tamr/
poste restante	پست امانات	/pos-te ʔa-mɑː-nɑːt/
priority mail	پست پیشتاز	/pos-te piːʃ-tɑːz/
receipt	قبض رسید	/ɢab-ze ra-siːd/
registered	سفارشی	/se-fɑː-re-ʃiː/
stamp	تمبر	/tamr/
telefax	پست تصویری	/pos-te tas-viː-riː/
telegram	تلگرام	/te-leg-rɑːm/
telegram form	فرم تلگرام	/for-me te-leg-rɑːm/

How much is an airmail to Italy? ....
.... /ha-ziː-ne pos-te ha-vvː-ʔi: be ʔiː-tvː-lɪ-jvː tʃe-ɢadr ʔast/
هزینهٔ پست هوایی به ایتالیا چقدر است؟
How much must I pay for postage? ....
/tʃe-ɢadr bvː-jad ba-rvː-je tamr be-par-dvː-zam/ چقدر باید برای تمبر بپردازم؟
I want to register this letter. ....
.../lot-fan nvː-me-je ma-rvː se-fvː-re-ʃi: ko-niːd/ لطفاً نامهٔ مرا سفارشی کنید
I want to send money. ....
.... /miː-xvː-ham puːl be-fe-res-tam/ می‌خواهم پول بفرستم.
I want to send money abroad. ....
/miː-xvː-ham be xvː-redʒ puːl be-fe-res-tam/ می‌خواهم به خارج پول بفرستم.
When's the post office open (close)? ....
.........../post-xvː-ne kej bvz (bas-te) ʔast/ پستخانه کی باز (بسته) است؟
Where can I get a telegram form? ....
.... /ko-dʒvː miː-ta-vvː-nam for-me te-leg-rvːm be-giː-ram/
کجا می‌توانم فرم تلگرام بگیرم؟
Where can I send a telegram? ....
................../ko-dʒvː miː-ta-vvː-nam te-leg-rvːm be-fe-res-tam/
کجا می‌توانم تلگرام بفرستم؟
Where's the post box around here? ....
/ʔɪn ta-ra-fvː san-duː-ɢe post ko-dʒvːst/ این طرفها، صندوق پست کجاست؟ .
Where's the poste restante counter? ....
..... /bvː-dʒe-je ʔa-mvː-nvː-te pos-tiː ko-dʒvːst/ باجهٔ امانات پستی کجاست؟
Where's the nearest post office? ....
.... /naz-diːk-ta-rɪn post-xvː-ne ko-dʒvːst/ نزدیکترین پستخانه کجاست؟
Where's the post office? ... /post-xvː-ne ko-dʒvːst/ پستخانه کجاست؟
Where's the stamp window? .... /bvː-dʒe-je tamr ko-dʒvːst/
باجهٔ تمبر کجاست؟

4-7
TELEPHONE

dialing	/ʃo-mɑ:-re ge-ref-tan/	شماره گرفتن
receiver	/gu:-ʃi:/	گوشی
reduced rate	/ner-xe tax-fi:f/	نرخ تخفیف
public phone	/te-le-fo-ne ʔe-mu:-mi:/	تلفن عمومی
telephone directory	/daf-ta-re rɑ:h-ne-mɑ:-je te-le-fon/	دفتر راهنمای تلفن
telephone number	/ʃo-mɑ:-re te-le-fon/	شماره تلفن

Could I talk to Farzad, please?
/mi:-ʃa-vad lot-fan bɑ: far-zɑ:d soh-bat ko-nam/ می‌شود لطفاً با فرزاد صحبت کنم؟

Give me a phone directory, please.
/lot-fan jek daf-ta-re rɑ:h-ne-mɑ:-je te-le-fon be man be-da-hi:d/
لطفاً یک دفتر راهنمای تلفن به من بدهید.

Hang on a moment. /jek lah-ze gu:-ʃi: xed-ma-te-tɑn bɑ:-ʃad/
یک لحظه گوشی خدمتتان باشد.

162 Beginner's Persian

Hello! I'm listening. .... /ʔa-lo be-far-mɑː-ʔiːd/ الو بفرمایید.
Hold the line, please. ....
.... /lot-fan guː-ʃiː xed-ma-te-tʌn bɑː-ʃad/. لطفاً گوشی خدمتتان باشد.
How can I phone the hotel information desk? ....
/tʃe-towr miː-ʃa-vad be daf-ta-re rɑːh-ne-mɑː-je ho-tel zaŋ be-za-nam/
چطور می‌شود به دفتر راهنمای هتل زنگ بزنم؟
How can I phone to Shiraz? ....
.... /tʃe-towr miː-ta-vɑː-nam be ʃiː-rɑːz zaŋ be-za-nam/
چطور می‌توانم به شیراز زنگ بزنم؟
I can't hear you very well. ....
../sa-dɑː-je-tʌn xuːb ʃe-niː-de ne-miː-ʃa-vad/. صدایتان خوب شنیده نمی‌شود.
I have to call NewYork. ....
./man bɑː-jad be nɪ-jo-jork te-le-fon ko-nam/. من باید به نیویورک تلفن کنم.
I telephoned my friend last night. ....
.... /diː-ʃab be duːs-tam te-le-fon kar-dam/. دیشب به دوستم تلفن کردم.
I told him the news by telephone. ....
.... /xa-bar rɑː te-le-fo-ni be ʔu: gof-tam/. خبر را تلفنی به او گفتم.
Please answer the telephone. ....
.... /lot-fan te-le-fon rɑː dʒa-vɑːb da-hiːd/. لطفاً تلفن را جواب دهید.
Speak louder, please. ....
.... /lot-fan bo-lan-tar soh-bat ko-niːd/. لطفاً بلندتر صحبت کنید.
There is no answer. .... /te-le-fon dʒa-vɑːb ne-miː-da-had/
تلفن جواب نمی‌دهد.
The line is engaged. ...... /te-le-fon ʔeʃ-ɢɑːl ʔast/. تلفن اشغال است.
What's your extension number? ....
../ʃo-mɑː-re-je dɑː-xe-lɪ-je ʃo-mɑː tʃand ʔast/؟ شمارهٔ داخلی شما چند است؟
What's your phone number? ....
... /ʃo-mɑː-re-je te-le-fo-ne ʃo-mɑː tʃand ʔast/؟ شمارهٔ تلفن شما چند است؟
Where is the nearest public phone? ....
/naz-diːk-ta-rɪn bɑː-dʒe-je te-le-fon ko-dʒɑːst/؟ نزدیکترین باجه تلفن کجاست؟
What number are you calling? ....
.... /be tʃe ʃo-mɑː-re-ʔi: miː-xɑː-hiːd te-le-fon ko-niːd/
به چه شماره‌ای می‌خواهید تلفن کنید؟

Would you tell her/him I rang. ....
..../be ʔi:-ʃʌn be-gu:-ʔi:d mʌn zaŋ za-dam/. به ایشان بگویید من زنگ زدم
You've got the wrong number. ....
......../ʃo-mv:-re rv: ʔeʃ-te-bv:h ge-ref-te-ʔi:d/. شماره را اشتباه گرفته‌اید

4-8
RESTAURANT
(MENU, ...)

MENU	/suː-ra-te ɢa-zɑː/	صورت غذا
1. breakfast	/sob-hɑː-ne/	۱. صبحانه
bread	/nʌn/	نان
butter	/ka-re/	کره
cake	/kejk/	کیک
cheese	/pa-niːr/	پنیر
fried eggs	/niːm-ruː/	نیمرو
honey	/ʔa-sal/	عسل
jam	/mo-rab-bɑː/	مربّا
milk	/ʃiːr/	شیر
omelette	/ʔom-let/	املت

2.lunch/dinner .... /nɑ:-hɑ:r (ʃɑ:m)/ ناهار (شام).۲

broth .... /ʔɑ:b-gu:ʃt/	آبگوشت
chelow-gheimeh .... /tʃe-low ɢej-me/	چلو قیمه
chelow-kabab .... /tʃe-low ka-bɑ:b/	چلو کباب
chelow-khoresht .... /tʃe-low xo-reʃt/	چلو خورشت
chelow-morgh .... /tʃe-low morɢ/	چلو مرغ
chicken breast .... /si:-ne-je morɢ/	سینهٔ مرغ
chicken leg .... /rɑ:-ne morɢ/	ران مرغ
liver .... /dʒe-gar/	جگر
mashed meat .... /ku:-bi:-de/	کوبیده
rice .... /be-rendʒ/	برنج
roast meat(kabab) .... /ka-bɑ:b/	کباب
steak .... /bar-ge/	برگه
stuffing .... /ɢej-me/	قیمه

3.soup .... /su:p/ سوپ .۳

barley soup .... /su:-pe dʒow/	سوپ جو
chicken soup .... /su:-pe dʒu:-dʒe/	سوپ جوجه
noodle soup .... /su:-pe reʃ-te/	سوپ رشته
vegetable soup .... /ʔɑ:ʃ/	آش

4.drinkables .... /nu:-ʃi:-da-ni:/ نوشیدنی .۴

beer .... /ʔɑ:b-dʒo/	آبجو
Canadadry .... /kɑ:-nɑ:-dɑ:/	کانادا
coffe .... /ɢah-ve/	قهوه
Coke .... /ko-kɑ:/	کوکا
doogh .... /du:ɢ/	دوغ
fruit juice .... /ʔɑ:b mi:-ve/	آب میوه
7-up .... /se-ven ʔɑ:p/	سون آپ
sherbet .... /ʃar-bat/	شربت

In Town 167

tea .... /tʃɑː-ʔiː/ چایی
water .... /ʔɑːb/ آب

5. dessert .... /de-ser/ دسر ۵.

chocolate icecream .... /bas-ta-nɪ-je ʃo-ko-lɑː-tiː/ بستنی شکلاتی
icecream .... /bas-ta-niː/ بستنی
olives .... /zej-tʊn/ زیتون
salad .... /sɑː-lɑːd/ سالاد
strawberry icecream .... /bas-ta-nɪ-je tuːt-fa-ran-giː/ بستنی توت فرنگی
vanilla icecream .... /bas-ta-nɪ-je vɑː-niː-liː/ بستنی وانیلی

6. juice .... /ʔɑːb-miː-ve/ آبمیوه ۶.

apple juice .... /ʔɑː-be siːb/ آب سیب
banana juice .... /ʃiː-re moz/ شیرموز
carrot juice .... /ʔɑː-be ha-viːdʒ/ آب هویج
grape juice .... /ʔɑː-be ʔan-guːr/ آب انگور
mixed juice .... /maʔ-dʒʊn/ معجون
pomegranate juice .... /ʔɑː-be ʔa-nɑːr/ آب انار

bill .... /suː-rat-he-sɑːb/ صورتحساب
bottle .... /bot-riː/ بطری
corkscrew .... /dar-bɑːz-kon/ دربازکن
cup .... /fen-dʒɑn/ فنجان
dessertspoon .... /ɢɑː-ʃo-ɢe de-ser-xo-riː/ قاشق دسرخوری
fork .... /tʃan-ɢɑːl/ چنگال
knife .... /kɑːrd/ کارد
mayonnaise sauce .... /so-se mɑː-jo-nez/ سس مایونز
napkin .... /dast-mɑːl/ دستمال
pepper .... /fel-fe-le sɪ-jɑːh/ فلفل سیاه
plate .... /boʃ-ɢɑːb/ بشقاب
salt .... /na-mak/ نمک

sauce	/sos/	سس
spoon	/ɢɒː-ʃog/	قاشق
tablespoon	/ɢɒː-ʃo-ɢe ɢa-zɒː-xo-riː/	قاشق غذاخوری
teaspoon	/ɢɒː-ʃo-ɢe tʃɒːj-xo-riː/	قاشق چایخوری
water	/ʔɒːb/	آب
bitter	/talx/	تلخ
cold	/sard/	سرد
hot	/garm/	گرم
piquant	/tond/	تند
salty	/ʃuːr/	شور
sour	/towrʃ/	ترش
sweet	/ʃiː-rɪn/	شیرین
tasty	/xoʃ-ma-ze/	خوشمزه

A menu, please. ..../liːs-te ɢa-zɒː lot-fan/ لیست غذا، لطفاً.
Bring me some water. .../ka-miː ba-rɒː-je man ʔɒːb bɪ-jɒː-va-riːd/
کمی برای من آب بیاورید.
Bring us this, please. .../lot-fan ʔɪn rɒː ba-rɒː-je-mʌn bɪ-jɒː-va-riːd/
لطفاً، این را برایمان بیاورید.
Do you have rice? ..../be-rendʒ dɒː-riːd/ برنج دارید؟
Give me tea, please. . /lot-fan tʃɒː-ʔiː bɪ-jɒː-va-riːd/ لطفاً چایی بیاورید.
hand me that plate, please. ....
/lot-fan ʔɒn boʃ-ɢɒːb rɒː be man be-da-hiːd/ لطفاً آن بشقاب را به من بدهید.
Help yourself. .... /be-far-mɒː-ʔiːd/ بفرمایید.
I feel like a cup of coffee. ....
.../ha-va-se jek fen-dʒʌn ɢah-ve kar-de-ʔam/ هوس یک فنجان قهوه کرده‌ام.
I'd like omelette. ..../man ʔom-let miː-xɒː-ham/ من املت می‌خواهم.
Is breakfast ready? ..../sob-hɒː-ne hɒː-zer ʔast/ صبحانه حاضر است؟
Is there a restaurant near here? ....
/dar naz-diː-ke ʔɪn-dʒɒː ɢa-zɒː-xo-riː hast/ در نزدیکی اینجا غذاخوری هست؟
Just take it to please me. ..../be xɒː-te-re man be-xo-riːd/
به خاطر من بخورید.

More cheese, please. ... /pa-ni:-re ʔe-zv:-fi: lot-fan/ پنیر اضافی، لطفاً.
This dish is overdone. . /ʔin Ga-zv: su:x-te ʔast/ این غذا سوخته است.
This dish is too salty. ..... /ʔin Ga-zv: ʃu:r ʔast/ این غذا شور است.
This dish is underdone. .... /ʔin Gazv: sorx na-ʃo-de ʔast/ این غذا سرخ نشده است.
Two teas, please. ..... /do fen-dʒʌn tʃv:j lot-fan/ دو فنجان چای لطفاً.
What do you want to order? ....
.... /ʃo-mv: tʃe se-fv:-reʃ mi:-da-hi:d/ شما چه سفارش می‌دهید؟
What for dessert? ....
.... /ba-rv:-je de-ser tʃe mejl dv:-ri:d/ برای دسر چه میل دارید؟
What's your dish for the day? ....
.... /Ga-zv:-je ru:-ze ʃo-mv: tʃi:st/ غذای روز شما چیست؟
What's the speciality of the house? ....
.... /Ga-zv:-je max-su:-se ʃo-mv: tʃi:st/ غذای مخصوص شما چیست؟
What meat dishes have you? ....
...... /tʃe noʔ Ga-zv:-hv:-je guʃ-ti: dv:-ri:d/ چه نوع غذاهای گوشتی دارید؟
What would you like to drink? ..... /tʃe mi:-nu:-ʃi:d/ چه می‌نوشید؟
Wouldn't you like? .... /mejl na-dv:-ri:d/ میل ندارید؟

snackbar .... /sʌn-di:-vi:-tʃi:/ ساندویچی
cheeseburger .... /tʃi:z ber-ger/ چیزبرگر
cutlet .... /kot-let/ کتلت
frankfurter (wiener) .... /frʌnk-for-ter/ فرانکفورتر
ham .... /ʒʌn-bon/ ژانبون
hamburger .... /ham-ber-ger/ همبرگر
hotdog .... /so-si:s kok-tel/ سوسیس کتل
sausage .... /so-si:s/ سوسیس

A hamburger, please. .... /jek ham-ber-ger lot-fan/ یک همبرگر، لطفاً.
Two sausages, please. .... /do so-si:s lot-fan/ دو سوسیس، لطفاً.

4-9
MUSEUM

anthropological museum .... /muː-ze-je ʔen-sʌn ʃe-nvː-siː/
موزهٔ انسان شناسی
archeological find ..... /kaʃ-fe bɐːs-tʌn-ʃe-nvː-siː/ کشف باستانشناسی
art .... /ho-nar/ هنر
artist .... /ho-nar-mand/ هنرمند
black and white reproduction ./nos-xe-je tʃvː-pɪ-je sɪ-jvː ho se-fiːd/
نسخهٔ چاپی سیاه و سفید
caricature .... /kvː-riː-kvː-tor/ کاریکاتور
cityscape .... /man-za-re-je ʃahr/ منظرهٔ شهر
collection .... /ko-lek-sɪ-jon/ کلکسیون
collection of coins .... /ko-lek-sɪ-jo-ne sek-ke/ کلکسیون سکّه
collection of painting ... /ko-lek-sɪ-jo-ne nɑG-Gvː-ʃiː/ کلکسیون نقّاشی
colour .... /raŋ/ رنگ
colour reproduction ... /nos-xe-je tʃvː-pɪ-je raŋ-giː/ نسخهٔ چاپی رنگی
colouring .... /raŋ-gvː-miː-ziː/ رنگآمیزی
drawing .... /tas-viːr/ تصویر

172 Beginner's Persian

English	Persian	Transcription
entrance ticket	بلیط ورودی	/be-li:-te vo-ru:-di:/
etching	حکّاری	/hak-kɑ:-ri:/
exhibit	شیئی نمایشی	/ʃej-ʔi: ne-mɑ:-je-ʃi:/
exhibition	نمایشگاه	/ne-mɑ:-jeʃ-gɑ:h/
fine arts	هنرهای زیبا	/ho-nar-hɑ:-je zi:-bɑ:/
fresco	نقاشی دیواری	/nɑG-Gɑ:-ʃi-je di:-vɑ:-ri:/
graphic arts	هنرهای ترسیمی	/ho-nar-hɑ:-je tar-si:-mi:/
guidebook	کتاب راهنما	/ke-tɑ:-be rɑ:h-ne-mɑ:/
history museum	موزهٔ تاریخ	/mu:-ze-je tɑ:-ri:x/
Iranian art	هنر ایرانی	/ho-na-re ʔi:-rɑ:-ni:/
literary museum	موزهٔ ادبیات	/mu:-ze-je ʔa-da-bɪj-jɑ:t/
memorical museum	موزهٔ یادبودها	/mu:-ze-je jɑ:d-bu:d-hɑ:/
miniature	مینیاتور	/mi:-nɪ-jɑ:-tu:r/
mosaic	موزاییک	/mu:-zɑ:-ʔi:k/
museum	موزه	/mu:-ze/
museum of applied arts	موزهٔ هنرهای تجربی	/mu:-ze-je ho-nar-hɑ:-je tadʒ-ro-bi:/
museum of fine arts	موزهٔ هنرهای زیبا	/mu:-ze-je ho-nar-hɑ:-je zi:-bɑ:/
museum-reserve	موزهٔ باستانشناسی	/mu:-ze-je bɑ:s-tʌn-ʃe-nɑ:-si:/
natural-science museum	موزهٔ علوم طبیعی	/mu:-ze-je ʔe-lu:-me ta-bi:-ʔi:/
oriental art	هنر مشرق زمین	/ho-na-re maʃ-reG za-mɪn/
painter	نقّاش	/nɑG-Gɑ:ʃ/
painting	نقّاشی	/nɑG-Gɑ:-ʃi:/
panel	بوم نقّاشی	/bu:-me nɑG-Gɑ:-ʃi:/
photographic art	هنر عکّاسی	/ho-na-re ʔak-kɑ:-si:/
picture	عکس	/ʔaks/
picture-gallery	گالری نقّاشی	/gɑ:-le-rɪ-je nɑG-Gɑ:-ʃi:/
polytechnic museum	موزهٔ صنعتی	/mu:-ze-je san-ʔa-ti:/
portrait	تک‌چهره	/tak tʃeh-re/
poster	پُستر	/pos-ter/
reproduction	نسخهٔ چاپی	/nos-xe-je tʃɑ:-pi:/
restorer	مرمّت‌کننده	/ma-rem-mat ko-nan-de/
sculpture	مجسّمه‌سازی	/mo-dʒas-sa-me sɑ:-zi:/

In Town

seascape	/man-za-re-je dar-jɒː/	منظرهٔ دریا
stained glass window	/viːt-rɒːj/	ویترای
still life	/ta-biː-ʔa-te biː-dʒʌn/	طبیعت بی‌جان
tapestry	/guːb-lan/	گوبلن
visitor's book	/daf-ta-re jɒːd-buːd/	دفتر یادبود
water colour	/ʔɒːb-raŋ/	آبرنگ
woodcut	/kan-de-kɒːriː/	کنده‌کاری
work of art	/ʔa-sa-re ho-na-riː/	اثر هنری

How much is the admission fee? ....
/Gej-ma-te be-liː-te vo-ruː-di: tʃe-Gadr ʔast/ قیمت بلیط ورودی چقدر است؟
I'm interested in architecture. ....
....../man be meʔ-mɒː-riː ʔa-lɒː-Ge-man-dam/. من به معماری علاقمندم
I'm interested in miniatures. ....
....../man be miː-nɪ-jɒː-tuːr ʔa-lɒː-Ge-man-dam/. من به مینیاتور علاقمندم
I'm interested in mosaics. ....
....../man be muː-zɒː-ʔiːk ʔa-lɒː-Ge-man-dam/. من به موزائیک علاقمندم
I'm interested in painting. ....
........../man be naG-Gɒː-ʃiː ʔa-lɒː-Ge-man-dam/. من به نقّاشی علاقمندم
I'm interested in sculpture. ....
............../man be mo-dʒas-sa-me sɒː-zi: ʔa-lɒː-Ge-man-dam/
من به مجسّمه‌سازی علاقمندم.
I'm interested in the graphic arts. ....
........../man be ge-rɒː-fiːk ʔa-lɒː-Ge-man-dam/. من به گرافیک علاقمندم
I like this picture. ..../man ʔaz ʔɪn tas-viːr xo-ʃam miː-ʔɒː-jad/
من از این تصویر خوشم می‌آید.
I like this subject. ...../man ʔaz ʔɪn mo-zuːʔ xo-ʃam miː-ʔɒː-jad/
من از این موضوع خوشم می‌آید.
Is this the original or a copy? ....
........................./ʔɪn ʔasl ʔast jɒː ko-piː/ این اصل است یا کپی؟
What school does he/she belong to? ....
................/kɒː-re ʔuː be ko-dɒːm mak-tab ta-ʔal-loG dɒː-rad/
کار او به کدام مکتب تعلّق دارد؟

174　Beginner's Persian

What trend in art are you most interested in? ....
............./ʃo-mɑ: ʔaz ko-dɑ:m sabk biːʃ-tar xo-ʃe-tʌn miː-ʔv:-jad/
شما از کدام سبک بیشتر خوشتان می‌آید؟

When did he/she live? ....
.... /ʔu: tʃe za-mɑ:-ni: zen-de-gi: miː-kard/ او چه زمانی زندگی می‌کرد؟

When is the museum open to the public? ....
................../muː-ze tʃe sv:-ʔa-ti: ʃo-ru:ʔ be kv:r miː-ko-nad/
موزه چه ساعتی شروع به کار می‌کند؟

Where are the miniatures painting? ....
................./sv:-lo-ne naG-Gv:-ʃiː-hv:-je miː-nı-jv:-tu:r ko-dʒv:st/
سالن نقاشی های مینیاتور کجاست؟

Where can I get a catalogue? ....
............./ʔaz ko-dʒv: miː-ta-vv:-nam kv:-tv:-lu:g ta-hıj-je ko-nam/
از کجا می‌توانم کاتالوگ تهیه کنم؟

Where is the archeological section? ....
..../Ges-ma-te bv:s-tʌn ʃe-nv:-si: ko-dʒv:st/ قسمت باستان‌شناسی کجاست؟

Where is the exit? .../da-re xo-ru:-dʒi: ko-dʒv:st/ در خروجی کجاست؟

Who painted this picture? ./ʔın tv:b-lo rv: tʃe ka-si: ke-ʃiː-de ʔast/
این تابلو را چه کسی کشیده است؟

Whose work is this? ..../ʔın kv:-re kiːst/ این کار کیست؟

4 - 10
FACTORY

designer	/tar-rɒ:h/	طرّاح
engineer	/mo-han-des/	مهندس
factory	/kɒ:r-xɒ:-ne/	کارخانه
foreman	/sar kɒ:r-gar/	سرکارگر
foundry worker	/kɒ:r-ga-re ri:x-te-gar/	کارگر ریخته‌گر
holiday	/mo-ra-xa-si:/	مرخصی
ironsmith	/ʔɒ:-haŋ-gar/	آهنگر
machine-operator	/mo-ta-sad-dɪ-je mɒ:-ʃɪn ʔɒ:-lɒ:t/	متصدّی ماشین‌آلات
mechanic	/me-kɒ:-ni:k/	مکانیک
occupation	/her-fe/	حرفه
paid holiday	/mo-ra-xaˌsi: bɒ: ho-Gu:G/	مرخصی با حقوق
plant	/kɒ:r-xɒ:-ne/	کارخانه
safety measures	/ʔeG-dɒ:-mɒ:-te ʔi: me-ni:/	اقدامات ایمنی
social security	/bi:-me-je ʔedʒ-te-mɒ:-ʔi:/	بیمهٔ اجتماعی
steel worker	/kɒ:r-ga-re fu:-lɒ:d-ri:z/	کارگر فولادریز
trade union	/ʔet-te-hɒ:-dɪ-je-je kɒ:r-ga-ri:/	اتّحادیهٔ کارگری

176 Beginner's Persian

trade union member	....	
	/ʔoz-ve ʔet-te-hʌ:-dɪ-je-je kʌ:r-ga-ri:/	عضو اتّحادیهٔ کارگری
turner	/te-rʌ:ʃ-kʌ:r/	تراشکار
wage	/ho-ɢu:ɢ/	حقوق
welder	/dʒu:ʃ-kʌ:r/	جوشکار
worker	/kʌ:r-gar/	کارگر
workshop	/kʌ:r-gʌ:h/	کارگاه

Are you a union member? ....
.............../ʃo-mʌ: ʔoz-ve ʔet-te-hʌ:-dɪ-je-je kʌ:r-ga-ri: has-ti:d/
شما عضو اتّحادیهٔ کارگری هستید؟

How long are the holiday? /mod-da-te mo-ra-xa-si: tʃe-ɢadr ʔast/
مدّت مرخصی چقدر است؟

How many hours a day do you work? ....
...................../ʃo-mʌ: tʃand sʌ:-ʔat dar ru:z kʌ:r mi:-ko-ni:d/
شما چند ساعت در روز کار می‌کنید؟

How many hours a week do you work? ....
................./ʃo-mʌ: tʃand sʌ:-ʔat dar haf-te kʌ:r mi:-ko-ni:d/
شما چند ساعت در هفته کار می‌کنید؟

How much do you earn? .... /tʃe-ɢadr ho-ɢu:ɢ mi:-gi:-ri:d/
چقدر حقوق می‌گیرید؟

The workers are on strike. ....
......../kʌ:r-ga-rʌn dar ʔeʔ-te-sʌ:b has-tand/
کارگران در اعتصاب هستند.

There is a strike at the factory. ....
............./dar kʌ:r-xʌ:-ne ʔeʔ-te-sʌ:b ʔast/
در کارخانه اعتصاب است.

What are the important industries in the town? ....
.........../sa-nʌ:-je-ʔe mo-hem-me ʃahr tʃi:st/
صنایع مهمّ شهر چیست؟

What is your occupation? ../ʃoɢ-le ʃo-mʌ: tʃi:st/
شغل شما چیست؟

We'д like to visit a steel works. ....
...../mʌ: mi:-xʌ:-hi:m ʔaz kʌ:r-xʌ:-ne-je zob ʔʌ:-han di:-dan ko-ni:m/
ما می‌خواهیم از کارخانهٔ ذوب آهن دیدن کنیم.

We'd like to visit an auto works. ....
/mv: mi:-xv:-hi:m ʔaz kv:r-xv:-ne-je ʔo-to-mo-bi:l sv:-zi: di:-dan ko-ni:m/

ما می‌خواهیم از کارخانهٔ اتومبیل‌سازی دیدن کنیم.

We'd like to visit an engineering works. ....
... /mv: mi:-xv:-hi:m ʔaz kv:r-xv:-ne-je mv:-ʃin sv:-zi: di:-dan ko-ni:m/

ما می‌خواهیم از کارخانهٔ ماشین‌سازی دیدن کنیم.

Which division of the factory do you work in? ....
.... /ʃo-mv: dar ko-dv:m Ges-ma-te kv:r-xv:-ne kv:r mi:-ko-ni:d/

شما در کدام قسمت کارخانه کار می‌کنید؟

SECTION 5

GENERAL NEEDS

- 5-1 SUPER MARKET/GROCERY
- 5-2 FRUIT/VEGETABLES
- 5-3 CLOTHING SHOP
- 5-4 CLOTHING REPAIR
- 5-5 HAIRDRESSER
- 5-6 LAUNDRY/DRY CLEANING
- 5-7 SHOE
- 5-8 SHOE REPAIR
- 5-9 BOOK/MAGAZINE
- 5-10 PHOTOGRAPHER

KITCHEN

5-1
SUPERMARKET
GROCERY

a box of matches	یک قوطی کبریت	/jek Gu:-ti: keb-ri:t/
bar of chocolate	بسته شکلات	/bas-te ʃo-ko-lv:t/
butter	کره	/ka-re/
candy	آبنبات	/ʔv:b na-bv:t/
cheese	پنیر	/pa-ni:r/
chocolate	شکلات	/ʃo-ko-lv:t/
cigarette	سیگار	/si:-gv:r/
cigarette lighter	فندک	/fan-dak/
cocoa	کاکائو	/kv:-kv:-ʔu:/
coffee	قهوه	/Gah-ve/
conserve	کنسرو	/kon-serv/
cream	خامه (سرشیر)	/xv:-me (sar-ʃi:r)/
battery	باتری	/bv:t-ri:/

egg	/tox-me morɢ/	تخم‌مرغ
fruit juice	/ʔɒ:b mi:-ve/	آب‌میوه
honey	/ʔa-sal/	عسل
lump suger	/ɢand/	قند
macaroni	/mɒ:-kɒ:-ro-ni:/	ماکارونی
marzipan	/kej-ke bɒ:-dɒ:-mi:/	کیک بادامی
milk	/ʃi:r/	شیر
mushroom	/ɢɒ:rtʃ/	قارچ
mustard	/xar-dal/	خردل
noodles	/reʃ-te/	رشته
rice	/be-rendʒ/	برنج
salt	/na-mak/	نمک
soap	/sɒ:-bun/	صابون
spaghetti	/ʔes-bɒ:-ge-ti:/	اسپاگتی
stewed apple	/kom-pu:-te si:b/	کمپوت سیب
stewed apricot	/kom-pu:-te zard ʔɒ:-lu:/	کمپوت زردآلو
stewed morello	/kom-pu:-te gi:-lɒ:s/	کمپوت گیلاس
stewed peach	/kom-pu:-te hu:-lu:/	کمپوت هلو
stewed pear	/kom-pu:-te go-lɒ:-bi:/	کمپوت گلابی
stewed quince	/kom-pu:-te be/	کمپوت به
stewed strawberries	/kom-pu:-te tu:t-fa-ran-gi:/	کمپوت توت‌فرنگی
suger	/ʃa-kar/	شکر
sweet	/ʃi:-ri:-ni:/	شیرینی
toffee	/tɒ:-fi:/	تافی
vegetable oil	/ro-ɢa-ne na-bɒ:-ti:/	روغن‌نباتی
vinegar	/ser-ke/	سرکه

SHEER

A bottle of milk, please. /jek bot-ri: ʃi:r lot-fan/. یک بطری شیر، لطفاً

A bottle of yogurt, please. ....
.................../jek bot-ri: mɒ:st lot-fan/. یک بطری ماست، لطفاً

A jar of cucumbers, please. ....
../lot-fan jek ʃi:-ʃe xɪ-jɒ:r ʃu:r be-da-hi:d/. لطفاً یک شیشه خیارشور بدهید

General Needs

A jar of honey, please. ....
.... /lot-fan jek ʃi:-ʃe ʔa-sal be-da-hi:d/ .لطفاً یک شیشه عسل بدهید
A jar of jam, please. ....
...... /lot-fan jek ʃi:-ʃe mo-rab-bɒ: be-da-hi:d/ .لطفاً یک شیشه مربّا بدهید
I should like a packet of biscuites. ....
.. /lot-fan jek bas-te bi:s-ku:-ʔi:t be-da-hi:d/ .لطفاً یک بسته بیسکویت بدهید
I should like a packet of coffee. ....
.... /lot-fan jek bas-te ɢah-ve be-da-hi:d/ .لطفاً یک بسته قهوه بدهید
I should like a packet of tea. ....
.... /lot-fan jek bas-te tʃɒ:j be-da-hi:d/ .لطفاً یک بسته چای بدهید
How much is this? .... /ʔɪn tʃand ʔast/ ؟این چند است
Give me a bottle of milk. /jek bot-ri: ʃi:r be-da-hi:d/. یک بطری شیر بدهید
Give me a box of matches. ....
.... /jek ɢu:-ti: keb-ri:t be-da-hi:d/ .یک قوطی کبریت بدهید
Give me a kilo of cheese. ....
.... /jek ki:-lo pa-ni:r be-da-hi:d/ .یک کیلو پنیر بدهید
Give me half kilo of suger. ....
.... /ni:m ki:-lo ʃa-kar be-da-hi:d/ .نیم کیلو شکر بدهید
Give me 250 grams mustard. ....
.... /di:-vi:s to pan-dʒɒ:h ge-ram xar-dal be-da-hi:d/ .۲۵۰ گرم خردل بدهید
What does charge for this chocolate? ....
.... /ɢej-ma-te ʔɪn ʃo-ko-lɒ:t tʃat ʔast/ ؟قیمت این شکلات چند است
What's the price of coffee? ....
.... /ɢej-ma-te ɢah-ve tʃe-ɢadr ʔast/ ؟قیمت قهوه چقدر است
What's the price of that? ....
.... /he-sɒ:-be ʔʌn tʃe-ɢadr mi:-ʃa-vad/ ؟حساب آن چقدر می‌شود

5-2
FRUITS
VEGETABLES

1. Fruit .... /mi:-ve/ ميوه .١

apple	/si:b/	سیب
apricot	/zard-ʔv:-lu:/	زردآلو
banana	/moz/	موز
bilberry	/zo-ɢv:-le ʔax-te/	زغال اخته
blackberry	/ta-meʃ-ke vah-ʃi:/	تمشک وحشی
cantaloupe	/tv:-le-bi:/	طالبی
cherry	/gi:-lv:s/	گیلاس
citron	/to-randʒ/	ترنج
coconut	/nv:r-gi:l/	نارگیل
cucumber	/xɪ-jv:r/	خیار
fig	/ʔan-dʒi:r/	انجیر

186 Beginner's Persian

grape	/ʔan-guːr/	انگور
grape fruit	/giː-riːp-fruːt/	گریپ‌فروت
goosberry	/xvːr-tuːt/	خارتوت
lemon	/liː-mu: torʃ/	لیموترش
mulberry	/tuːt/	توت
muskmelon	/xar-bo-ze/	خربزه
orange	/por-ta-Gvːl/	پرتقال
peach	/huː-luː/	هلو
pear	/go-lvː-biː/	گلابی
persimmon	/xor-mvː-lu/	خرمالو
pine apple	/ʔvː-nvː-nvːs/	آناناس
plum	/gow-dʒe/	گوجه
pomegranate	/ʔa-nvːr/	انار
quince	/be/	به
raspberry	/ta-meʃk/	تمشک
blackcherry	/ʔvːl-bvː-luː/	آلبالو
strawberry	/tuːt-fa-ran-giː/	توت‌فرنگی
sweet lemon	/liː-mu: ʃiː-rɪn/	لیموشیرین
tangerine	/nvː-ren-giː/	نارنگی
watermelon	/hen-de-vvː-ne/	هندوانه

2. Nut .... /miː-ve-je ger-duː-ʔiː/ میوهٔ گردویی ۲.

almond	/bvː-dvːm/	بادام
hazelnut	/fan-doG/	فندق
peanut	/bvː-dvːm-za-miː-niː/	بادام‌زمینی
pistachio	/pes-te/	پسته
walnut	/ger-du:/	گردو

3. Vegetables .... /sab-zi:-dʒvːt/ سبزیجات ۳.

asparagus	/mvːr-tʃuː-be/	مارچوبه
aubergine	/bvː-dem-dʒʌn/	بادمجان
beans	/luː-bɪ-jvː/	لوبیا

General Needs 187

beetroot	چغندر /tʃo-Gon-dar/	
broad been	باقلا /bv:G-lv:/	
cabbage	كلم /ka-lam/	
carrot	هویج /ha-vi:dʒ/	
cauliflower	گل‌كلم /gol-ka-lam/	
celery	كرفس /ka-rafs/	
coriander	گشنیز /geʃ-ni:z/	
cress	شاهی /ʃv:-hi:/	
dill	شوید /ʃe-vi:d/	
garlic	سیر /si:r/	
green beans	لوبیاسبز /lu:-bɪ-jv: sabz/	
green peas	نخودسبز /no-xod sabz/	
leek	تره /ta-re/	
lentil	عدس /ʔa-das/	
lettuce	كاهو /kv:-hu:/	
marjoram	گلپر (مرزنجوش) /gol-par (mar-zan-dʒu:ʃ)/	
marrow	كدو /ka-du:/	
mint	نعناع /naʔ-nv:ʔ/	
mushroom	قارچ /Gv:rtʃ/	
onion	پیاز /pɪ-jv:z/	
parsley	جعفری /dʒaʔ-fa-ri:/	
pea	نخود /no-xod/	
pepper	فلفل /fel-fel/	
potato	سیب‌زمینی /si:b-za-mi:-ni:/	
radish	تربچه /to-rob-tʃe/	
rhubarb	ریواس /ri:-vv:s/	
spinage	اسفناج /ʔes-fa-nv:dʒ/	
split peas	لپه /la-pe/	
sweet basil	ریحان /rej-hʌn/	
sweet fennel	مرزه /mar-ze/	
tarragon	ترخون /tar-xʊn/	
tomato	گوجه‌فرنگی /gow-dʒe fa-ran-gi:/	
turnip	شلغم /ʃal-Gam/	

Give good ones. .... /xu:-baʃ rv: be-da-hi:d/. خوبش را بدهید.
Give me a kilo of banana. /jek ki:-lo moz be-da-hi:d/. یک کیلو موز بدهید.
Have you got apples? .... /si:b dv:-ri:d/ ؟سیب دارید
How much are half kilo of lemons? ....
.... /ni:m ki:-lo li:-mu: tʃand mi:-ʃa-vad/ ؟نیم کیلو لیمو چند می‌شود
How much are they? ...... /Gej-ma-taʃ tʃand Past/ ؟قیمتش چند است
I want ten of oranges. ../man dah ʔa-dad por-ta-Gv:l mi:-xv:-ham/
من ده عدد پرتقال می‌خواهم.
That's too expensive. .... /xej-li: ge-rʌn Past/. خیلی گران است.
This is green. .... /ʔɪn kv:l Past/. این کال است.

5-3 CLOTHING SHOP

Size .... /?an-dv:-ze/ اندازه

WOMEN /BLOUSES/DRESSES/SUITS/

USA	8	10	12	14	16	18
Metric (Iranian)	38	40	42	44	46	48

MEN /SUITS/

USA	36	38	40	42	44	46
Metric (Iranian)	38	40	42	44	46	48

MEN /SHIRTS/

USA	15	16	17	18
Metric (Iranian)	38	41	43	45

belt	/ka-mar band/	کمربند
bikini	/mɒ:-jo za-nɒ:-ne/	مایو زنانه
blouse	/bu:-lu:z/	بلوز
brassiere(bra)	/kor-set/	کرست
briefs	/ʃort/	شورت
buttom	/doɒ-me/	دگمه
chequered shirt	/pi:-rɒ:-ha-ne tʃɒ:-hɒ:r xɒ:-ne/	پیراهن چهارخانه
coat	/kot/	کت
colorful clothes	/le-bɒ:s-hɒ:-je ran-gɒ:-raŋ/	لباسهای رنگارنگ
cutton	/na-xi:/	نخی
dress of cotton	/le-bɒ:-se na-xi:/	لباس نخی
elegent clothes	/le-bɒ:-se ʃi:k/	لباس شیک
flax	/ka-tɒ:-ni:/	کتانی
fur coat	/pɒ:l-to xaz/	پالتو خز
glove	/dast-keʃ/	دستکش
hand bag	/ki:-fe das-ti:/	کیف دستی
hat	/ko-lɒ:h/	کلاه
jeans	/dʒɪn/	جین
leather coat	/ko-te tʃar-mi:/	کت چرمی
night gown	/le-bɒ:-se ʃab/	لباس شب
night shirt	/pi:-rɒ:-ha-ne ʃab/	پیراهن شب
overcoat	/ʔo-ver-kot/	اورکت
panties	/ʃor-te za-nɒ:-ne/	شورت زنانه
pants	/ʃal-vɒ:r/	شلوار
pullover	/po-li:-ver/	پلیور
raincoat	/bɒ:-rɒ:-ni:/	بارانی
shirt	/pi:-rɒ:-han/	پیراهن
simple clothes	/le-bɒ:-se sɒ:-de/	لباس ساده
skirt	/dɒ:-man/	دامن
sock	/dʒu:-rɒ:-be ku:-tɒ:h/	جوراب کوتاه
stocking	/dʒu:-rɒ:-be bo-land/	جوراب بلند
striped dress	/le-bɒ:-se row-ʃan/	لباس روشن
T-shirt	/ti:-ʃert/	تی شرت
tie	/ke-rɒ:-vɒ:t/	کراوات

General Needs

tights	/dʒuː-rʌːb ʃal-vvː-riː/	جوراب‌شلواری
velvet	/max-mal/	مخمل
vest	/dʒe-liː-ɢe (ziːr-puːʃ)/	جليقه (زيرپوش)
white dress	/le-bʌː-se row-ʃan/	لباس روشن
woolen	/paʃ-miː/	پشمی

Can I see it?	/miː-ta-vvː-nam ʔʌn rʌ be-biː-nam/	می‌توانم آن را ببينم؟
Have you a cheaper one?	/je-ki: ʔar-zʌn-tar dʌː-riːd/	يكی ارزانتر داريد؟
How much is it?	/ɢej-ma-taʃ tʃand ʔast/	قيمتش چند است؟
How much is my bill?	/he-sʌː-be man tʃe-ɢadr miː-ʃa-vad/	حساب من چقدر می‌شود؟
Give me a size larger.	/jek ʔan-dʌː-ze bo-zorg-tar be-da-hiːd/	يك اندازه بزرگتر بدهيد.
Give me that one.	/ʔʌn je-ki: rʌ be-da-hiːd/	آن يكی را بدهيد.
Give two sizes smaller, please.	/do ʔan-dʌː-ze kuː-tʃek-tar be-da-hiːd lot-fan/	دو اندازه كوچكتر بدهيد،لطفا.
I don't like this color.	/ʔin raŋ rʌ duːst na-dʌː-ram/	اين رنگ را دوست ندارم.
I want another style.	/no-ʔe diː-ga-riː miː-xvː-ham/	نوع ديگری را می‌خواهم.
Let me have that.	/ʔʌn rʌ be man be-da-hiːd/	آن را به من بدهيد.
That dress is in the latest style.	/ʔʌn le-bʌːs ʔʌː-xa-rin mod ʔast/	آن لباس آخرين مد است.
That down one.	/ʔʌn pʌː-ʔiː-niː/	آن پائينی.
That left one.	/ʔʌn sam-te tʃa-piː/	آن سمت چپی.
That red one.	/ʔʌn ke ɢer-mez ʔast/	آن كه قرمزاست.
That right one.	/sam-te rʌːs-tiː/	سمت راستی.
This color is too dark.	/ʔin raŋ xej-liː tiː-re ʔast/	اين رنگ خيلی تيره است.
This is tight.	/ʔin taŋ ʔast/	اين تنگ است.
This is too bright.	/ʔin xej-liː row-ʃan ʔast/	اين خيلی روشن است.
This is too dark.	/ʔin xej-liː tiː-re ʔast/	اين خيلی تيره است.

This is too large. ....../ʔɪn xej-li: bo-zorg ʔast/	این خیلی بزرگ است.
This is loose. ..../ʔɪn go-ʃvːd ʔast/	این گشاد است.
What a nice skirt! ..../tʃe dvː-ma-ne ɢa-ʃan-gi:/	چه دامن قشنگی!
What's your suit size?	
...../ʔan-dvː-ze-je le-bvː-se ʃo-mvː tʃand ʔast/	اندازهٔ لباس شما چند است؟
What kind would you like?	
.............../tʃe now-ʔi: rvː duːst dvː-riːd/	چه نوعی را دوست دارید؟
Where's locker? .... /raxt-kan ko-dʒvːst/	رختکن کجاست؟

5-4 CLOTHING REPAIR

button .... دگمه /dog-me/
collar .... یقه /ja-Ge/
mend .... تعمیر کردن /taʔ-miːr kar-dan/
sew on .... دوختن /duːx-tan/
sleeve .... آستین /ʔvːs-tɪn/

Here is a split in my trousers. ....
.../ʔɪn-dʒvː-je ʃal-vvː-ram pvː-re ʃo-de ʔast/ اینجای شلوارم پاره شده است.
I would like these buttons sewn on. ....
.... /miː-xvː-ham ʔɪn dog-me-hvː duːx-te ʃa-vad/
میخواهم این دگمه ها دوخته شود.

I would like this zipper changed. ....
.... /miː-xvː-ham ʔɪn ziːp ʔa-vaz ʃa-vad/ .می‌خواهم این زیپ عوض شود
Make this skirt longer. ....
.... /ʔɪn dvː-man rvː bo-lan-tar ko-niːd/ .این دامن را بلندتر کنید
Make this trousers shorter. ....
.... /ʔɪn ʃal-vvːr rvː kuː-tvːh-tar ko-niːd/ .این شلوار را کوتاهتر کنید
Take this to be repaired, please. ....
.. /lot-fan ʔɪn rvː ba-rvː-je taʔ-miːr be-da-hiːd/ .لطفاً این را برای تعمیر بدهید
The lining of my coat is torn. ....
.... /ʔvːs-ta-re ko-tam pvː-re ʃo-de/ .آستر کتم پاره شده
Where is the tailor's? .... /xaj-jvː-tiː ko-dʒvːst/ ؟خیّاطی کجاست

5-5

HAIRDRESSER

barber's	/sal-mɒ:-nɪ-je mar-dɒ:-ne/	سلمانی مردانه
beard	/ri:ʃ/	ریش
beauty parlour	/sɒ:-lo-ne zi:-bɒ:-ʔi:/	سالن زیبایی
curlers	/bi:-gu:-di:/	بیگودی
curly hair	/mu:-je fer/	موی فر
eau-de-cologne	/ʔod-ko-lon/	ادکلن
eyebrow	/ʔab-ru:/	ابرو
eyelashe	/mo-ʒe/	مژه
hair	/mu:/	مو
hair-cut	/ʔes-lɒ:h/	اصلاح
hair-cut with scissors	/ʔes-lɒ:h bɒ Gej-tʃi:/	اصلاح با قیچی
hair-cut with razor	/ʔes-lɒ:h bɒ: ti:G/	اصلاح با تیغ
hair-do	/ʔɒ:-rɒ:-je-ʃe mu:/	آرایش مو
hairdresser	/ʔɒ:-rɒ:-jeʃ-gar/	آرایشگر
hair-dryer	/se-ʃu:-wɒ:r/	سشوار
hair grip	/gi:-re-je sar/	گیرهٔ سر

hairpin	/san-dʒɒː-Ge sar/	سنجاق سر
hair-restorer	/fer bɒːz kon/	فربازکن
hair-set	/ʔɒː-rɒː-je-ʃe mu:/	آرایش مو
hair spray	/fi:k-sɒː-tu:r/	فیکساتور
lady's salon	/sɒː-lo-ne za-nɒː-ne/	سالن زنانه
lotion	/lo-sɪ-jon/	لوسیون
manicure	/mɒː-ni:-kor/	مانیکور
massage	/mɒː-sɒːʒ/	ماساژ
mirror	/ʔɒːj-ne/	آینه
moustache	/si:-bi:l/	سبیل
nail	/nɒː-xon/	ناخن
parting	/far-Ge sar/	فرق سر
razor	/xod-ta-rɒːʃ/	خودتراش
razor blade	/ti:G/	تیغ
shampoo	/ʃos-te-ʃu:-je sar/	شستشوی سر
shave	/ʔes-lɒː-he su:-rat/	اصلاح صورت
temple	/xat-te ri:ʃ/	خط ریش
wig	/ko-lɒːh gi:s/	کلاه‌گیس

I should like a shampoo, please. ....
.... /lot-fan sa-ram rɒː be-ʃu:-ʔi:d/ لطفاً سرم را بشویید
I want a hair cut. ../mi:-xɒː-ham ʔes-lɒːh ko-nam/ می‌خواهم اصلاح کنم
I want a shave, please. ....
.... /lot-fan su:-ra-tam rɒː ʔes-lɒːh ko-ni:d/ لطفاً صورتم را اصلاح کنید
Make it shorter, please . /lot-fan ku:-tɒːh-tar ko-ni:d/ لطفاً کوتاه‌تر کنید
Make the parting on the left/right. ....
.... /lot-fan far-Ge sa-ram rɒː be tʃap (rɒːst) ʃɒː-ne ko-ni:d/
لطفاً فرق سرم را به چپ (راست) شانه کنید
Not too short, please. ....
.... /lot-fan zɪ-jɒːd ku:-tɒːh na-ko-ni:d/ لطفاً زیاد کوتاه نکنید
Please trim the back. /lot-fan mu:-hɒː-je poʃt rɒː mo-rat-tab ko-ni:d/
لطفاً موهای پشت را مرتّب کنید

Please trim the front. ....
/lot-fan mu:-hɑ:-je dʒe-low rɑ: mo-rat-tab ko-ni:d/ .لطفاً موهای جلو را مرتّب کنید
Please trim my beard/moustache. ....
............/lot-fan ri:ʃ-hɑ:-je (si:-bi:l-hɑ:-je) ma-rɑ: ʔes-lɑ:h ko-ni:d/
لطفاً ریشهای (سبیلهای) مرا اصلاح کنید.
Where is the barber's? .../ʔɑ:-rɑ:-jeʃ-gɑ:h ko-dʋ:st/؟آرایشگاه کجاست
Where is the nearest barber's? ....
..../naz-di:k-ta-rın ʔɑ:-rɑ:-jeʃ-gɑ:h ko-dʒʋ:st/ ؟نزدیکترین آرایشگاه کجاست

5-6
LAUNDRY
DRY CLEANING

coat	/kot/	کت
dress	/le-bɒːs/	لباس
dry-cleaning	/xoʃ-ʃuː-ʔiː/	خشکشویی
linen	/ma-lɒː-fe/	ملافه
lining	/lɒː-ʔiː/	لایی
shirt	/piː-rɒː-han/	پیراهن
skirt	/dɒː-man/	دامن
stain	/la-ke/	لکه
stain remover	/la-ke-giː-riː/	لکه‌گیری
trousers	/ʃal-vɒːr/	شلوار

I need my things for today. ....
.... /le-bɑ:s-hɑ:-jam rɑ: ʔem-ru:z ʔeh-tɪ-jɑ:dʒ dɑ:-ram/
لباسهایم را امروز احتیاج دارم.
I need my things for tomorrow. ....
/le-bɑ:s-hɑ:-jam rɑ: far-dɑ: ʔeh-tɪ-jɑ:dʒ dɑ:-ram/ لباسهایم را فردا احتیاج دارم.
I want to have my clothes pressed. ....
. ./lot-fan le-bɑ:s-hɑ:-je ma-rɑ: ʔo-tu: be-za-ni:d/ لطفاً لباسهای مرا اتو بزنید.
I'd like to have my clothes drycleaned. ....
......../lot-fan le-bɑ:s-hɑ:-je ma-rɑ: be-ʃu:-ʔi:d/ لطفاً لباسهای مرا بشویید.
When can I have my clothes back? ....
.... /le-bɑ:s-hɑ:-jam rɑ: kej mi:-ta-vv:-nam pas be-gi:-ram/
لباسهایم را کی می‌توانم پس بگیرم؟
Where can I have my things dry-cleaned? ....
. /ko-dʒɑ: mi:-ta-vv:-nam le-bɑ:s-hɑ:-jam rɑ: ba-rɑ:-je xoʃ-ʃu:-ʔi: be-da-ham/
کجا می‌توانم لباسهایم را برای خشکشویی بدهم؟
Where can I have my things pressed? ....
. ./ko-dʒɑ: mi:-ta-vv:-nam le-bɑ:s-hɑ:-jam rɑ: ba-rɑ:-je ʔo-tu: be-da-ham/
کجا می‌توانم لباسهایم را برای اتو بدهم؟
Where can I have my things washed? ....
/ko-dʒɑ: mi:-ta-vv:-nam le-bɑ:s-hɑ:-jam rɑ: ba-rɑ:-je ʃos-tan be-da-ham/
کجا می‌توانم لباسهایم را برای شستن بدهم؟
Where is the nearest dry cleaning? ....
....../naz-di:k-ta-rɪn xoʃ-ʃu:-ʔi: ko-dʒɑ:st/ نزدیکترین خشکشویی کجاست؟
Please remove this stain. ..../lot-fan ʔɪn la-ke rɑ: pɑ:k ko-ni:d/
لطفاً این لکه را پاک کنید.
This is not mine. ..../ʔɪn mɑ:-le man ni:st/ این مال من نیست.

5-7
SHOES

WOMEN /SHOES/

USA	6	7	8	9
Metric (Iranian)	37	38	40	41

MEN /SHOES/

USA	1	2	3	4	5	6	7	8	8/5	9	9/5	10	11
Metric (Ir.)	33	34/35	36	37	38	39	41	42	43	43	44	44	45

boot ..../tʃak-me/ چکمه
hiking boot ..../puː-tiː-ne kuːh na-var-diː/ پوتین کوهنوردی
laced shoes ..../kaf-ʃe ban-diː/ کفش بندی
leather shoes ..../kaf-ʃe tʃar-miː/ کفش چرمی
mule ..../dam-pvː-ʔiː/ دمپایی
open toe mule ..../dam-pvː-ʔi-je dʒe-low bvːz/ دمپایی جلوباز
shoes with high heels ....../kaf-ʃe pvːʃ-ne bo-land/ کفش پاشنه‌بلند

slipper	/kaf-ʃe rɑ:-ha-ti:/	کفش راحتی
sport shoe	/kaf-ʃe var-ze-ʃi:/	کفش ورزشی
trainer	/kaf-ʃe var-ze-ʃi:/	کفش ورزشی

Have you slippers? ..... /kaf-ʃe rɑ:-ha-ti: dɑ:-ri:d/ ؟کفش راحتی دارید
I want a pair of shoes. ....
.... /jek dʒoft kafʃ mi:-xɑ:-ham/ .یک جفت کفش می‌خواهم
I wear size 43. ....
.... /man ʔan-dɑ:-ze-je tʃe-hel ʔo se mi:-pu:-ʃam/ من اندازهٔ ۴۳ می‌پوشم.
This shoe is tight. .... /ʔɪn kafʃ taŋ ʔast/ این کفش تنگ است.
What are these a pair? ./ʔɪn-hɑ: dʒof-ti: tʃand ʔast/؟ اینها جفتی چند است
What size of shoes do you want? ....
.... /tʃe ʔan-dɑ:-ze kafʃ mi:-xɑ:-hi:d/ ؟چه اندازه کفش می‌خواهید
These are too large. .... /ʔɪn-hɑ: ba-rɑ:-je man bo-zor-gand/
اینها برای من بزرگند.

5-8 SHOES REPAIR

boot	/tʃak-me/	چکمه
heel	/pɒːʃ-ne/	پاشنه
heel plate	/niːm-taxt/	نیم‌تخت
nail	/miːx/	میخ
shoe	/kafʃ/	کفش
shoe lace	/ban-de kafʃ/	بند کفش
shoe polish	/vːks/	واکس

Could you repair my shoes? ....
.... /miː-ta-vːː-niːd kafʃ-hɒː-je ma-rɒː taʔ-miːr ko-niːd/
می‌توانید کفشهای مرا تعمیر کنید؟

Fasten the heel on please. ....
/lot-fan pv:ʃ-ne-je kaʃ rv: moh-kam ko-ni:d/ لطفاً پاشنهٔ کفش را محکم کنید.
How long will it take? ....
................../tʃe mod-dat tu:l mi:-ke-ʃad/ چه مدّت طول می‌کشد؟
How much does it cost? ...... /tʃe-Gadr mi:-ʃa-vad/ چقدر می‌شود؟
I need my shoes as soon as possible. ....
.... /man kaʃʃ-hv:-jam rv: xej-li: zu:d ʔeh-tɪ-jv:dʒ dv:-ram/
من کفشهایم را خیلی زود احتیاج دارم.
I need to have my shoes mended. ....
/kaʃʃ-hv:-je man nɪ-jv:z be taʔ-mi:r dv:-rad/ کفشهای من نیاز به تعمیر دارد.
I need to have my shoes polished. ....
.. /kaʃʃ-hv:-je man nɪ-jv:z be vv:ks dv:-rad/ کفشهای من نیاز به واکس دارد.
Please put heel plate on my shoes. ....
/lot-fan ni:m-taxt be ta-he kaf-ʃam be-za-ni:d/ لطفاً نیم‌تخت به ته کفشم بزنید.
When it will be ready? ....
.... /kej ʔv:-mv:-de mi:-ʃa-vad/ کی آماده می‌شود؟

5-9 BOOK MAGAZINE

article	/ma-ɢɑː-le/	مقاله
author	/mo-ʔal-lef/	مؤلّف
catalogue	/kɑː-tɑː-luːg/	کاتالوگ
collected works	/madʒ-muː-ʔe-je ʔɑː-sɑːr/	مجموعهٔ آثار
collection	/madʒ-muː-ʔe/	مجموعه
copy	/ko-piː/	کپی
correspondent	/xa-bar-ne-gɑːr/	خبرنگار
dictionary	/far-haŋ-ge lo-ɢat/	فرهنگ لغت
English-Persian dictionary	/far-haŋ-ge ʔeŋ-giː-liː-siː be fɑːr-siː/	فرهنگ انگلیسی به فارسی
pocket dictionary	/far-haŋ-ge dʒiː-biː/	فرهنگ جیبی
edition	/viː-rɑː-jeʃ/	ویرایش
editor	/viː-rɑːs-tɑːr (sar-da-biːr)/	ویراستار (سردبیر)

editorial	/sar-ma-ɢᴀ̆ː-le/	سرمقاله
editorial board	/hej-ʔa-te tah-riː-rı-je/	هیئت تحریریه
fashion magazine	/ma-dʒal-le-je mod/	مجلّهٔ مُد
guide book	/ke-tᴀ̆ː-be rᴀ̆ːh-ne-mᴀ̆ː/	کتاب راهنما
humorous magazine	/ma-dʒal-le-je fo-kᴀ̆ː-hiː/	مجلّهٔ فکاهی
illustrated magazine	/ma-dʒal-le-je mo-sav-var/	مجلّهٔ مصوّر
journalist	/ruːz-nᴀ̆ː-me ne-gᴀ̆ːr/	روزنامه‌نگار
library	/ke-tᴀ̆ːb-xᴀ̆ː-ne/	کتابخانه
litrary magazine	/ma-dʒal-le-je ʔa-da-biː/	مجلّهٔ ادبی
magazine	/ma-dʒal-le/	مجلّه
newspaper	/ruːz-nᴀ̆ː-me/	روزنامه
news-stand	/kı-juːs-ke ruːz-nᴀ̆ː-me/	کیوسک روزنامه
novel	/ro-mᴀn/	رمان
Persian-English dictionary	/far-haŋ-ge fᴀ̆ːr-si: be ʔiːŋ-giː-liː-siː/	فرهنگ فارسی به انگلیسی
poem	/ʃeʔr/	شعر
poet	/ʃᴀ̆ː-ʔer/	شاعر
printing house	/ʃᴀ̆ːp-xᴀ̆ː-ne/	چاپخانه
prose-writer	/nasr ne-viːs/	نثرنویس
public library	/ke-tᴀ̆ːb-xᴀ̆ː-ne-je ʔe-mu:-miː/	کتابخانهٔ عمومی
publications	/ʔen-te-ʃᴀ̆ː-rᴀ̆ːt/	انتشارات
publisher	/nᴀ̆ː-ʃer/	ناشر
reader	/xᴀ̆v-nan-de/	خواننده
scientific magazine	/ma-dʒal-le-je ʔel-miː/	مجلّهٔ علمی
socio-political magazine	/ma-dʒal-le-je sı-jᴀ̆ː-si: ʔedʒ-te-mᴀ̆ː-ʔiː/	مجلّهٔ سیاسی - اجتماعی
story	/dᴀ̆ːs-tᴀn/	داستان
technical magazine	/ma-dʒal-le-je fan-niː/	مجلّهٔ فنّی
translation	/tar-dʒo-me/	ترجمه
translator	/mo-tar-dʒem/	مترجم
writer	/ne-viː-san-de/	نویسنده

Where is the nearest library? ....
..... /naz-di:k-ta-rın ke-tɒ:b xɒ:-ne ko-dʒɒ:st/ نزدیکترین کتابخانه کجاست؟
When dose the library open? ....
.... /ke-tɒ:b xɒ:-ne kej bɒ:z ʔast/. کتابخانه کی باز است؟
How can one join the library? ....
.... /tʃe-towr mi:-ʃa-vad ʔoz-ve ke-tɒ:b xɒ:-ne ʃod/
چطور می‌شود عضو کتابخانه شد؟
When does the library close? ....
.... /ke-tɒ:b xɒ:-ne kej mi:-ban-dad/؟ کتابخانه کی می‌بندد
I'd like a book on Persian literature. ....
....../man ke-tɒ:-bi: dar mo-re-de ʔa-da-bıj-jɒ:-te fɒ:r-si: mi:-xɒ:-ham/
من کتابی در مورد ادبیّات فارسی می‌خواهم
Where can I get a newspapar? ....
.... /ʔaz ko-dʒɒ: mi:-ta-vɒ:-nam ru:z-nɒ:-me be-xa-ram/
از کجا می‌توانم روزنامه بخرم؟
How much is this magazine? ....
........../Gej-ma-te ʔın ma-dʒal-le tʃand ʔast/. قیمت این مجلّه چند است؟
How much is this newspapar? ....
.... /Gej-ma-te ʔın ru:z-nɒ:-me tʃand ʔast/ قیمت این روزنامه چند است؟
Are this the latest magazines? ....
.... /ʔın ʔɒ:-xa-rın ʃo-mɒ:-re ʔast/؟ این آخرین شماره است
What English magazines do you have? ....
.... /tʃe ma-dʒal-le-hɒ:-ʔi: be ʔeŋ-gi:-li:-si: dɒ:-ri:d/
چه مجلّه‌هایی به انگلیسی دارید؟
What English newspapers do you have? ....
.... /tʃe ru:z-nɒ:-me-hɒ:-ʔi: be ʔeŋ-gi:-li:-si: dɒ:-ri:d/
چه روزنامه‌هایی به انگلیسی دارید؟

5 - 10
PHOTOGRAPHER

camera	دوربین عکّاسی	/duːr-biː-ne ʔak-kvː-siː/
develope	ظهور	/ze-huːr/
film	فیلم	/fiːlm/
photo	عکس	/ʔaks/
slide	اسلاید	/ʔes-lvːjd/

I want to have a full-face. ....
................../man miː-xvː-ham ʔak-se ta-mvːm rox be-giː-ram/
من می‌خواهم عکس تمام‌رخ بگیرم.

I want to have a full-length. ....
................../man miː-xvː-ham ʔak-se ta-mvːm ɢad be-giː-ram/
من می‌خواهم عکس تمام‌قد بگیرم.

I want to have a half-length. ....
.................../man miː-xvː-ham ʔak-se niːm ɢad be-giː-ram/
من می‌خواهم عکس نیم‌قد بگیرم.

I want to have a profile. ....
.... /man mi:-xv:-ham ʔak-se ni:m rox be-gi:-ram/
من می‌خواهم عکس نیم‌رخ بگیرم.
I want to have my photo taken. ....
.... /man mi:-xv:-ham ʔaks be-gi:-ram/ من می‌خواهم عکس بگیرم.
I want to have this photograph enlarged. ....
.... /ʔın ʔaks rv: ba-rv:-je man bo-zorg tʃv:p ko-ni:d/
این عکس را برای من بزرگ چاپ کنید.
I should like to have half a dozen photos. ....
.... /man ʃeʃ ʔaks mi:-xv:-ham/ من شش عکس می‌خواهم.
I should like to have this film developed. ....
.... /lot-fan ʔın fi:lm rv: zv:-her ko-ni:d/ لطفاً این فیلم را ظاهر کنید.
I would like black-and-white prints. ....
.... /man ʔak-se sı-jv:h se-fi:d mi:-xv:-ham/ من عکس سیاه‌سفید می‌خواهم.
I would like colour prints. .... /man ʔak-se raŋ-gi: mi:-xv:-ham/
من عکس رنگی می‌خواهم.
Please make prints from this film. ....
/lot-fan ʔaz ru:-je ʔın fi:lm tʃv:p ko-ni:d/ لطفاً از روی این فیلم چاپ کنید.
Please send the photos to this address. ....
.... /lot-fan ʔaks-hv: rv: be ʔın ne-ʃv:-ni: be-fe-res-ti:d/
لطفاً عکس‌ها را به این نشانی بفرستید.
Six by four, please. /ʔaks ʃeʃ dar tʃv:-hv:r bv:-ʃad/. عکس ۶ در ۴ باشد.
What size do you like? ....
.... /tʃe ʔan-dv:-ze-ʔi: mi:-xv:-hi:d/ چه اندازه‌ای می‌خواهید؟
We want to have our photos taken. ....
.... /mv: mi:-xv:-hi:m ʔaks be-gi:-ri:m/ ما می‌خواهیم عکس بگیریم.

H E A L T H

6-1   PARTS OF THE BODY
6-2   DOCTOR/CLINIC
6-3   DENTIST
6-4   PHARMACY

6-1
PARTS OF THE BODY

ankle	/mo-tʃe pɒ:/	مچ پا
anus	/maG-ʔad/	مقعد
arm	/bɒ:-zu:/	بازو
beard	/ri:ʃ/	ریش
bladder	/ma-sɒ:-ne/	مثانه
blood	/xʊn/	خون
body	/ba-dan/	بدن
bone	/ʔos-to-xʌn/	استخوان
brain	/maGz/	مغز
breast	/pes-tʌn/	پستان
cheek	/gu:-ne/	گونه
chest	/si:-ne/	سینه
chin	/tʃɒ:-ne/	چانه

ear	گوش	/guːʃ/
eardrum	پردهٔ گوش	/par-de-je guːʃ/
elbow	آرنج	/ʔv:-randy/
eye	چشم	/tʃeʃm/
eyebrow	ابرو	/ʔab-ruː/
eyelash	پلک	/pelk/
face	صورت	/suː-rat/
finger	انگشت دست	/ʔaŋ-goʃ-te dast/
flesh	گوشت	/guːʃt/
foot	پا	/pv:/
forehead	پیشانی	/piː-ʃv:-niː/
gall	صفرا	/saf-rv:/
gland	غدّه	/God-de/
gum	لثه	/la-se/
hair	مو	/muː/
hand	دست	/dast/
head	سر	/sar/
heart	قلب	/Galb/
heel	پاشنه	/pv:ʃ-ne/
hip	باسن	/bv:-san/
index finger	انگشت اشاره	/ʔaŋ-goʃ-te ʔe-ʃv:-rc/
intestine	روده	/ruː-de/
jaw	فک	/fak/
joint	مفصل	/maf-sal/
kidney	کلیه	/ko-lɪ-je/
knee	زانو	/zv:-nuː/
leg	پا	/pv:/
lip	لب	/lab/
little finger	انگشت کوچک	/ʔaŋ-goʃ-te kuː-tʃak/
liver	کبد	/ka-bad/
lung	شُش	/ʃoʃ/
middle finger	انگشت وسط	/ʔaŋ-goʃ-te va-sat/
mouth	دهان	/da-hʌn/
muscle	ماهیچه	/mv:-hiː-tʃe/

Health

mustache	/siː-biːl/	سبیل
nail	/nʌ-xon/	ناخن
neck	/gar-dan/	گردن
nerve	/ʔa-sab/	عصب
nipple	/nuː-ke pes-tʌn/	نوک پستان
nose	/biː-niː/	بینی
noseril	/suː-rʌ-xe biː-niː/	سوراخ بینی
palate	/saɢ-fe da-hʌn/	سقف دهان
palm	/ka-fe dast/	کف دست
pupil	/mar-do-mak/	مردمک
rectum	/rʌst ruː-de/	راست روده
rib	/dan-de/	دنده
ring finger	/ʔaŋ-goʃ-te ʔaŋ-goʃ-tar/	انگشت انگشتر
shoulder	/ʃʌ-ne/	شانه
skin	/puːst/	پوست
skull	/dʒom-dʒo-me/	جمجمه
spine	/so-tuː-ne fa-ɢa-rʌt/	ستون فقرات
spleen	/ta-hʌl/	طحال
stomach	/meʔ-de/	معده
thigh	/rʌn/	ران
throat	/ga-luː/	گلو
thumb	/ʔaŋ-goʃ-te ʃast/	انگشت شست
toe	/ʔaŋ-goʃ-te pʌ/	انگشت پا
tongue	/za-bʌn/	زبان
tonsil	/low-ze/	لوزه
tooth	/dan-dʌn/	دندان
trachea	/nʌj/	نای
vagina	/mah-bel/	مهبل
vein	/rag/	رگ
waist	/ka-mar/	کمر
wrist	/motʃ/	مچ

6-2

DOCTOR CLINIC

clinic	/matab, ki:-li:-ni:k/	مطب، کلینیک
cough	/sor-fe/	سرفه
diet	/re-ʒi:m/	رژیم
examination	/mo-ʔv:-je-ne/	معاینه
first aid	/ko-mak-hv:-je ʔav-va-lıj-je/	کمکهای اولیّه
first-aid post	/mar-ka-ze ko-mak-hv:-je ʔav-va-lıj-je/	مرکز کمکهای اوّلیه
hospital	/bi:-mv:-res-tʌn/	بیمارستان
illness	/bi:-mv:-ri:/	بیماری
laboratory	/ʔv:z-mv:-jeʃ-gv:h/	آزمایشگاه
operation	/ʔa-ma-le dʒar-rv:-hi:/	عمل جرّاحی
optician	/ʔej-nak sv:z/	عینک ساز
pain	/dard/	درد
pharmacy	/dv:-ru:-xv:-ne/	داروخانه

218 Beginner's Persian

scratch	/xa-rʌːʃ/	خراش
sneese	/ʔat-se/	عطسه
surgery	/dʒar-rʌː-hiː/	جرّاحی
wound	/zaxm/	زخم
x-ray room	/rʌː-diːo-lo-ʒiː/	رادیولوژی

۱. **Medical occupations** /ʃoGl-hʌː-je pe-zeʃ-kiː/ شغلهای پزشکی

chief doctor	/pe-zeʃ-ke ʔar-ʃad/	پزشک ارشد
dentist	/dan-dʌn pe-zeʃk/	دندانپزشک
doctor	/pe-zeʃk/	پزشک
general practitionar	/pe-zeʃ-ke dʌː-xe-liː/	پزشک داخلی
gynaecologist	/mo-ta-xas-se-se za-nʌn/	متخصّص زنان
neuropathologist	/mo-ta-xas-se-se ʔaʔ-sʌːb/	متخصّص اعصاب
nurse	/pa-ras-tʌːr/	پرستار
oculist	/tʃeʃm pe-zeʃk/	چشم‌پزشک
orthopedist	/mo-ta-xas-se-se ʃe-kas-te-band/	متخصص شکسته‌بندی
pediatrician	/mo-ta-xas-se-se kuː-da-kʌn/	متخصّص کودکان
psychologist	/ra-vʌn-pe-zeʃk/	روانپزشک
surgeon	/dʒar-rʌːh/	جرّاح
throat specialist	/mo-ta-xas-se-se gu: ʃo hal Go biː-niː/	متخصّص گوش و حلق و بینی
urologist	/mo-ta-xas-se-se ma-dʒʌː-rɪ-je ʔed-rʌːr/	متخصّص مجاری ادرار

۲. **diseases** /biː-mʌː-riː-hʌː/ بیماریها

anemia	/kam xuː-niː/	کم‌خونی
angina	/ʔʌn-ʒɪn/	آنژین
asthr	/ʔʌsm/	آسم
backache	/poʃt dard/	پشت درد
biliousness	/nʌː-rʌː-ha-tɪ-je kiː-se-je saf-rʌː/	ناراحتیِ کیسهٔ صفرا
blood pressure	/fe-ʃʌː-re xʊn/	فشار خون

boil	/ku:rk/	كورك
bronchitis	/bron-ʃi:t/	برونشیت
cancer	/sa-ra-tʌn/	سرطان
cold	/sar-mʌ: xor-de-gi:/	سرماخوردگى
constipation	/je-bu:-sat/	يبوست
corn	/mi:x-tʃe/	ميخچه
cramp	/ge-ref-te-gɪ-je ʔa-zo-lʌ-ni:/	گرفتگى عضلانى
dangerous disease	/bi:-mʌ:-rɪ-je xa-tar-nʌ:k/	بيمارى خطرناك
diabetes	/ma-ra-ze ɢand/	مرض قند
diarrhoea	/ʔes-hʌ:l/	اسهال
diphtheria	/di:f-tri:/	ديفترى
dislocation	/dar raf-te-gi:/	دررفتگى
dizziness	/sar-gi:-dʒe/	سرگيجه
earache	/gu:ʃ-dard/	گوش‌درد
epilepsy	/serʔ/	صرع
faint	/zaʔf (bi:-hʌ:-li:)/	ضعف (بى‌حالى)
flu	/ʔʌn-fu:-lʌn-zʌ:/	آنفولانزا
fracture	/ʃe-kas-te-gi:/	شكستگى
haemerrhoids	/ba-vʌ:-si:r/	بواسير
heart attack	/ham-le-je ɢal-bi:/	حملهٔ قلبى
heart trouble	/nʌ:-rʌ:-ha-tɪ-je ɢal-bi:/	ناراحتى قلبى
indisposition	/bi:-hʌ:-li:/	بى‌حالى
infectious disease	/bi:-mʌ:-rɪ-je ʔe-fu:-ni:/	بيمارى عفونى
insectbite	/ga-zi:-de-gɪ-je ha-ʃa-rʌ:t/	گزيدگى حشرات
insomnia	/bi:-xʌ:-bi:/	بى‌خوابى
internal disease	/bi:-mʌ:-rɪ-je dʌ:-xe-li:/	بيمارى داخلى
jaundice	/ja-ra-ɢʌn/	يرقان
kidney trouble	/nʌ:-rʌ:-ha-tɪ-je kol-ja-vi:/	ناراحتى كليوى
liver trouble	/nʌ:-rʌ:-ha-tɪ-je ka-ba-di:/	ناراحتى كبدى
lumbago	/ka-mar-dard/	كمردرد
lung trouble	/nʌ:-rʌ:-ha-tɪ-je rɪ-ja-vi:/	ناراحتى ريوى
malaria	/mʌ:-lʌ:-rɪ-jʌ:/	مالاريا
measles	/sor-xak/	سرخك
migraine	/mi:g-ren/	ميگرن

mumps	/ʔor-jon/	اریون
nervous illness	/biː-mɒː-rɪ-je ʔa-sa-biː/	بیماری عصبی
neuralgia	/dar-de ʔaʔ-sɒːb/	درد اعصاب
nose bleeding	/xʊn-da-mɒːɢ/	خون دماغ
palpitation	/ta-pe-ʃe ɢalb/	تپش قلب
pneumonia	/zɒː-tol-rɪ-je/	ذات الریه
poisoning	/mas-muː-mɪj-jat/	مسمومیّت
pulse	/nabz/	نبض
rabies	/hɒː-riː/	هاری
reduction	/dʒɒː ʔan-dɒːx-te-gi/	جاانداختن
rheumatism	/ro-mɒː-tiːsm/	رماتیسم
scar	/dʒɒː-je zaxm/	جای زخم
scarlet fever	/max-ma-lak/	مخملک
serious disease	/biː-mɒː-rɪ-je va-xiːm/	بیماری وخیم
slight illness	/biː-mɒː-rɪ-je xa-fiːf/	بیماری خفیف
smallpox	/ʔɒː-be-le mor-ɢʌn/	آبله مرغان
spasm	/ge-ref-te-giː/	گرفتگی
strain	/ke-ʃiː-de-giː/	کشیدگی
stomach bleeding	/xʊn-riː-zɪ-je meʔ-de/	خونریزی معده
stomach trouble	/ʔam-rɒː-ze ʃe-ka-miː/	امراض شکمی
toothache	/dan-dʌn-dard/	دندان درد
typhoid	/has-be/	حصبه

۲. 2. Examination .... /mo-ʔɒː-je-ne/ معاینه

Breathe deeply. ...... /na-fa-se ʔa-miːɢ be-ke-ʃiːd/ نفس عمیق بکشید.
Come to see me in 2 days. ....
...../baʔd ʔaz do ruːz mo-rɒː-dʒe-ʔe ko-niːd/ بعد از دو روز مراجعه کنید.
How can I get to the clinic? ....
.... /tʃe-towr miː-ta-vɒː-nam be kiː-liː-niːk be-ra-vam/
چطور می‌توانم به کلینیک بروم؟

Health 221

How can I get to the hospital? ....
............/tʃe-towr miː-ta-vvː-nam be biː-mvː-res-tʌn be-ra-vam/
چطور می‌توانم به بیمارستان بروم؟
How long have you had it? ....
/tʃe mod-dat ʔɪn nvː-rvː-ha-tiː rv dvːʃ-te-ʔiːd/ چه مدّت این ناراحتی را داشته‌اید؟
I ache all over. ..../ta-mvː-me ba-da-nam dard miː-ko-nad/
تمام بدنم درد می‌کند.
I'm afraid I have neuralgic problem. ....
........../miː-tar-sam mob-ta-lvː be nvː-rvː-ha-tɪ-je ʔa-sa-biː bvː-ʃam/
می‌ترسم مبتلا به ناراحتی عصبی باشم.
I'm not well. .... /hvː-lam xuːb niːst/. حالم خوب نیست.
I can't breathe easily. ....
............./man ne-miː-ta-vvː-nam be rvː-ha-tiː ta-naf-fos ko-nam/
من نمی‌توانم به راحتی تنفّس کنم.
I caught a cold. ..../sar-mvː xor-de-ʔam/. سرما خورده‌ام.
I complain of insomnia. .... /ʔaz biː-xvː-biː nvː-rvː-ha-tam/
از بیخوابی ناراحتم.
I dislocated my arm. ... /das-tam dar raf-te ʔast/. دستم در رفته است.
I dislocated my leg. ...... /pvː-jam dar raf-te ʔast/. پایم در رفته است.
I don't feel well at all. ./hiːtʃ hvː-lam xuːb niːst/. هیچ حالم خوب نیست.
I feel ill. ..../nvː-xo-ʃam/. ناخوشم.
I feel quite exhausted. .... /xej-liː ʔch-svː-se xas-te-gi miː-ko-nam/
خیلی احساس خستگی می‌کنم.
I feel very weak. ....
..../ʔch-svː-se zaʔ-fe ʃa-diː-di miː-ko-nam/. احساس ضعف شدیدی می‌کنم.
I feel dizzy. ..../sa-ram gidʒ miː-ra-vad/. سرم گیج می‌رود.
I've a headache. ..../sar-dard dvː-ram/. سردرد دارم.
I've a nausea. .... /hvː-lam xa-rvːb ʔast/. حالم خراب است.
I've a pain in my left side. ./dar-di dar pah-luː-je tʃa-pam dvː-ram/
دردی در پهلوی چپم دارم.
I've a sore throat. .... /ga-lu: dard dvː-ram/. گلو درد دارم.
I've cut my finger. ../ʔaŋ-goʃ-tam rvː bo-riː-de-ʔam/. انگشتم را بریده‌ام.
I've diarrhoea. .... /ʔes-hvːl dvː-ram/. اسهال دارم.
I've fever. .... /tab dvː-ram/. تب دارم.

I've had a bad cold. .... /bad dʒuː-riː sar-mɑː xor-de-ʔam/
بدجوری سرما خورده‌ام.
I've indigestion. .... /suː-ʔe hɑː-ze-me dɑː-ram/ سوءهاضمه دارم.
I've no appetite. .... /ʔeʃ-te-hɑː na-dɑː-ram/ اشتها ندارم.
I've pain here. ..... /ʔɪn-dʒɑː-jam dard miː-ko-nad/ اینجایم درد می‌کند.
I keep feeling dizzy. ..../mo-rat-tab sa-ram giːdʒ miː-ra-vad/
مرتّب سرم گیج می‌رود.
I need a doctor. ....
........../man be pe-zeʃk ʔeh-tɪ-jɑːdʒ dɑː-ram/ من به پزشک احتیاج دارم.
I often have attacks of giddiness. ....
................/ʔaG-lab sa-ram giːdʒ miː-ra-vad/ اغلب سرم گیج می‌رود.
I'll have to send you to hospital. ....
................/ʃo-mɑː bɑː-jad be biː-mɑː-res-tʌn ʔeʔ-zɑːm ʃa-viːd/
شما باید به بیمارستان اعزام شوید.
Is it curable? .... /Gɑː-be-le ʔa-lɑːdʒ ʔast/ قابل علاج است؟
Is it dangerous? .... /xa-tar-nɑːk ʔast/ خطرناک است؟
My back aches. .... /poʃ-tam dard miː-ko-nad/ پشتم درد می‌کند.
My stomach is out of order. ..../meʔ-de-ʔam nɑː-rɑː-hat ʔast/
معده‌ام ناراحت است.
Please call an ambulance. ....
...../lot-fan jek ʔʌm-buː-lʌns se-dɑː ko-niːd/ لطفاً یک آمبولانس صدا کنید.
What should I do? .... /tʃe bɑː-jad be-ko-nam/ چه باید بکنم؟
Where is the pain? .... /ko-dʒɑː dard miː-ko-nad/ کجا درد می‌کند؟
Would you please check me up? ....
.... /mom-ken ʔast ma-rɑː mo-ʔɑː-je-ne-je kɑː-mel ko-niːd/
ممکن است مرا معاینهٔ کامل کنید؟
You must have an injection. ....
.............../ʃo-mɑː bɑː-jad ʔʌm-puːl be-za-niːd/ شما باید آمپول بزنید.
You must take the medicine. ....
......./ʃo-mɑː bɑː-jad dɑː-ru mas-raf ko-niːd/ شما باید دارو مصرف کنید.

6-3
DENTIST

I have a broken tooth. ....
.... /dan-dɑ:-nam ʃe-kas-te ʔast/. دندانم شکسته است.
I have a swollen gum. ..../ta-var-ro-me la-se dɑ:-ram/. تورّم لثه دارم.
I have a toothache. .... /dan-dʌn-dard dɑ:-ram/. دندان درد دارم.
I have my tooth filled. . /dan-dɑ:-nam por ʃo-de ʔast/. دندانم پر شده است.
Open your mouth. ./da-hɑ:-ne-tʌn rɑ: bɑ:z ko-ni:d/. دهانتان را باز کنید.
Please do something for the pain. ....
............/lot-fan dar-daʃ rɑ: ʔɑ:-rɑ:m ko-ni:d/. لطفاً دردش را آرام کنید.
Please extract this tooth. ....
............/lot-fan ʔin dan-dʌn rɑ: be-ke-ʃi:d/. لطفاً این دندان را بکشید.
Please fill this tooth. ....
............/lot-fan dan-dɑ:-nam rɑ: por ko-ni:d/. لطفاً دندانم را پر کنید.
Rinse your mouth. ./da-hɑ:-ne xod rɑ: be-ʃu:-ʔi:d/. دهان خود را بشویید.
Spit out. .... /ʔɑ:-be da-hʌn rɑ: xɑ:-redʒ ko-ni:d/. آب دهان را خارج کنید.
Which tooth is troubling you? ....
......./ko-dɑ:m dan-dɑ:-ne-tʌn dard mi:-ko-nad/؟ کدام دندانتان درد می‌کند؟

6-4
PHARMACY

adhesive plaster	/na-vɑ:r zaxm/	نوار زخم
antifever	/tab-bor/	تب بر
antiseptic	/dɑ:-ru:-je zed-de ʔe-fu:-ni:/	داروی ضدّعفونی
aspirin	/ʔɑ:s-pi:-rɪn/	آسپرین
bandage	/bʌn-dɑ:ʒ/	بانداژ
caution	/ʔeh-tɪ-jɑ:t/	احتیاط
comb	/ʃɑ:-ne/	شانه
corn ointment	/po-mɑ:-de mi:x-tʃe/	پماد میخچه
cotton	/pan-be/	پنبه
cough mixture	/ʃar-ba-te sor-fe/	شربت سرفه
drop	/ɢat-re/	قطره
drug	/dɑ:-ru:/	دارو
eau de cologne	/ʔod-ko-lon/	ادکلن
first aid	/ko-mak-hɑ:-je ʔav-va-lɪj-je/	کمکهای اولیّه
for the baby	/batʃ-tʃe-gɑ:-ne/	بچّه گانه

for the ear	/ba-rɑ:-je gu:ʃ/	برای گوش
for the eye	/ba-rɑ:-je tʃe-ʃm/	برای چشم
for the nose	/ba-rɑ:-je bi:-ni:/	برای بینی
glycerine	/gi:-li:-si:-rɪn/	گلیسیرین
hair brush	/bo-re-se mu:/	برس مو
nail clipper	/nɑ:-xon-gi:r/	ناخنگیر
ointment	/po-mɑ:d/	پماد
ointment for burns	/po-mɑ:-de su:x-te-gi:/	پماد سوختگی
oxygen water	/ʔɑ:-be ʔok-si:-ʒe-ne/	آب اکسیژنه
pain relieving medicine	/dɑ:-ru:-je mo-sak-ken/	داروی مسکّن
pill	/Gors/	قرص
powder	/pu:dr/	پودر
razor	/ti:G/	تیغ
sedative	/ʔɑ:-rɑ:m-baxʃ/	آرامبخش
shaving cream	/xa-mi:-re ri:ʃ/	خمیرریش
skin cream	/ke-re-me pu:st/	کرم پوست
sleeping pill	/Gor-se xɑ:-bɑ:-var/	قرص خواب‌آور
soap	/sɑ:-bun/	صابون
stain remover	/dɑ:-ru:-je zed-de lak/	داروی ضدلک
syrup	/ʃar-bat/	شربت
tampon	/na-vɑ:r beh-dɑ:ʃ-ti:/	نوار بهداشتی
toilet paper	/kɑ:-Ga-ze tu:-vɑ:-let/	کاغذ توالت
toilet soap	/sɑ:-bu:-ne tu:-vɑ:-let/	صابون توالت
tooth brush	/mes-vɑ:k/	مسواک
tooth paste	/xa-mi:r dan-dʌn/	خمیردندان
tooth pick	/xe-lɑ:l dan-dʌn/	خلال دندان
vaseline	/vɑ:-ze-lɪn/	وازلین

How much is this medicine? ....
.................../Gej-ma-te ʔɪn dɑ:-ru: tʃand ʔast/ قیمت این دارو چند است؟
I'd like to have this prescription. ....
...................../ʔɪn nos-xe rɑ: be-pi:-tʃi:d/ این نسخه را بپیچید

Please give me something for a headache. ....
/lot-fan tʃi:-zi: ba-rv:-je sar-dard be-da-hi:d/ .لطفاً چیزی برای سردرد بدهید
Please give me something for a burn. ....
.... /lot-fan tʃi:-zi: ba-rv:-je su:x-te-gi: be-da-hi:d/
لطفاً چیزی برای سوختگی بدهید.
Please give me something for a cold. ....
.... /lot-fan tʃi:-zi: ba-rv:-je sar-mv: xor-de-gi: be-da-hi:d/
لطفاً چیزی برای سرماخوردگی بدهید.
Please give me something for toothache. ....
.... /lot-fan tʃi:-zi: ba-rv:-je dan-dʌn-dard be-da-hi:d/
لطفاً چیزی برای دندان‌درد بدهید.
What have you for cold? . /ba-rv:-je sar-mv:-xor-de-gi: tʃe dv:-ri:d/
برای سرماخوردگی چه دارید؟
What's good for sore throat? ....
/ba-rv:-je ga-lu:-dard tʃe xu:b ʔast/ ؟برای گلودرد چه خوب است
What's this good for? ....
................../ʔɪn ba-rv:-je tʃe xu:b ʔast/ ؟این برای چه خوب است
What is this medicine called? .... /ʔes-me ʔɪn dv:-ru: tʃi:st/
اسم این دارو چیست؟
Where is the pharmacy? . /dv:-ru:-xv:-ne ko-dʒv:st/ ؟داروخانه کجاست

SECTION 7
AMUSEMENTS

7-1 SPORTS

7-2 TELEVISION/RADIO

7-3 CINEMA

7-4 THEATRE

7-5 CONCERT

7-6 HOBBIES

7-7 MAMALS/BIRDS/FISH/
     INSECTS/AMPHIANS/
     REPTILES

7-1
SPORTS

American football	/fu:t-bɒ:l ʔɒ:m-ri:-kɒ:-ʔi:/	فوتبال امریکایی
badminton	/bad-mın-ton/	بدمینتون
badminton racket	/rɒ:-ke-te bad-mın-ton/	راکت بدمینتون
basketball	/bas-ket-bɒ:l/	بسکتبال
boxing	/boks/	بوکس
car racing	/mo-sɒ:-be-Ge-je ʔo-to-mo-bi:l sa-vɒ:-ri:/	مسابقهٔ اتومبیل‌سواری
champion	/Gah-ra-mʌn/	قهرمان
climbing	/ku:h-na-var-di:/	کوهنوردی
cycle racing	/mo-sɒ:-be-Ge-je do-tʃar-xe sa-vɒ:-ri:/	مسابقهٔ دوچرخه‌سواری
defeat	/bɒ:xt/	باخت
fencing	/ʃam-ʃi:r bɒ:-zi:/	شمشیربازی
final	/fi:-nɒ:l/	نهایی
football	/fu:t-bɒ:l/	فوتبال
football world cup	/dʒɒ:-me dʒa-hɒ:-ni-je fu:t-bɒ:l/	جام جهانی فوتبال
free exercises	/nar-meʃ-hɒ:-je sa-bok/	نرمشهای سبک
friendly match	/bɒ:-zi-je du:s-tɒ:-ne/	بازی دوستانه

golf	گلف	/golf/
golf ball	توپ گلف	/tu:-pe golf/
gymnastic	ژیمناستیک	/ʒi:m-nɑ:s-ti:k/
gymnasium	باشگاه ورزشی	/bɑ:ʃ-gɑ:-he var-ze-ʃi:/
handball	هندبال	/hand-bɑ:l/
hockey	چوگان	/tʃow-gʌn/
horse racing	اسب‌دوانی	/ʔasb da-vɑ:-ni:/
ice hockey	چوگان روی یخ	/tʃow-gɑ:-ne ru:-je jax/
judo	جودو	/ju:-do/
jumping	پرش	/pa-reʃ/
karate	کاراته	/kɑ:-rɑ:-te/
long jump	پرش طول	/pa-re-ʃe tu:l/
national champion	قهرمان کشور	/ɢah-ra-mɑ:-ne keʃ-var/
motor sport	موتورسواری	/mo-tor sa-vɑ:-ri:/
Olympic champion	قهرمان المپیک	/ɢah-ra-mɑ:-ne ʔo-lam-pi:k/
Olympic games	بازیهای المپیک	/bɑ:-zi:-hɑ:-je ʔo-lam-pi:k/
polevault	پرش با نیزه	/pa-reʃ bɑ: nej-ze/
record	رکورد	/re-kord/
referee	داور	/dɑ:-var/
rugby	راگبی	/rɑ:g-bi:/
running	دو	/dow/
semi-final	نیمه‌نهایی	/ni:-me na-hɑ:-ʔi:/
shot put	پرتاب وزنه	/par-tɑ:-be nej-ze/
skate	اسکیت	/ʔes-kejt/
skiing	اسکی	/ʔes-ki:/
sport	ورزش	/var-zeʃ/
sport dress	لباس ورزشی	/le-bɑ:-se var-ze-ʃi:/
sport shoe	کفش ورزشی	/kaf-ʃe var-ze-ʃi:/
squash	اسکواش	/ʔes-ko-vɑ:ʃ/
stadium	استادیوم	/ʔes-tɑ:-dɪ-jom/
swimming	شنا	/ʃe-nɑ:/
table tennis	تنیس روی میز	/te-ni:-se ru:-je mi:z/
table tennis net	تور تنیس روی میز	/tu:-re te-ni:-se ru:-je mi:z/
table tennis racket	راکت تنیس روی میز	/rɑ:-ke-te te-ni:-se ru:-je mi:z/

Amusements 233

table tennis table	.... /miː-ze te-niː-se ruː-je miːz/	میز تنیس روی میز
tennis	/te-niːs/	تنیس
tennis ball	/tuː-pe te-niːs/	توپ تنیس
tennis racket	/rvː-ke-te te-niːs/	راکت تنیس
track suit	..... /garm-kon (ʃal-vvː-re var-ze-ʃiː)/	گرمکن (شلوار ورزشی)
trainer	/kaf-ʃe var-ze-ʃiː/	کفش ورزشی
training	/tam-rɪn/	تمرین
volleyball	/vvː-liː-bvːl/	والیبال
walking	/rvːh pej-mvː-ʔiː/	راهپیمایی
waterpolo	/vvː-ter-po-lo/	واترپلو
weight lifting	/vaz-ne bar-dvː-riː/	وزنه‌برداری
win	/bord/	برد
world champion	/Gah-ra-mvː-ne dʒa-hʌn/	قهرمان جهان
wrestling	/koʃ-tiː/	کشتی
yachting	/mo-svː-be-Ge-je ka-ra-dʒi: rvː-niː/	مسابقهٔ کرجی‌رانی
yoga	/juː-gvː/	یوگا

How about going for a bike ride? ....
................/tʃe-towr ʔast ka-mi: do-tʃar-xe sa-vvː-ri: ko-niːm/
چطور است کمی دوچرخه‌سواری کنیم؟
How many stadiums are there in your town? ....
.... /ʃah-re ʃo-mvː tʃand tvː ʔes-tvː-dɪ-jom dvː-rad/
شهر شما چند تا استادیم دارد؟
How many years have you been active in sport? ....
../tʃand svːl ʔast ke var-zeʃ miː-ko-niːd/ چند سال است که ورزش می‌کنید؟
I came second in the race .. /dar mo-svː-be-Ge dov-vom ʃo-dam/
در مسابقه دوّم شدم.
I usually go in riding. ....
................../man maʔ-muː-lan do-tʃar-xe sa-vvː-ri: miː-ko-nam/
من معمولاً دوچرخه‌سواری می‌کنم.
I play football twice a week. ....
................../man haf-te-ʔi: do bvːr fuːt-bvːl bvː-zi: miː-ko-nam/
من هفته‌ای دو بار فوتبال بازی می‌کنم.

It's a friendly game between Iran and Japan. ....
......../mo-sʌ:-be-Ge-ʔi: du:s-tʌ:-ne bej-ne ʔi:-rʌn va ʒʌ:-pon ʔast/
مسابقه‌ای دوستانه بین ایران و ژاپن است.
Let's go swimming. ..../bɪ-jʌ: be-ra-vi:m ʃe-nʌ:/ بیا برویم شنا
Our team won ten points. ....
................/ti:-me mʌ: dah ʔem-tɪ-jʌ:z bord/ تیم ما ده امتیاز برد.
Runing is good exercise. ....
..................../dow var-ze-ʃe xu:-bi: ʔast/ دو ورزش خوبی است.
There's a football game today. ....
/ʔem-ru:z jek mo-sʌ:-be-Ge-je fu:t-bʌ:l hast/ امروز یک مسابقه فوتبال هست.
What's your best result? ....
............../beh-ta-rɪn ma-Gʌ:-mi: ke be dast ʔʌ:-var-de-ʔi:d tʃi:st/
بهترین مقامی که به‌دست آورده‌اید چیست؟
What's your favorite team? ....
................./ti:-me mo-re-de ʔa-lʌ:-Ge-je ʃo-mʌ: ko-dʌ:m ʔast/
تیم مورد علاقهٔ شما کدام است؟
What kind of a game is it? ....
............../tʃe noʔ mo-sʌ:-be-Ge-ʔi: ʔast/ چه نوع مسابقه‌ای است؟
What kind of sport do you go in for? ....
............../ʃo-mʌ: tʃe var-ze-ʃi: mi:-ko-ni:d/ شما چه ورزشی می‌کنید؟
What sports are popular in your country? ....
........../tʃe var-ze-ʃi: dar keʃ-va-re ʃo-mʌ: mah-bu:-bɪj-jat dʌ:-rad/
چه ورزشی در کشور شما محبوبیّت دارد؟
When does the competition start? ....
........../mo-sʌ:-be-Ge kej ʃo-ru:ʔ mi:-ʃa-vad/ مسابقه کی شروع می‌شود؟
Would you like to go running? ....
................./mʌ:-je-li: be-ra-vi:m be-do-vi:m/ مایلی برویم، بدویم؟

7-2
TELEVISION
RADIO

antenna	/ʔʌn-ten/	آنتن
announcer	/guː-jan-de/	گوینده
battery	/bɒːt-riː/	باتری
black-and-white television		
	/te-le-viː-zɪ-jo-ne sɪ-jɒːh se-fiːd/	تلویزیون سیاه سفید
broadcast	/pax-ʃe bar-nɒː-me/	پخش برنامه
channel	/kɒː-nɒːl/	کانال
colour television	/te-le-viː-zɪ-jo-ne raŋ-giː/	تلویزیون رنگی
FM	/ʔef ʔem/	اف.ام.
interference	/ta-dɒː-xol/	تداخل
picture	/tas-viːr/	تصویر
knob	/dog-me/	دگمه
latest news	/ʔɒː-xa-rɪn ʔax-bɒːr/	آخرین اخبار

long wave	/mow-dʒe bo-land/	موج بلند
medium wave(MW)	/mow-dʒe mo-ta-vas-set/	موج متوسّط
news commentor	/mo-fas-se-re ʔax-bɑ:r/	مفسّر اخبار
program guide	/feh-res-te bar-nɑ:-me/	فهرست برنامه
radio	/rɑ:-dɪ-jo/	رادیو
radio network	/ʃa-ba-ke-je rɑ:-dɪ-jo-ʔi:/	شبکهٔ رادیویی
sound	/sa-dɑ:/	صدا
short wave(SW)	/mow-dʒe ku:-tɑ:h/	موج کوتاه
TV network	/ʃa-ba-ke-je te-le-vi:-zɪ-jo-ni:/	شبکهٔ تلویزیونی
TV screen	/saf-he-je te-le-vi:-zɪ-jon/	صفحهٔ تلویزیون
transmission	/mo-xɑ:-be-re/	مخابره
tuning	/tan-zi:m/	تنظیم
tuning scale	/saf-he-je tan-zi:m/	صفحهٔ تنظیم
UHF	/ʔu: ʔetʃ ʔef/	یو.اچ.اف.
VHF	/vi: ʔetʃ ʔef/	وی.اچ.اف.
volume	/vo-lu:m/	ولوم
waves	/ʔam-vɑ:dʒ/	امواج
weather report	/go-zɑ:-re-ʃe vaz-ʔe ha-vɑ:/	گزارش وضع هوا

Adjust the radio set for short wave. ....
.... /lot-fan rɑ:-dɪ-jo rɑ: ru:-je mow-dʒe ku:-tɑ:h tan-zi:m ko-ni:d/
لطفاً رادیو را روی موج کوتاه تنظیم کنید.
Please adjust the brightness. ....
/lot-fan row-ʃa-nɑ:-ʔi: rɑ: tan-zi:m ko-ni:d/. لطفاً روشنایی را تنظیم کنید.
Please adjust the contrast. ....
..... /lot-fan kon-te-rɑ:st rɑ: tan-zi:m ko-ni:d/. لطفاً کنتراست را تنظیم کنید.
please turn off the radio. ....
.... /lot-fan rɑ:-dɪ-jo rɑ: xɑ:-mu:ʃ ko-ni:d/. لطفاً رادیو را خاموش کنید.
please turn on the TV. /lot-fan te-le-vi:-zɪ-jon rɑ: row-ʃan ko-ni:d/
لطفاً تلویزیون را روشن کنید.
Switch over to the other channel, please. ....
.... /lot-fan kɑ:-nɑ:l rɑ: ʔa-vaz ko-ni:d/. لطفاً کانال را عوض کنید.

Turn it down, please. .... /lot-fan se-dɑ:-jaʃ rɑ: kam ko-ni:d/
لطفاً صدایش را کم کنید.
Turn it up, please. .... /lot-fan se-dɑ:-jaʃ rɑ: zi-jɑ:d ko-ni:d/
لطفاً صدایش را زیاد کنید.
What's on television tonight? ....
.... /ʔem-ʃab te-le-vi:-zi-jon tʃe bar-nɑ:-me-ʔi: dɑ:-rad/
امشب تلویزیون چه برنامه‌ای دارد؟
When is a musical broadcast on? ....
.... /bar-nɑ:-me-je mu:-se-Gi: kej paxʃ mi:-ʃa-vad/
برنامهٔ موسیقی کی پخش می‌شود؟
When is a news bulletin on? ..... /ʔax-bɑ:r kej paxʃ mi:-ʃa-vad/
اخبار کی پخش می‌شود؟
When is a sports broadcast on? ....
.... /bar-nɑ:-me-je var-ze-ʃi: kej paxʃ mi:-ʃa-vad/
برنامهٔ ورزشی کی پخش می‌شود؟

7-3
CINEMA

actor	/ho-nar-pi:-ʃe/	هنرپیشه
actress	/ho-nar-pi:-ʃe-je zan/	هنرپیشهٔ زن
afternoon showing	/se-ʔʌn-se ru:z/	سئانس روز
bill-board	/ʔeʔ-lʌn/	اعلان
black and white film	/fi:l-me sI-jv:h se-fi:d/	فیلم سیاه سفید
cameraman	/fi:lm-bar-dv:r/	فیلم‌بردار
cartoon	/kv:r-tʊn/	کارتون
cinema	/si:-ne-mv:/	سینما
composer	/ʔv:-haŋ-sv:z/	آهنگساز
director	/kv:r-gar-dʌn/	کارگردان
documentary film	/fi:l-me mos-ta-nad/	فیلم مستند
dubbed film	/fi:l-me du:b-le ʃo-de/	فیلم دوبله شده
evening showing	/se-ʔʌn-se ʃab/	سئانس شب
feature film	/fi:l-me ho-na-ri:/	فیلم هنری
festival	/dʒaʃn-vv:-re-je fi:lm/	جشنوارهٔ فیلم
film	/fi:lm/	فیلم

film studio	/ʔes-to-dɪ-jo-je fiːlm bar-dɑ̆ː-riː/	استودیوی فیلمبرداری
full-length film	/fiːl-me siː-na-mɑ̆ː-ʔiː/	فیلم سینمایی
horror movies	/fiːlm-hɑ̆ː-je tars-nɑ̆ːk/	فیلمهای ترسناک
leading role	/naɢ-ʃe ʔas-liː/	نقش اصلی
newsreel	/ʔɑ̆ːr-ʃiː-ve fiːlm/	آرشیو فیلم
popular film	/fiːl-me xɑ̆ː-ne-vɑ̆ː-de-gi/	فیلم خانوادگی
role	/naɢʃ/	نقش
science fiction movies	/fiːlm-hɑ̆ː-je ʔel-miː ta-xaj-jo-liː/	فیلمهای علمی_تخیلی
screen	/par-de-je siː-na-mɑ̆ː/	پردهٔ سینما
script	/se-nɑ̆ː-rɪ-jo/	سناریو
script-writer	/se-nɑ̆ː-rɪ-jo ne-viːs/	سناریونویس
short film	/fiːl-me kuː-tɑ̆ːh/	فیلم کوتاه
shot	/kɑ̆ːdr/	کادر
showing	/se-ʔɑ̆ːns/	سئانس
showing times	/ʃo-ruː-ʔe se-ʔɑ̆ːns/	شروع سئانس
showing today	/fiːlm bar ruː-je ʔek-rɑn/	فیلم بر روی اکران

Did you like this film?	/ʔaz fiːlm xo-ʃe-tɑn ʔɑ̆ː-mad/	از فیلم خوشتان آمد؟
Do you like movie?	/fiːlm rɑ̆ː duːst dɑ̆ː-riːd/	فیلم را دوست دارید؟
How long does the film last?	/mod-da-te fiːlm tʃe-ɢadr ʔast/	مدت فیلم چقدر است؟
How would you like to go to movie tonight?	/tʃe-towr ʔast ʔem-ʃab be jek fiːlm be-ra-viːm/	چطور است امشب به یک فیلم برویم؟
I like adventure movies.	/man fiːlm-hɑ̆ː-je mɑ̆ː-dʒa-rɑ̆ː-ʔi rɑ̆ː duːst dɑ̆ː-ram/	من فیلمهای ماجرایی را دوست دارم.
I like comedy movies.	/man fiːlm-hɑ̆ː-je ko-me-diː rɑ̆ː duːst dɑ̆ː-ram/	من فیلمهای کمدی را دوست دارم.
Let's go to the cinema tonight.	/bɪ-jɑ̆ː ʔem-ʃab be siː-na-mɑ̆ː be-ra-viːm/	بیا امشب به سینما برویم.

One ticket for the next showing, please. ....
.... /jek be-li:t ba-rɑ̃:-je se-ʔʌn-se baʔ-di: lot-fan/
یک بلیط برای سئانس بعدی، لطفاً.
The film had an exciting plot. ....
.... /fi:lm su:-ʒe-je dʒɑ̃:-le-bi: dɑ̃:-ʃt/ فیلم سوژهٔ جالبی داشت.
What's your favorite movie? ....
.... /fi:l-me mow-re-de ʔa-lɑ̃:-Ge-je ʃo-mɑ̃: ko-dɑ̃:m ʔast/
فیلم مورد علاقهٔ شما کدام است؟
What kind of film do you like? ....
.... /tʃe noʔ fi:l-mi: rɑ̃: du:st dɑ̃:-ri:d/ چه نوع فیلمی را دوست دارید؟
When does the next showing start? ....
/se-ʔʌn-se baʔ-di: kej ʃo-ru:ʔ mi:-ʃa-vad/ سئانس بعدی کی شروع می‌شود؟
Who directed this film? ....
/kɑ̃:r-gar-dɑ̃:-ne ʔɪn fi:lm tʃe ka-si: ʔast/ کارگردان این فیلم چه کسی است؟
Who wrote the script? ....
/se-nɑ̃:-rɪ-jo rɑ̃: tʃe ka-si: ne-veʃ-te ʔast/ سناریو را چه کسی نوشته است؟
Who's your favorate actor/actress? ....
.... /ho-nar-pi:-ʃe-je mo-re-de ʔa-lɑ̃:-Ge-je ʃo-mɑ̃: ki:st/
هنرپیشهٔ مورد علاقهٔ شما کیست؟

7-4
THEATRE

act	/par-de/	پرده
acting	/bɒ:-zi:/	بازی
actor	/ho-nar pi:-ʃe/	هنرپیشه
actress	/ho-nar-pi:-ʃe-je zan/	هنرپیشهٔ زن
amphitheatre	/ʔɒ:m-fi: tɒ:-ʔɒ:tr/	آمفی تئاتر
applause	/dast za-dan/	دست زدن
balcony	/bɒ:l-kon/	بالکن
ballet	/bɒ:-le/	باله
box	/loʒ/	لژ
box-office	/gi:-ʃe/	گیشه
cast	/bɒ:-zi:-ga-rʌn/	بازیگران
charecter	/ʃax-sɪj-jat/	شخصیّت
chorus	/kor/	کُر
comedy	/ko-me-di:/	کمدی
company	/go-ru:-he (ho-nar-pi:-ʃe-gʌn)/	گروه (هنرپیشگان)
composer	/ʔɒ:-haŋ-sɒ:z/	آهنگساز

conductor	رهبر اركستر	/rah-ba-re ʔor-kes-ter/
costume	لباس	/le-bɒ:s/
curtain	پرده	/par-de/
decor	دكور	/de-kor/
drama	درام	/de-rɒ:m/
dramatic art	هنرهای دراماتیک	/ho-nar-hɒ:-je de-rɒ:-mɒ:-ti:k/
front stalls	ردیف جلو	/ra-di:-fe dʒe-low/
honoured art worker	شخصیّت بارز هنری	/ʃax-sɪj-ja-te bɒ:-re-ze ho-na-ri:/
interval	تنفّس	/ta-naf-fos/
leading role	نقش اصلی	/naG-ʃe ʔas-li:/
leading man/lady	هنرپیشهٔ اصلی	/ho-nar-pi:-ʃe-je ʔas-li:/
matinee	نمایش بعدازظهر	/ne-mɒ:-je-ʃe baʔd ʔaz zohr/
opera	اپرا	/ʔo-pe-rɒ:/
overture	پیش‌درآمد	/pi:ʃ da-rɒ:-mad/
performance	اجرا	/ʔedʒ-rɒ:/
play	نمایش	/ne-mɒ:-jeʃ/
playwright	درامنویس	/de-rɒ:m ne-vi:s/
premiere	اولین اجرا	/ʔav-va-lɪn ʔedʒ-rɒ:/
producer	تهیّه کننده	/ta-hɪj-je ko-nan-de/
program	برنامه	/bar-nɒ:-me/
puppet theatre	تئاتر عروسکی	/tɒ:-ʔɒt-re ʔa-ru:-sa-ki:/
repertoire	برنامهٔ نمایش	/bar-nɒ:-me-je ne-mɒ:-jeʃ/
scene	سِن	/sen/
scene designer	دکوراتور	/de-ko-rɒ:-towr/
seat	صندلی	/san-da-li:/
show	نمایش	/ne-mɒ:-jeʃ/
singer	آوازخوان	/ʔɒ:-vɒ:z-xɒn/
soloist	تکنواز	/tak-na-vɒ:-zi:/
theatre	تئاتر	/tɒ:-ʔɒ:tr/
tonight's show	نمایش امشب	/ne-mɒ:-je-ʃe ʔem-ʃab/
variety theatre	تئاتر متنوّع	/tɒ:-ʔɒ:t-re mo-ta-nav-veʔ/
the stalls	جایگاه	/dʒɒ:j-gɒ:h/

Amusements 245

Did you like the show? ....
............./ʔaz ne-mɒː-jeʃ xo-ʃe-tʌn ʔɒː-mad/ ؟از نمایش خوشتان آمد
Have you ticket for today for the theatre? ....
../be-li:-te tɒː-ʔɒːtr ba-rɒː-je ʔem-ru:z dɒː-ri:d/ بلیط تئاتر برای امروز دارید؟
How long is the interval? ....
............./mod-da-te ta-naf-fos tʃe-ɢadr ʔast/ مدّت تنفّس چقدر است؟
How much is the ticket? ..../ɢej-ma-te be-li:t tʃe-ɢadr ʔast/
قیمت بلیط چقدر است؟
I enjoyed it very much. ..../man xej-li: laz-zat bor-dam/
من خیلی لذّت بردم.
I feel like going to the puppet. ....
............./de-lam mi:-xɒː-had be tɒː-ʔɒːt-re ʔa-ru:-sa-ki: be-ra-vam/
دلم می‌خواهد به تئاتر عروسکی بروم.
Let's go to the buffet. . /bɪ-jɒː be bu:-fe be-ra-vi:m/. بیا به بوفه برویم.
Show me my seat, please. ./lot-fan dʒɒː-je ma-rɒː ne-ʃʌn da-hi:d/
لطفاً جای مرا نشان دهید.
What's on tonight at the central pupppet theatre? ....
... /bar-nɒː-me-je ʔem-ʃa-be tɒː-ʔɒːt-re mar-ka-zɪ-je ʔa-ru:-sa-ki: tʃi:st/
برنامهٔ امشب تئاتر مرکزی عروسکی چیست؟
Where are the boxes, please? ..../be-bax-ʃi:d loʒ ko-dʒɒːst/
ببخشید، لژ کجاست؟
Who is playing today? ..../ʔem-ru:z tʃe ka-si: bɒː-zi: mi:-ko-nad/
امروز چه کسی بازی می‌کند؟
Who is in the leading role? ....
.................../tʃe ka-si: naɢ-ʃe ʔas-li: rɒː ʔi:-fɒː mi:-ko-nad/
چه کسی نقش اصلی را ایفا می‌کند؟
Who wrote the play? . /ne-vi:-san-de-je ʔɪn ne-mɒː-jeʃ-nɒː-me ki:st/
نویسندهٔ این نمایشنامه کیست؟

7-5
CONCERT

accompanist	/ham-rɑ:-hi: ko-nan-de/	همراهی کننده
cello	/vɪ-jo-lon-sel/	ویولنسل
chorus	/ham-xʌn kor/	همخوان، کُر
classic music	/mu:-si:-ɢɪ-je ke-lɑ:-si:k/	موسیقی کلاسیک
composer	/ʔɑ:-haŋ-sɑ:z/	آهنگساز
concert	/kon-sert/	کنسرت
conductor	/rah-ba-re ʔor-kes-ter/	رهبر ارکستر
drums	/ʤɑ:z/	جاز
drums player	/ʤɑ:-zi:st/	جازیست
ensemble	/gu:-ru:-he mu:-si:-ɢi:/	گروه موسیقی
flute	/nej/	نی
folk music	/mu:-si:-ɢɪ-je ma-hal-li:/	موسیقی محلّی
guitar	/gi:-tɑ:r/	گیتار
guitarist	/gi:-tɑ:r zan/	گیتارزن
jazz music	/mu:-si:-ɢɪ-je ʤɑ:z/	موسیقی جاز
keyboard	/ʔor-ge ʔe-lek-te-ro-ni:-ki:/	ارگ الکترونیکی

light music .... /mu:-si:-GI-je ʔɒ:-rɒ:m/ موسیقی آرام
music .... /mu:-si:-Gi:/ موسیقی
music disc .... /di:s-ke mu:-si:-Gi:/ دیسک موسیقی
music tape .... /na-vv:-re mu:-si:-Gi:/ نوار موسیقی
musician .... /mu:-si:-Gi:-dʌn/ موسیقیدان
orchestera .... /ʔor-kes-ter/ ارکستر
organ .... /ʔorg/ ارگ
performer(MC) .... /modʒ-ri:/ مجری
pianist .... /pɪ-jv:-ni:st/ پیانیست
piano .... /pɪ-jv:-no/ پیانو
pop music .... /mu:-si:-GI-je pv:p/ موسیقی پاپ
rock music .... /mu:-si:-GI-je rv:k/ موسیقی راک
snap music .... /mu:-si:-GI-je ʔes-nap/ موسیقی اسنپ
song .... /ʔv:-vv:z/ آواز
symphony .... /san-fo-ni:/ سنفونی
symphony music .... /mu:-si:-GI-je san-fo-ni:k/ موسیقی سنفونیک
traditional music .... /mu:-si:-GI-je son-na-ti:/ موسیقی سنّتی
violin .... /vɪ-jo-lon/ ویلن
violinist .... /vɪ-jo-lon-zan/ ویلن‌زن

Did you like the concert? .... /ʔaz kon-sert xo-ʃe-tʌn ʔv:-mad/
از کنسرت خوشتان آمد؟
Do you like listening to jazz? . /du:st dv:-ri: be dʒv:z gu:ʃ ko-ni:/
دوست داری به جاز گوش کنی؟
Do you like music? .... /ʔaz mu:-si:-Gi: xo-ʃe-tʌn mi:-ʔv:-jad/
از موسیقی خوشتان می‌آید؟
Do you like pop music? ....
.... /mu:-si:-GI-je pv:p rv: du:st dv:-ri:d/ موسیقی پاپ را دوست دارید؟
Do you like popular music? ....
/mu:-si:-GI-je maʔ-mu:-li: rv: du:st dv:-ri:d/ موسیقی معمولی را دوست دارید؟
Do you often go to conserts? .... /zɪ-jv:d be kon-sert mi:-ra-vi:d/
زیاد به کنسرت می‌روید؟

Do you play any musical instrument? /ʃo-mɑ: sɑ:-zi: mi:-za-ni:d/
شما سازی می‌زنید؟
He is a bass. .... /ʔu: sa-dɑ:-jaʃ bam ʔast/ او صدایش بم است.
I like Iranian folk songs. ....
.... /man ʔaz ʔɑ:-vɑ:z-hɑ:-je ma-hal-lɪ-je ʔi:-rɑ:-ni: xo-ʃam mi:-ʔɑ:-jad/
من از آوازهای محلّی ایرانی خوشم می‌آید.
I play accordion. . /man ʔɑ:-kɑ:r-de-ʔon mi:-za-nam/. من آکاردئون می‌زنم.
I play guitar. .... /man gi:-tɑ:r mi:-za-nam/ من گیتار می‌زنم.
I play keyboard. .... /man ʔorg mi:-za-nam/ من ارگ می‌زنم.
I play piano. .... /man pɪ-jɑ:-no mi:-za-nam/ من پیانو می‌زنم.
She is a soprano. ..../ʔu: sa-dɑ:-jaʃ su:p-rɑ:-no ʔast/
او صدایش سوپرانو است.
That song was a hit last year. ....
../pɑ:r-sɑ:l ʔɑn ʔɑ:-vɑ:z ʔɑ:-me-pa-sand ʃod/ پارسال آن آواز عامه‌پسند شد.
What Iranian songs do you know? ....
....................../tʃe ʔɑ:-vɑ:z-hɑ:-je ʔi:-rɑ:-ni: rɑ: mi:-ʃe-nɑ:-si:d/
چه آوازهای ایرانی را می‌شناسید؟
What kind of music does he/she play? ....
......./ʔu: tʃe noʔ mu:-si:-ɢi: mi:-na-vɑ:-zad/ او چه نوع موسیقی می‌نوازد؟
What's program today? ....
...................../bar-nɑ:-me-je ʔem-ru:z tʃi:st/ برنامهٔ امروز چیست؟
Who is conducting? .... /tʃe ka-si: rah-ba-re ʔor-kes-ter ʔast/
چه کسی رهبر ارکستر است؟
Who is the soloist? ..../tʃe ka-si: tak-na-vɑ:-zi: mi:-ko-nad/
چه کسی تکنوازی می‌کند؟
Who is your favourite composer? ....
......................./ʔɑ:-haŋ-sɑ:-ze mo-re-de ʔa-lɑ:-ɢe-je ʃo-mɑ: ki:st/
آهنگساز مورد علاقه شما کیست؟
Who is your favourite singer? ....
...................../xɑ:-nan-de-je mo-re-de ʔa-lɑ:-ɢe-je ʃo-mɑ: ki:st/
خوانندهٔ مورد علاقهٔ شما کیست؟

7-6
H O B B I E S

book	/ke-tɒ:b/	کتاب
cinema	/si:-ne-mɒ:/	سینما
classical music	/mu:-si:-ɢɪ-je ke-lɒ:-si:k/	موسیقی کلاسیک
dance	/raɢs/	رقص
folk music	/mu:-si:-ɢɪ-je ma-hal-li:/	موسیقی محلّی
handicrafts	/sa-nɒ:-jeʔ das-ti:/	صنایع دستی
historical novels	/ro-mʌn-hɒ:-je tɒ:-ri:-xi:/	رمانهای تاریخی
horror movies	/fi:lm-hɒ:-je tars-nɒ:k/	فیلمهای ترسناک
jazz	/mu:-si:-ɢɪ-je dʒɒ:z/	موسیقی جاز
light music	/mu:-si:-ɢɪ-je ʔɒ:-rɒ:m/	موسیقی آرام
love stories	/dɒ:s-tʌn-hɒ:-je ʔɒ:-ʃe-ɢɒ:-ne/	داستانهای عاشقانه
magazine	/ma-dʒal-le/	مجلّه
movie	/fi:lm/	فیلم
museum	/mu:-ze/	موزه
music	/mu:-si:-ɢi:/	موسیقی
music disc	/di:s-ke mu:-si:-ɢi:/	دیسک موسیقی

music tape .... /na-vɑ:-re mu:-si:-ɢi:/ نوار موسیقی
mystery stories .... /dɑːs-tɑn-hɑ:-je mar-mu:z/ داستانهای مرموز
newspaper .... /ru:z-nɑ:-me/ روزنامه
novel .... /ro-mɑn/ رمان
painting .... /naɢ-ɢɑ:-ʃi:/ نقاشی
park .... /pɑ:rk/ پارک
picture .... /tɑ:b-lo/ تابلو
poem .... /ʃeʔr/ شعر
pop music .... /mu:-si:-ɢi-je pɑ:p/ موسیقی پاپ
rock music .... /mu:-si:-ɢi-je rɑ:k/ موسیقی راک
science fiction movies .... /fi:lm-hɑ:-je ʔel-mi: ta-xaj-jo-li:/
فیلمهای علمی-تخیّلی
science fiction stories ....
.... /dɑ:s-tɑn-hɑ:-je ʔel-mi: ta-xaj-jo-li:/ داستانهای علمی-تخیّلی
sculpture .... /mo-dʒas-sa-me sɑ:-zi:/ مجسّمه‌سازی
statue .... /mo-dʒas-sa-me/ مجسّمه
theatre .... /tɑ:-ʔɑ:tr/ تئاتر
traditional music .... /mu:-si:-ɢi-je son-na-ti:/ موسیقی سنّتی

Are you satisfied? .... /rɑ:-zi: has-ti:d/ راضی هستید؟
Can I bring Maria? ....
......./mi:-ta-vɑ:-nam mɑ:-ri-jɑ: rɑ: bi-jɑ:-va-ram/ میتوانم ماریا را بیاورم؟
Can I bring my friend along? ....
................/mi:-ta-vɑ:-nam du:s-tam rɑ: ham-rɑ:h bi-jɑ:-va-ram/
میتوانم دوستم را همراه بیاورم؟
Dancing is his/her favorate activity. ....
/raɢ-si:-dan sar-gar-mi-je del-xɑ:-he ʔust/. رقصیدن سرگرمی دلخواه اوست
Did you enjoy it? .... /xo-ʃe-tɑn ʔɑ:-mad/؟ خوشتان آمد
Do you like listening to jazz? ....
..... 'du:st dɑ:-ri: be dʒɑ:z gu:ʃ ko-ni:/ دوست داری به جاز گوش کنی؟
Do you like movie? .... /fi:lm du:st dɑ:-ri:d/ فیلم دوست دارید؟
Do you like pop music? ....
.... /mu:-si:-ɢi-je pɑ:p rɑ: du:st dɑ:-ri:d/ موسیقی پاپ را دوست دارید؟

Do you like popular music? ....
................./muː-siː-ɢı-je ʔvː-me-pa-sand rv: duːst dvː-riːd/
موسیقی عامه‌پسند را دوست دارید؟
Have you any plans for this evening? ....
........./ba-rvː-je ʔasr bar-nvː-me-ʔi: dvː-riːd/ برای عصر برنامه‌ای دارید؟
His/Her dancing was superb. .. /ʔvː-li: miː-raɢ-siːd/ عالی می‌رقصید.
How about going for hiking? ....
........./tʃe-towr ʔast ka-mi: dar biː-ruː-ne ʃahr ɢa-dam be-za-niːm/
چطور است کمی در بیرون شهر قدم بزنیم؟
How would you like to go to movie tonight? ....
.................../tʃe-towr ʔast ʔem-ʃab be jek fiːlm be-ra-viːm/
چطور است امشب به یک فیلم برویم؟
I'm going to the museum. ...../miː-xvː-ham be mu-ze be-ra-vam/
می‌خواهم به موزه بروم.
I'm looking forward to you. .../mon-ta-ze-rat has-tam/. منتظرت هستم.
I like it here. .. /ʔaz ʔın-dʒv: xo-ʃam miː-ʔvː-jad/ از اینجا خوشم می‌آید.
It sounds good to me. ..../be na-za-ram xuːb miː-ʔvː-jad/
به نظرم خوب می‌آید.
Let me change. ./ʔe-dʒv:-ze be-de le-bvːs-hvː-jam rv: ʔa-vaz ko-nam/
اجازه بده لباس‌هایم را عوض کنم.
Let us go this way. ....
................./bı-jv: ʔaz ʔın ta-raf be-ra-viːm/. بیا از این طرف برویم.
Let us go to the park and have fun. ....
..../bı-jv: be-ra-viːm pvːr ko taf-riːh ko-niːd/. بیا برویم پارک و تفریح کنیم.
Shall we go out for a walk? ....../be-ra-viːm biː-run be-gar-diːm/
برویم بیرون بگردیم؟
That's fine. ....,/xuːb ʔast/. خوب است.
That song was a hit last year. ....
../pvːr-svːl ʔʌn ʔvː-vvːz ʔvː-me-pa-sand ʃod/. پارسال آن آواز عامه‌پسند شد.
That sounds like a good idea. ....
........../fek-re xuː-bi: be na-zar miː-re-sad/. فکر خوبی به نظر می‌رسد.
The scenery in the mountains is very beautiful. ....
.........../man-za-re kuːh-hvː xej-li: ziː-bvːst/. منظره کوه‌ها خیلی زیباست.

We had a good time at the party. ....
...... /dar meh-mɒː-ni: be mɒ: xoʃ go-zaʃt/. در مهمانی به ما خوش گذشت.
What a magnificent building! ....
.... /tʃe ba-nɒː-je mo-dʒal-la-li:/ ! چه بنای مجلّی!
What are we going to do today? ....
.... /bar-nɒː-me-je ʔem-ru:-ze mɒ: tʃi:st/ ? برنامهٔ امروز ما چیست؟
What are you going to do next friday? ....
.... /dʒom-ʔe-je ʔɒː-jan-de tʃe-kɒːr xɒː-hi: kard/
جمعهٔ آینده چه کار خواهی کرد؟
What building is this? ....
.... /ʔɪn tʃe sɒːx-te-mɒː-ni: ʔast/ ? این چه ساختمانی است؟
What's your favorite music band? ....
... /gu:-ru:-he mu:-si:-ɢi:-je mo-re-de ʔa-lɒː-ɢe-je ʃo-mɒ: ko-dɒːm ʔast/
گروه موسیقی مورد علاقهٔ شما کدام است؟
What's your favorite book? ....
/ke-tɒː-be mo-re-de ʔa-lɒː-ɢe-je ʃo-mɒ: tʃi:st/? کتاب مورد علاقهٔ شما چیست
What's your favorite movie? ....
.... /fi:l-me mo-re-de ʔa-lɒː-ɢe ʃo-mɒ: ko-dɒːm ʔast/
فیلم مورد علاقهٔ شما کدام است؟
What kind of music do you like? ....
..... /tʃe noʔ mu:-si:-ɢi: rɒ: du:st dɒː-ri:d/ ? چه نوع موسیقی را دوست دارید
Where would you like to go? ....
.... /mi:-xɒː-hi: ko-dʒɒ: be-ra-vi:/ ? می‌خواهی کجا بروی
Who's this statue by? ....
.... /ʔɪn mo-dʒas-sa-me ʔa-sa-re ki:st/ ? این مجسمه اثر کیست
Who's your favorate actor/actress? ....
.... /ho-nar-pi:-ʃe-je mo-re-de ʔa-lɒː-ɢe-je ʃo-mɒ: ki:st/
هنرپیشهٔ مورد علاقهٔ شما کیست؟
Who's your favorite singer? ....
.... /xɒː-nan-de-je mo-re-de ʔa-lɒː-ɢe-je ʃo-mɒ: ki:st/
خوانندهٔ مورد علاقهٔ شما کیست؟
Would you like to come with us? ....
.... /du:st dɒː-ri: bɒː mɒ: bɪ-jɒː-ʔi:/ ? دوست داری با ما بیایی

7-7

MAMALS / BIRDS
FISH / INSECTS
AMPHIANS/REPTILES

1. Mamals .... /pes-tʌn-dɑ:-rʌn/ پستانداران .۱

bear .... /xers/	خرس
buffalo .... /gɑ:v-mi:ʃ/	گاومیش
calf .... /gu:-sɑ:-le/	گوساله
camel .... /ʃo-tor/	شتر
cat .... /gor-be/	گربه
cow .... /gɑ:v/	گاو
deer .... /ʔɑ:-hu:/	آهو
dog .... /sag/	سگ

English	Persian	Transcription
elephant	فیل	/fi:l/
fawn	بچه‌آهو	/batʃ-tʃe ʔɒ:-hu:/
fox	روباه	/ru:-bɒ:h/
giraffe	زرافه	/zar-rɒ:-fe/
goat	بز	/boz/
hippopotamus	اسب آبی	/ʔas-be ʔɒ:-bi:/
horse	اسب	/ʔasb/
hyena	کفتار	/kaf-tɒ:r/
ibex	بز وحشی	/bo-ze-vah-ʃi:/
jackal	شغال	/ʃo-ɢɒ:l/
jaguar	جگوار	/dʒag-vɒ:r/
kangaroo	کانگورو	/kʌn-go-ro/
kid	بزغاله	/boz-ɢɒ:-le/
kitten	بچه‌گربه	/batʃ-tʃe gor-be/
lamb	بره	/bar-re/
leopard	پلنگ خالدار	/pa-laŋ-ge xɒ:l-dɒ:r/
lion	شیر	/ʃi:r/
lynx	سیاه‌گوش	/sɪ-jɒ:h gu:ʃ/
marten	سمور	/sa-mu:r/
monkey	میمون	/mej-mʊn/
mouse	موش	/mu:ʃ/
ox	گاو نر	/ɢɒ:-ve nar/
pig	خوک	/xu:k/
porcupine	جوجه‌تیغی	/dʒu:-dʒe ti:-ɢi:/
puppy	توله‌سگ	/tu:-le sag/
rabbit	خرگوش	/xar-gu:ʃ/
raccoon	راکون	/rɒ:-kon/
rat	موش صحرایی	/mu:-ʃe sah-rɒ:-ʔi:/
reindeer	گوزن	/ga-vazn/
rhino	کرگدن	/kar-ga-dan/
sheep	گوسفند	/gu:-se-fand/
squirrel	سنجاب	/san-dʒɒ:b/
tapir	خوک خرطوم‌دار	/xu:-ke xor-tu:m-dɒ:r/
tiger	ببر	/babr/

weasel	/rɒ:-su:/	راسو
wolf	/gorg/	گرگ
yak	/gɒ:v-mi:ʃ/	گاومیش
zebra	/gu:-re-xar/	گورخر

2.Birds   /pa-ran-de-gʌn/ پرندگان .٢

barn owl	/mor-Ge haGG/	مرغ حق
bat	/xof-fɒ:ʃ/	خفاش
canary	/Ga-nɒ:-ri:/	قناری
chick	/dʒu:-dʒe/	جوجه
chicken	/dʒu:-dʒe morG/	جوجه‌مرغ
condor	/ʃɒ:h-rox/	شاهرخ
crane	/dor-nɒ:/	درنا
crow	/ka-lɒ:G/	کلاغ
cuckoo	/fɒ:x-te/	فاخته
duck	/ʔor-dak/	اردک
eagle	/ʔo-Gɒ:b/	عقاب
emu	/ʃo-tor-mor-Ge ʔos-to-rɒ:-lɪ-jɒ:-ʔi:/	شترمرغ استرالیایی
falcon	/bɒ:z/	باز
flamingo	/mor-Ge ɒ:-ta-ʃi: (fe-lɒ:-mi:n-go)/	مرغ آتشی(فلامینگو)
goose	/Gɒ:z/	غاز
grouse	/bɒ:-Gar-Ga-re/	باقرقره
hawk	/ʃɒ:-hɪn/	شاهین
hen	/morG/	مرغ
hoopoe	/hod-hod/	هدهد
lark	/tʃa-kɒ:-vak/	چکاوک
nightingale	/bol-bol/	بلبل
ostrich	/ʃo-tor-morG/	شترمرغ
owl	/dʒoGd/	جغد
parrot	/tu:-ti:/	طوطی
partidage	/kabk/	کبک
peacock	/tɒ:-vu:s/	طاووس

pelican	/pe-li:-kʌn/	پليكان
penguin	/pan-gu:-ʔan/	پنگوئن
pheasant	/ɢar-ɢv:-vol/	قرقاول
pigeon	/ka-bu:-tar/	كبوتر
guail	/bel-der-tʃɪn/	بلدرچين
seagull	/mor-ɢe dar-jv:-ʔi:/	مرغ دريايی
sparrow	/gon-dʒeʃk/	گنجشك
stork	/lak-lak/	لكلك
swallow	/pa-ras-tu:/	پرستو
swan	/gu:/	قو
turkey	/bu:-ɢa-la-mʊn/	بوقلمون
wild duck	/mor-ɢv:-bɪ-je vah-ʃi:/	مرغابی وحشی
woodpecker	/dv:r-ku:b/	داركوب

3.Fish .... /mv:-hi:-hv:/ ۲. ماهيها

carp	/mv:-hɪ-je ɢa-nv:t/	ماهی قنات
eel	/mv:r-mv:-hi:/	مارماهی
octopus	/haʃt-pv:/	هشت پا
perch	/mv:-hɪ-je se-fi:d/	ماهی سفيد
prawn	/mej-gu:/	ميگو
salmon	/mv:-hɪ-je ʔv:-zv:d/	ماهی آزاد
shark	/ku:-se/	كوسه
shell	/sa-daf/	صدف
smoked salmon	/mv:-hɪ-je du:-di:/	ماهی دودی
sword fish	/ʔar-re-mv:-hi:/	ازه ماهی
trout	/ɢe-zel-ʔv:-lv:/	قزل آلا
tunna	/mv:-hɪ-je ton/	ماهی تن
whale	/bv:-lon/	بالن

Amusements 259

4.Insects .... /ha-ʃa-rɐːt/ ۴. حشرات

ant .... /muːr-tʃe/ مورچه
bee .... /zan-buːr/ زنبور
bug .... /sɐːs/ ساس
butterfly .... /par-vɐː-ne/ پروانه
cockrooch .... /suːsk/ سوسک
cricket .... /dʒiːr-dʒiː-rak/ جیرجیرک
dragon fly .... /san-dʒɐː-ɢak/ سنجاقک
fly .... /ma-gas/ مگس
honey bee .... /zan-buː-re ʔa-sal/ زنبورعسل
horse fly .... /xar-ma-gas/ خرمگس
insect .... /ha-ʃa-re/ حشره
lady bird .... /kafʃ-duː-zak/ کفش‌دوزک
leech .... /zɐː-luː/ زالو
locust .... /ma-lax/ ملخ
louse .... /ʃe-peʃ/ شپش
milliped .... /he-zɐːr-pɐː/ هزارپا
moth .... /biːd/ بید
mosquito .... /paʃ-ʃe/ پشه
scorpion .... /ʔa-ɢa-rab/ عقرب
silk worm .... /ker-me ʔab-riː-ʃam/ کرم ابریشم
snail .... /ha-la-zʊn/ حلزون
spider .... /ʔan-ka-buːt/ عنکبوت
worm .... /kerm/ کرم
weevil .... /ʃe-pe-ʃak/ شپشک

5.Amphians/Reptiles /do-ziːs-tʌn , xa-zan-de-gʌn/ ۵.دوزیستان، خزندگان

chameleon .... /ʔɐːf-tɐːb-pa-rast/ آفتاب‌پرست
crab .... /xar-tʃaŋ/ خرچنگ
crocodile .... /tem-sɐːh/ تمساح
frog .... /ɢuːr-bɐː-ɢe/ قورباغه

lizard	/mɑ:r-mu:-lak/	مارمولک
snake	/mɑ:r/	مار
turtle	/lɑ:k-poʃt/	لاک‌پشت
viper	/ʔaf-ʔi:/	افعی

Part Three

GEOGRAPHY

I.I   GENERAL PROFILE

I.II   THE CLIMATE

I.III   AGE DISTRIBUTION

I.IV   LANGUAGE

I.V   OCCUPATION

I.VI   RELIGION

Geography 265

I.I GENERAL PROFILE

Area .... 1,648,000 sq.km

Population 60,000,000

Ratio of lands. Agricultural Regions 54.9%
Desert Regions and
arid Lands 20.7%
Forest Regions 14.4%
Town Regions 7.6%
Habitable Lakes .... 2.4 %

Urbanization .... 54 %

I-II CLIMATE

The climate is dry tropical in most parts of the plateau between the Caspian Sea and the Persian Gulf. It's bracing and mild in the valley, and rigorous in winter in the northwest and higher valleys.

Temperature Low: Tabriz .... (-15/+27)
High: Ahwaz .... (+7/+47)
Average: Tehran .... (-3/+37)

Annual Rainfall

Max. 2000 mm .... in Guilan (Caspian shores)
Min. 100 mm .... in Central Regions
Average 275mm

I-III AGE DISTRIBUTION

```
0 - 19 ..................................................... 53.5 %
20 - 39 .................................................... 27.3 %
40 - 59 .................................................... 13.7 %
60+ .......................................................... 5.5 %
```

I.IV LANGUAGE

Native Languages:

Farsi(Persian), Azarbaijani(Turkey), Kurdish, Lori, Mazandarani, Guilaki, Baluchi, Turkmen, Arabic, Armenian and other.

Official Language:

Official Language is Farsi(Persian). English and French are common among the educated.

I.V OCCUPATION

```
services ..................................................... 45.5 %
Agriculture ................................................ 29.2 %
Industry .................................................... 25.3 %
```

1.6 RELIGION

```
Muslim ...................................................... 99 %
other ......................................................... 1 %
```

SECTION II
TRAVEL

II.I   TRAVELING TO IRAN
II.II INLAND TRIPS
II.III ROAD AND MOTORING
II.IV TRANSPORTATION
II.V   ADAPTATION AND HOSPITALITY
II.VI NATIONAL IRANIAN DISHES
II.VII OPENING AND CLOSING TIMES

II.I TRAVELING TO IRAN

AIR................The best way to travel to Iran is by air.

LAND..............One can also travel to Iran by land. The main highways which join Iran with the neighbouring countries are:

1. The Iran-Turkey highway from Bazargan in the northwest of Iran.

2. The Zahedan-Mirjaveh highway on the Pakistan border.

3. The Taybad-Herat highway on the Afghan border.

4. The Astara-Sarakhs and the Jolfa highway to the Azarbaijan.

SEA................Iran also possesses sea-routes from the southern Ports to Bahrein, Kuwait, Omman and the UAE.

II.II INLAND TRIPS

BY LAND.........Travel by land is by bus, hired cars and rail.

BY AIR............There are regular air services between Tehran and other major cities in Iran.

II.III ROAD AND MOTORING

The road system of Iran is radial. The Asian Highway from London to Singapore enters Iran at Bazargan on the Iran-Turkey frontier and passes through Tabriz, Zanjan, Tehran, Semnan, Mashhad and Taybad on the Afghan border. Iran's internal road system covers over 40,000 km and further building is underway. Projects recently completed include the CENTO Pakistan-Tabriz -Bazargan highway, the Tehran-Gazvin freeway and the Heraz route to the Caspian (Tehran-Amol). The Iranian section of the Asian highway is complete and work has begun on a new highway between Bandar-e-Abbas and the Afghan frontier. Two highways are scheduled between Tehran and the Caspian Sea coast and an extension to the proposed Tehran-Isfahan freeway to Shiraz to calm traffic congestion from the Shiraz Refinery.

II.IV TRANSPORTATION

CAR................There is no need for carrying extra petrol. The cost of fuel for the means of transport makes up a small part of travelling payments, and It's much lower than other countries.

TRAIN............The main cities of Iran like Ahwaz, Gorgan, Isfahan, Khorramshahr, Mashhad, Tabriz and Tehran are available by rail road.

AIRCRAFT.......Iran Air(Homa), Aseman and Kish airlines have regular flight to all the big cities and even to smaller towns in faraway parts of Iran. The fare for internal flights, too, is relatively low compared with that of other countries. Air ticket can be obtained either directly from sale bureaus or through private agencies which are active as a wide network in Tehran and other major cities.

II.V ADAPTATION AND HOSPITALITY CENTERS

HOTEL/INN......There are many hotels and inns of different gradings as adaptation placings in large and medium sized cities.

HOSPITALITY CENTERS

Hospitality centers are lots in Iran. There are many restaurants in the cities. Chelow-kabab lodges and other eating places which offer all type of Iranian and foreign dishes. The traditional hospitable centers are tea-houses which are usually called 'ghahve-khaneh' (coffee-house) which in addition to tea and waterpipe, offer a sort of Iranian stew dish called 'ab-goosht'. They serve as a gathering place for various social groups and a center for the exchange of information and news.

ON ROAD.........The main hospitality services between cities are provided by resraurants where Iranian and possibly a number of local dishes are offered. The quality of services of road restaurants are commonly lower than city resturants.

II.VI NATIONAL IRANIAN DISHES

DISH...............The most popular of these are 'chelow-kabab' (boiled rice and roasted meat), 'Ab-goosht' (lamb meat broth mixed with cereals, potato and spice), 'Chelo-morgh' (boiled rice and fowl meat), 'Chelow-khoresht' or 'chelow-gheimeh'(boiled rice and stuffing).

BREAD............There are four famous kinds of bread. 'lavash' (a thin, crispy variety), 'bar-bary' (the choice for breakfast), 'taftoon' (fresh, flat lunch bread), 'sangak' (bread baked on hotpebbles).

BEVERAGE......'Doogh' (yogurt mixed with mineral water) is a cold traditional beverage, sometimes mixed with some aromatic ground herbs, drunk at the table

II.VII OPENING AND CLOSING TIMES

LOCAL TIME:
GMT+3.5 hrs.

WEEKLY CLOSING DAYS:
Thursday afternoon and Friday (government offices non-commercial banks and certain other establishements close all day Thursday.)

COMMERICAL BANKS:
7:30 - 14:00 hours

COMMERICAL OFFICES:
8:00 - 14:00 hours

SHOP HOURS:
Usually 9:00 - 13:00 & 16:00 - 20:0 sat. thus.

RESTAURANT HOURS:
Usually 12:00 - 14:00 & 19:00 - 21:00

BAZAAR HOURS:
It's different in various cities but the common time is 10:00-13:00 and 17:00-20:30 (depend on the season)

SECTION III
SIGHTS

III.I	MAIN ATTRACTIONS
III.II	AZARBAIJAN
III.III	FARS
III.IV	HAMADAN
III.V	ILAM
III.VI	ISFAHAN
III.VII	KERMAN
III.VIII	KERMANSHAH
III.IX	KHORASSAN
III.X	KHUZESTAN
III.XI	KURDESTAN
III.XII	SOUTHERN COASTS AND PERSIAN GULF ISLANDS

III.XIII TEHRAN
III.XIV THE CASPIAN COAST
III.XV   YAZD
III.XVI SPORTS
III.XVII IRANIAN HANDICRAFTS

III.I MAIN ATTRACTIONS

Fascinating museums, historical and cultural interest, hunting and fishing, investment and contractor's potential, mountain and seaside resorts, Persian carpets and traditional arts, relics of Hakhamaneshian (Achaemenian), Sassanian and Islamic cultures, rich folklore, spectacular scenery, trade and weath of archaeological

III.II Azarbaijan

Ahar............Ghal'eh Babak(Fort of Babak) in Kaleibar

Ardabil..........A'zam Mosque, Bogh-e-je Sheikhsafi (the mausoleum of Sheikhsafi), peerles remedial hot spring such as Sareyn located 20 km from Ardabil, with their special components of sulphur and other salts own valuable medical effects, Savalan mountain

Jolfa............Asiab Kharabe(ruined watermill) in Alamdar-Gargar, Kelisa-Kharabe (ruined church)

Khoy............The Shams-e-tabrizi Tower

Maku............Tatavous Church in Siahcheshmeh

Maragheh.........	Borj-e-Kabud(The Blue Tower), The Observatory, Borj-e-Sorkh(The Red Tower), and Round Tower
Miyaneh........	Qhal'eh dokhtar(fort of doughter), Qhal'eh Zohak(fort of Zohak), and Pol-e-dokhtar(bridge of doughter)
Naqadeh.......	The Hassanlu hill and village
Tabriz...........	Ark(fort of Ark), Bagh-e-golestan(park of Golestan), Jom'eh Mosque, Khane-ye-Mashrutiyat(House of Mashrutiyat), Masjed-e-Kabood(blue mosque), The Bazaar, The modern bazaar of Shams, The promenade of Shahgoli, Maghbarat-ol-Sho'ara (Tomb of poets), traditional museum and Sahand mountain.
Takab...........	Takhte-Soleiman situated 45 kilometers north east of Takab.
Urumieh Lake.	Urumieh Lake with its plentiful island such as Arezu, Ashk-e-Daghi and Spiri is one of the most attractive zones of Azarbaijan. The towns located on the coast of this lake such as Golman khaneh, Rahmanlu, Agh-Gonbad and Sharaf-khaneh town lodging amenities for the aims of tourism.

III.III FARS

**Perspolis
(Takht-e-Jamshid)**
Takht-e-Jamshid, as invaluable archeological antiquities of the brilliance of ancient Iran, Perspolis, one of the capitals of the Achamenian Empire, was virtually a dynamic shrine.

Shiraz...........Armenian church, Atashkadeh-ye-Azarju(Azarju Firetemple) in Darab, Chehel-tanan and Haft-tanan monastries and its water reservoir, Darvazeh Quran(the Quran gate), Dasht-e-azadegan mountainous village, Madraseh-ye-Khan (Khan theological school), Kazerun, Masjed-e-no(new mosque), Mudan cave, Naghsh-e-Rostam, Naghsh-e-Shapoor, Narenjestan-e-Qavam (the Qavam Orangery), Masjed-e-Nasir-ol-molk (Nasir-ol-molk mosque), Pars Museum, Pazargad school and citalel of Vakil, shrine of Ahmad-ebne-Ja'far son of the seventh Imam, statue of Shapour I, the ancient Jom'eh mosque, the tomb of Hafez, the tomb of Saadi, Vakil Bazaar with bargains in kelims, copper inlaid woodwork, tribal jewellery, mosaic jewel and cigarette boxes, Vakil mosque.

III.IV HAMADAN

Hamadan......Dome of the Allahvis, Ganj-Nameh, Mausoleum of esther and Murdkhai, Shir-e-Sangi (stone lion), the famous caves of Ali-saadr, Hizag and Joogh Ghaleh, the village of Lalejin which is the center of the pottery industry with 50 workshops where all kinds of beautiful pots with different colors and designs are habitually being produced, tombs of Avicenna and Baba Taher.

III.V ILAM

Ilam............. Bridge of Bahram-e-chubin, the arch of Farhad and Shirin, the mountain-pass of chubin and palace of the Sassanian period.

III.VI ISFAHAN

Isfahan......... Aeineh khaneh park, Allahverdikhan Bridge, Chehel-Sotoon palace(forty columns palace) with many paintings on its inside walls, Imam square(former Nagsh-e-Jahan), Jom'eh Mosque of Isfahan with a fine collection of post-Islamic architecture, Khaju Bridge, park of Boostan-e-Mellat, shahrestan Bridge, shaking minarets, the building of Ali-Qapu, the church of Badakhm

Sight 281

(Beytol-Lahm), the church of Jolfa, the Gheisarieh Bazaar, the mosque of Imam (Masjed-e-shah), the mosque of Sheikh Lotfollah, the Zayandeh-Rood River, the Zoroustrian Firetemple, Vonk Armenian Cathedral.

Handicrafts.... Brocades, Carpet-weaving, Delicate manuscripts, Enamel, Engraving, Embroidery, Gilding, Hand block printed cloth, Inlay, miniature painting, Mosaic, Silver-work, skin-sewing.

III. VII KERMAN

Bam.............Bam is an example of a completely oriental town.

Kerman.........The Bazaar with a public bath which has now accepted the form of a museum Gonbade-jahelieh (the Dome of Jahelieh) which is an Atashkadeh related to Sassanian period, the Galeh Ardashir and Galeh Dokhtar related to the Sassanian period, the great Friday mosque, Gonbad-e-sabz (the Green Dome), the public bath and carvansara of Ganj-Alikhan located inside the bazaar, the tomb of the Gharakhtayan dynasty.

Mahan.......... The tomb of the great Sufi leader shah-Nematollah-e-Vali.

III.VIII KERMANSHAH

Ancient cities. .Kermanshah, Kerend, Paveh, Qasr-e-shirin, Songhor Eslamabad

Historical
relics............Bistoon (35Km east of the Kermanshah)is the famed Bistoon rock with its Akhamenian relief showing Darius as victor over pretender Gaumatas, and its several hundred lines of trilingual cuneiform inscription (Old Persian, Akkadian and Elamaite), one of the most important historical documents of ancient world, Taq-e-bostan (bas-reliefs of Ardeshir II, Shapour II and Sharpour III and Khosrow II), the ancient manuments of Qasr-e-shirin, the famous temple Anahita in Kangavar, the religious theater of Moaven-ol-molk in Bakhtaran.

III.IX KHORASSAN

Mashhad....... The museum of Imam-Reza in Mashhad holds one at the most extensive cultural and beautiful treasures in the whole country, Expressly with its manuscript books and paintings, the new market named the Reza Bazaar, tomb of Khajeh, traditional Bazaar of Mashhad, traditional wrestling at the Zurkhaneh Eyd-gah.

Neishabur......The tomb of great painter Kamal-ol- Molk, the tomb of sheikh Attar, the tomb of well-known poet Omar khaiyam.

Tus..............At Tus is the tomb of Ferdowsi, the great epic poet of Iran. His tomb honoured by those who acknowledge the poet's genius in keeping the Persian language as protected as possible from the influence of Arabic root-words.

III.X KHUZESTAN

Ahwaz.......... The monument of Masjed-e-Soleiman and Shooshtar from Achaemenian, Parthian and Sassanian period are in their turn of great value.

Shush...........Haft Tappeh(Ilami places, tablets and statues), the ancient city of Shush.

III.XI KURDESTAN

Sanandaj.......Cave of Karaftu near Saqqez, Dar-ol-Khan school, Jom'eh-Mosque, Sanandaj museum of Ganjineh Zeivieh.

Handicrafts.... Coarse carpet, Neadlework, embroidery and spangle work which attract great numbers of eager buyers, turned and wooden products.

III.XII SOUTHERN COASTS AND PERSIAN GULF ISLANDS

The well-known island of Hormoz with its ancient fort and reservoirs, the island of Qeshm with its plentiful ancient and local sights, and lastly the island of Kish with its great tourist accommodations and historical monuments, like the town of Harireh and the traditional reservoirs.

III.XIII TEHRAN

Tehran..........Abgineh museum, Archaeological museum, Azadi monument(tower), Bazaar of Tehran as the largest trade center of the country, carpet museum, college of Religion(Sepahsalar), Ethnological museum, Forest park of Chitgar, Forest park of Mirdamad, Forest park of Sorkhehesar, Golestan Palace with its internal and external compounds, Iranian museum of Anthropology, Marble Palace, Mosque of Imam, Mottahari Mosque, Museum of Decorative Arts, Museum of Jewels in the Bank Melli of Iran where the famous diamond of "Daryaye-nur" (sea of light) as well as the royal crowns and Jewels are kept, National Art Museum, Palace of Niavaran, Palace of Sa'd-Abad, Park of Daneshjue,

Park of Eram, Park of Gheitarieh, Park of Jamshidieh, Park of Laleh, Park of Mellat, Park of Niavaran, Park of Shahr, Reza Abbassi Museum, shrine of Abdol-Azim at Rey, Rudaki Hall

The most important centers of higher education, administrative, military, political, economic, commercial institutions and communications are centered in Tehran.

III.XIV THE CASPIAN COAST

The northern part of Iran borders on the Caspian Sea, where the clean, Shark-free waters are ideal for swimming and water sports. The resort towns between Babolsar and Bandar-e-Anzali are popular vacation spots for Iranians and the long coast line is developing in to a resort area with great tourist potential. The climate is sub-tropical and humid, in contrast to the dry main plateau.

III.XV YAZD

Yazd.............Alexander Prison, the Dowlat-Abad Garden, the Jomeh Mosque of Yazd, the khan Bazaar, the Khan Garden, the Khan square, the mosque of Amir Chakhmagh, Atash-Kadeh Yazdan(the Yazdan

Firetemple)
Yazd is the largest center of Iranian Zoroastrians who have inhabited this city for many centuries.

III.XVI SPORTS

House of strength

The people of Iran have always been great sportmen and nowhere is this better demonstrated than in the Zurkhaneh (House of Strength) once called the "Persian schools for Heroes". Found in most towns throughout the country, they have their origin in the rigid training of young Iranians in athletics, endurance and armed combat, as described by Herodotus and Strabo.

A visit to these ancient exercises, which are accompanied by chanting and ceremonial ritual, is highly recommended.

Wrestling....... Wrestling stemmed from the Zurkhaneh and was a national sport at least by the 8th century A.D. It's one which modern Iranians still excel.

Climbing......... The terrain of Iran is flanked by rugged oaks, and climbing is a favorite sport. Main climbing season is at the end of summer, but several winter ascents have been made. While the mountain presents few technical difficulties, the great height, the seepage of sulphurous gases and the absence of water near the summit make the ascent physically strenuous. Excursions by mule or horse into the mountains are also popular.

Skiing.......... There are several well-equipped skiing areas within easy reach of the capital, the best known being Ab-e-Ali, 50 Km from Tehran, with 15 ski-lifts. Shemshak, at the foot of Sarakchal mountains is Iran's highest ski resort, usually open for eight month a year.

Other sports... Facilities for badminton, basketball, football, golf, polo, racing, riding, water and mountain skiing, squash, swimming and tennis are all available in Iran. The Azadi stadium, just outside Tehran, which seats 100 000, is the focus of competitive sports. In country districts the old sports of cock fighting and howking still survive.

III.XVII IRANIAN HANDICRAFTS

Carpet.......... Bakhtiari, Bijar, Isfahan, Kerman, Nayin Tabriz, Turkman

Other........... Ceramics, Copper and Bronze products, Curriery, Enamel, Engraving, Glassblowing, Glazed tiles, Inlay and other delicate items made of metal, wood and bone, Miniature paiting, Mosaic, Pottery, Termeh (Cashmere), the jajim (a coarse woollen cloth used as a carpet) which is lighter and softer than a coarse carpet, and many metalic and wooden valuable handcrafts.

HIPPOCRENE BEGINNER'S SERIES

The Beginner's Series consists of basic language instruction: vocabulary, grammar, common phrases and review questions; along with cultural insights, interesting historical background, and hints about everyday life.

Beginner's Bulgarian
207 pp • 5 1/2 x 8 1/2 • 0-7818-0034-4 • $ 9.95 (76)

Beginner's Chinese
150 pp • 5 1/2 x 8 • 0-7818-0566-X • (690)

Beginner's Czech
200 pp • 5 1/2 x 8 1/2 • 0-7818-0231-8 • $9.95 (74)

Beginner's Hungarian
200 pp • 5 1/2 x 7 • 0-7818-0209-1 • $7.95 (68)

Beginner's Maori
120 pp • 5 1/2 x 8 1/2 • 0-7818-0605-4 • $8.95 (703)

Beginner's Persian
304 pp • 5 1/2 x 8 1/2 • 07818-0567-8 • $14.95 (696)

Beginner's Polish
200 pp • 5 1/2 x 8 1/2 • 0-7818-0299-7 • $ 9.95 (82)
2 cassettes: 0-7818-0330-6 • $12.95 (56)

Beginner's Romanian
200 pp • 5 1/2 x 8 1/2 • 0-7818-0208-3 • $7.95 (79)

Beginner's Swahili
200 pp • 5 1/2 x 8 1/2 • 0-7818-0209-1 • $9.95 (52)
2cassettes: 0-7818-0336-5 • $12.95 (55)

Beginner's Ukrainian
130 pp • 5 1/2 x 8 1/2 • 0-7818-0443-4 • $11.95 (88)

Beginner's Vietnamese
517 pp • 7 x 10 • 30 lessons • 0-7818-0411-6 • $19.95 (253)

Other Hippocrene Dictionaries and Language Books of Interest . . .

ARABIC-ENGLISH DICTIONARY
450 pages • 5½ x 8¼ • 15,000 entries • 0-7818-0153-2 • $14.95pb • (487)

ARABIC HANDY DICTIONARY
120 pages • 5 x 7¾ • 0-87052-960-9 • $8.95pb • (463)

ARABIC-ENGLISH/ ENGLISH-ARABIC STANDARD DICTIONARY
900 pages • 5½ x 8½ • 0-7818-0383-7 • $24.95pb • (195)

ARABIC-ENGLISH LEARNER'S DICTIONARY
467 pages • 18,000 entries • 0-87052-914-5 • $18.95pb • (flex plastic)

ENGLISH-ARABIC LEARNER'S DICTIONARY
1,242 pages • 20,000 entries • 0-87052-155-9 • $24.95pb • (flex plastic)

MODERN MILITARY DICTIONARY: ENGLISH-ARABIC/ ARABIC-ENGLISH
250 pages • 5½ x 8½ • 0-7818-0243-1 • $14.95pb • (214)

SAUDI ARABIC BASIC COURSE: URBAN HAJAZI DIALECT
288 pages • 6½ x 8½ • 50 lessons • 0-7818-0257-1 • $14.95pb • (171)

KURDISH-ENGLISH/ ENGLISH-KURDISH DICTIONARY
400 pages • 4 x 6 • 8,000 entries • 0-7818-0246-6 • $11.95pb • (218)

PERSIAN-ENGLISH STANDARD DICTIONARY
700 pages • 5½ x 8½ • 22,500 entries • 0-7818-0055-2 • $19.95pb • (350)

ENGLISH-PERSIAN STANDARD DICTIONARY
700 pages • 5½ x 8½ • 40,000 entries • 0-7818-0056-0 • $19.95pb • (365)

Tutorial
ARABIC GRAMMAR OF THE WRITTEN LANGUAGE
560 pages • 5½ x 8½ • 0-87052-101-2 • $19.95pb • (397)

ARABIC FOR BEGINNERS
186 pages • 5¼ x 8¼ • 0-7818-0114-1 • $9.95pb • (18)

LET US CONVERSE IN ARABIC
156 pages • 5 ½ • X 8½ • 0-7818-0562-7 • $11.95 • (702)

MASTERING ARABIC
320 pages • 5¼ x 8¼ • 0-87052-922-6 • $14.95pb • (501)
2 cassettes: 0-87052-984-6 • $12.95 • (507)

MALTESE-ENGLISH/ENGLISH-MALTESE DICTIONARY AND PHRASEBOOK
175 pages • 3 ¾ x 7 • 1,500 entries • 0-7818-0565-1 • $11.95pb • (697)

THE MODERN PUSHTU INSTRUCTOR
Script and romanized form
343 pages • 4 x 8 • 0-7818-0204-0 • $22.95 • (174)

handwritten: chom duzehr ast.
handwritten: beah bo-khor-eem - Let's eat

THE ART OF PERSIAN COOKING
by Forough Hekmat

This collection features such traditional Persian dishes as Abgushte Adas (Lentil soup), Mosamme Khoreshe (Egglplant Stew), Lamb Kebab, Cucumber Borani (Special Cucumber Salad), Sugar Halva and Gol Moraba (Flower Preserves).

From creating a holiday menu to determining which utensils to use, THE ART OF PERSIAN COOKING covers a wide array of practical information to help even the novice chef prepare elaborate Persian dishes. The exotic fare is further enhanced by rich descriptions of the cultural and culinary history of Persian cuisine in special sections entitled "The History of Persian Cuisine," "Food and Entertainment within the Persian Home," and "The Fundamentals of Classic Persian Cooking."

190 pages • 5 1/2 x 8 1/2 • 0-7818-0241-5 • $9.95pb • (125)

All prices subject to change. **TO PURCHASE HIPPOCRENE BOOKS** contact your local bookstore, call (718) 454-2366, or write to: HIPPOCRENE BOOKS, 171 Madison Avenue, New York, NY 10016. Please enclose check or money order, adding $5.00 shipping (UPS) for the first book and $.50 for each additional book.